The Shakespearean Stage 1574-1642

The
Shakespearean Stage
1574-1642

ANDREW GURR

Professor of English
University College Nairobi

CAMBRIDGE
AT THE UNIVERSITY PRESS
1970

Published by the Syndics of the Cambridge University Press
Bentley House, 200 Euston Road, London N.W.1
American Branch: 32 East 57th Street, New York, N.Y.10022

© Cambridge University Press 1970

Library of Congress Catalogue Card Number: 72 116747

Standard Book Number: 521 07816 4

Printed in Great Britain
at the University Printing House, Cambridge
(Brooke Crutchley, University Printer)

Contents

Illustrations

Preface

This book is primarily a summary of such books as E. K. Chambers's *Elizabethan Stage*, G. E. Bentley's *Jacobean and Caroline Stage* and other scholarly studies. It is meant to be a conspectus of the material background to Shakespearean drama, a picture of the society in which the drama flourished, of the acting companies, their theatres, and their acting and staging. A digest of eleven volumes of closely-packed information has no value as a reference work, of course, and the picture which this book tries to paint is therefore inevitably an impressionistic (not to say Fauviste) one. It has a selection of the details which are provided comprehensively in the reference works and in subsequent scholarly studies, and should be read as a preliminary, outlining, study of the background circumstances out of which the plays first appeared.

Background studies to Shakespearean drama are not the same thing as historical criticism, the kind of approach to the plays which was used by Schücking and others earlier this century. What Shakespeare's own contemporaries made of him and his works, the desideratum of such an approach, is not particularly important to later centuries. Every age will study its ancestors for its own different purposes, and these purposes are unlikely to be quite the same as those of the ancestors themselves. The business of Shakespeare criticism would have no point if it were not necessary to re-read him to suit the always-changing interests of the times. A picture of the background to the plays is useful to this business in a negative way; it minimises misunderstandings of the plays as they were originally composed. If this book can offer any help to readers of the plays in this respect, it will serve its purpose.

The term 'Shakespearean' is used to cover what are normally called the Elizabethan, Jacobean and Caroline periods—that is, the latter half of Elizabeth's reign, from the 1570s to 1603, the whole of the reign of James I, 1603–25, and the period of rule (as distinct from reign) of Charles I, 1625–42. Shakespeare's own contact with the London theatre world extended only from about 1590 to 1616, but he stands on its highest peak, and his name if anyone's has to be given to the period. The theatre conditions which supplied Shakespeare with the venue for his plays came into existence in the 1570s, and disappeared abruptly in 1642. The first official recognition of the London-based commercial acting companies was given in 1574; a total ban on playing was imposed in 1642, and was thoroughly enforced for the next eighteen years, long enough to destroy almost all traces of Shakespearean theatre conditions and traditions. The seventy years of acting in which Shakespeare's career was embedded needs to be seen as a whole, and the best single word for it is Shakespearean.

A number of the variables of the Shakespearean period have been regularised for convenience. The old-style system of dating, which began the calendar year in March instead of on 1 January, has been silently adjusted to the modern dating. The titles of plays and the names of players, which were spelt in various ways even by their owners, have been regularised in the forms adopted by Chambers and Bentley. In accordance with the general principle of supplying an authentic picture of the Shakespearean background, quotations are given wherever possible in the original spelling, except that the Elizabethan typographical conventions of i for j, initial v and medial u, have been altered to the modern usage. And to be consistent in the same principle, actors are normally called players, theatres are playhouses, and their product is the unserious business of playing.

ANDREW GURR

Leeds 1969

Acknowledgements

We should like to thank the following for permission to reproduce the plates: the University Library, Cambridge (Plate I), the Governors of Dulwich College Picture Gallery (Plates II–IV), the Bibliotheek der Rijksuniversiteit, Utrecht (Plate V), the Master and Fellows of Magdalene College, Cambridge (Plate VI), the Marquess of Bath (Plate VII), and the Trustees of the Chatsworth Settlement (Plate VIII).

1. Introduction

Hamlet, like any other Shakespearean nobleman, wore his hat indoors. When the foppish and murderous Osric came flourishing his head-gear with the invitation to fight Laertes, Hamlet undoubtedly doffed his bonnet in reply to Osric's flourish, and then put it back on. Osric's failure to follow suit led to Hamlet's reproof ('Put your bonnet to his right use, 'tis for the head'). The unbonneted Hamlet familiar to modern audiences is a creation of the indoor theatre and fourth-wall staging, where every scene is a room unless it is specified otherwise, and where everyone goes hatless accordingly. Hamlet in 1600 walked under the sky in an open amphitheatre, on a platform which felt out-of-doors in comparison with modern theatres, but which indifferently represented indoors or out to the Elizabethans. There was a wall at the back of the platform, fronting the 'tiring-house' or room where the players changed, the off-stage area. It gave access to the playing area by two or more doors and a balcony. These places of entry could equally well provide the imagination with the exterior doors and balcony of a house or the interior doors and gallery of a great hall. Hamlet's headgear was worn with equal indifference to the imagined scene.

The wearing of hats on stage is a minor matter in comparison with, say, Hamlet's use of a 'nighted colour' in his clothes, so far as the play's general concerns go. But unless we know Hamlet is himself bonneted the point of his verbal fencing with Osric may be missed. Hats are useful either to guard the wearer's face against the sun, or to keep the head warm. Hamlet's request that Osric should put his bonnet to its right use is taken by Osric to be made out of concern for the hot sun ('I thank your lordship, it is very hot'). Hamlet, having been too much 'in the "son"', denies this ('No, believe me, 'tis very cold, the wind is northerly'), an equally good reason for keeping his own hat on; and when Osric hastens to agree, catches him up on it ('But yet, methinks, it is very sultry and hot for my complexion'). He keeps his hat on with both reasons. Hamlet is not just making Osric look a fool. For Osric to keep his hat off in Hamlet's presence was excessively deferential, especially in a creature of the usurping King addressing that King's victim, and Hamlet ensures that the excess is made apparent. Shakespeare made stage business out of similar by-play with hats in *Love's Labour's Lost*, v.i, *A Midsummer Night's Dream*, iv.ii, and *As*

You Like It, III.iii. Unless we know that Hamlet kept his hat on while Osric continued to flourish his, we miss the real point of the incident. It also helps to know that a typical Elizabethan 'bonnet' in 1600 had a high crown, a narrow brim, and a round dome—a kind of elongated bowler hat—in order to visualise Horatio's image of Osric running off like a baby lapwing 'with the shell on his head'.

Hamlet makes highly sophisticated use of the theatre conditions of its time. The company of players who arrive in II.ii were real, not the caricatures of players found in *A Midsummer Night's Dream* or Marston's *Histriomastix*, and the specimen of their work which the leading player offers is a genuine, if deliberately archaic, set speech, an audition piece, not a parody. Despite Polonius's interruptions, the player delivers his 'passionate speech' about rugged Pyrrhus with such good inward accompaniment to his outward appearance of passion that he changes colour and tears come into his eyes. And all this, as Hamlet bitterly tells himself afterwards, is monstrously for a fiction, a 'dream of passion':

> what would he do,
> Had he the motive and the cue for passion
> That I have?

All that is really monstrous, of course, is that Hamlet has no more motive or cue for passion than the player; he himself is as much a fiction as the player. What Shakespeare is doing in this scene is to refine on the familiar Elizabethan joke of 'tragedy played in jest', the paradox which sees murders done for entertainment, and appearances pretending to be reality. The fictitious Hamlet rails at the fiction of the player. Shakespeare's refinement is to make this paradoxical situation not a joke but an emphatic assertion of Hamlet's reality.

There are many other details of the play's staging which depend on contemporary life, and which enlighten reading of the play. The disposition of the stage for the play-within-the-play, for instance, which has exercised the ingenuity of some commentators, must have followed the pattern for plays at Court: the performers of the play at the back of the stage by the largest opening in the tiring-house wall (the so-called discovery-space), King Claudius and Queen Gertrude on the 'state' or throne at the front of the stage in the middle of the amphi-theatre yard, Hamlet and Ophelia to one side with a view of both.[1] Another example is the dumb-show, the mimed plot-summary with which the play-within-the-play begins. Dumb-shows were a fairly archaic device by the time *Hamlet* was written, but not so archaic that Shakespeare's contemporaries hesitated to use them. Nor were they such rare devices that Hamlet could not have foreseen the players using one. The mistake in prematurely revealing the mousetrap through the dumb-show is partly due to Hamlet's lack of foresight, and his failure to allow for the players' stupidity is a component in the savagery with which he greets them when they come out to start the play itself. Again, when Polonius is stabbed through, as the Second Quarto and the schoolboy joke have it, the arras, it is worth knowing that the curtain behind which Polonius hid hung in front of a 'discovery-space', an alcove or similar structure deep enough to conceal quite substantial properties. The player of Polonius could have called out from the back of the alcove, leaving room for the player of Hamlet to make a full-blooded lunge through the curtain without fear of actually running his fellow through. Polonius could then safely come forward to become a corpse, before Hamlet drew the curtain back to reveal him. The duel at the climax in v.ii must have been similarly full-blooded. Fencing displays were a feature of the entertainment the stages offered to the Elizabethan public, and at least one player (Richard Tarlton the clown) was a Master of Fence. Though Hamlet claims in his opening soliloquy to be utterly unlike Hercules (the archetypal man of action), in the duel with Laertes he would certainly have been required to belie his words.

These and similar items of background information can enlarge the dimensions of any play of the period. The playhouses were not places for art or culture, and their poetry was the very impure poetry of money. It was entertainment, not art, and therefore written for an age, not for all time. The players in *Hamlet* were sent for to divert Hamlet's attention from whatever it was brought on his antic disposition. They were to provide a casual diversion from serious affairs. The supposition that this was their only function, their place in society, is an accurate reflection of society's estimation of the players and of the fare they provided. The fare was not therefore, except marginally, a 'literary' product; it was transient like the performances which embodied it, and it was dependent on the environment of the performances as few written works have ever been. This is the chief reason why the background to the plays repays study.

Playhouses were places of impure art, and in some eyes they were not even places of legitimate entertainment. William Harrison commented when the first playhouses were built in 1576 that 'It is an evident token of a wicked time when plaiers wexe so riche that they can build such houses'.[2] To Harrison the entertainment they offered was no better than that of 'houses of baudrie'. They were even built in the same neighbourhoods, as Prynne, the Puritan author of an attack on playing, wrote in 1633:

our Theaters if they are not Bawdy-houses, (as they may easily be, since many Players, *if reports be true, are common Panders,*) yet they are Cosin-germanes, at *leastwise neighbours to them*: Witnesse the *Cock-pit,* and *Drury-lane: Black-friers Play-house,* and *Duke-humfries;* the *Red-bull,* and *Turnball-street:* the *Globe,* and *Bank-side Brothel-houses,* with others of this nature.[3]

The poet and epigrammatist John Davies sketched the day of a typical playgoer, an idle gallant, in terms which also acknowledged the equivalent status of brothels and playhouses ('In Fuscum': *Epigrammes*, 39):

> *Fuscus* is free, and hath the world at will,
> Yet in the course of life that he doth leade,
> He's like a horse which turning rounde a mill,
> Doth alwaies in the selfe same circle treade:
> First he doth rise at 10. and at eleven
> He goes to *Gyls*, where he doth eate till one,
> Then sees a play til sixe, and sups at seaven,
> And after supper, straight to bed is gone,
> And there till tenne next day he doth remaine,
> And then he dines, then sees a commedy,
> And then he suppes, and goes to bed againe.
> Thus rounde he runs without variety:
> Save that sometimes he comes not to the play
> But falls into a whore-house by the way.

Such an idea of playgoing was hardly likely to create a devotional attitude to their art in the players. Playing was deplored by the authorities, in 1574 when the innyards were the venues, and the crowds were largely artisans and apprentices, just as it was deplored in 1633, when playhouses were in great halls in the heart of London, and the trouble was caused more by the coaches of the great than by tumultuous apprentices. In 1574 the city authorities described the scene in these words:

the inordynate hauntyinge of greate multitudes of people, speciallye youthe, to playes, enterludes, and shewes, namelye occasyon of ffrayes and quarrelles, eavell practizes of incontinencye in greate Innes, havinge chambers and secrete places adjoyninge to their open stagies and gallyries, inveglynge and alleurynge of maides, speciallye orphanes and good Cityzens Children under Age, to previe and unmete Contractes, the publishinge of unchaste uncomelye and unshamefaste speeches and doynges, withdrawinge of the Queenes Majesties Subjectes from dyvyne service on Sonndaies and hollydayes, at which Tymes suche playes weare Chefelye used, unthriftye waste of the moneye of the poore and fond persons, sondrye robberies by pyckinge and Cuttinge of purses, utteringe of popular busye and sedycious matters, and manie other Corruptions of youthe and other enormyties, besydes that allso soundrye slaughters and mayhemings of the Quenes Subjectes have happened by ruines of Skaffoldes, fframes, and Stagies, and by engynes, weapons, and powder used in plaies.[4]

The innyards were in the City jurisdiction, and by the turn of the century the City Fathers managed to close them to the players. The theatres designed and built as theatres were located just outside the City jurisdiction, and in 1633 it was the Privy Council, the executive instrument of the King's government, which had to intervene to impose traffic regulations in the vicinity of the leading playhouse. They declared that

Whereas ye Board hath taken consideracion of the great inconveniencs that growe by reason of the resort to the Play house of ye Blackffryars in Coaches, whereby the streets neare thereunto, are at the Playtime so stopped that his Ma^ts Subjects going about their necessarie affayres can hardly finde passage and are oftentymes endangered: Their lps remembring that there is an easie passage by water unto that playhouse w^thout troubling the streets, and that it is much more fit and reasonable that those wch goe thither should goe thither by water or else on foote rather than the necessarie businesses of all others, and the publique Commerce should be disturbed by their pleasure, doe therefore Order, that if anie p[er]son man or woman of what Condicion soever repaire to the aforesayd Playhouse in Coach so soone as they are gone out of their Coaches the Coach men shall departe thence and not retourne till the ende of the play, nor shall stay or retourne to fetch those whom they carryed anie nearer wth their Coaches then the farther parte of St Paules Church yarde on the one syde, and ffleet-Conduite on the other syde, and in ye tyme betweene their departure and returne shall either returne home or else abide in some other streets lesse frequented with passengers and so range their Coaches in those places that the way be not stopped, wch Order if anie Coachman disobey, the next Constable or Officer is hereby charged to commit him p^resently to Ludgate or Newgate; And the Lo: Mayor of ye Citie of London is required to see this carefully pfourmed by the Conestables and Officers to whom it apperteyneth and to punish every such Conestable or officer as shall be found negligent therein. And to the ende that none may p^retende ignorance hereof, it is lastly ordered that Copies of this Order, shalbe set up at Paules Chaine, by direction of the Lorde Mayor as also at the west ende of St Paules Church, at Ludgate and the Blackfryers Gate and Fleete Conduite.[5]

A contemporary noted that the regulations were duly enforced, but that, human flesh being what it is, they were effective for only two or three weeks.

The official records of course are only concerned with the troubles the players made. The other side of the story is suggested by the awed wonder with which foreign travellers described what they saw on the London stages, and the declarations of much-travelled Englishmen like Fynes Moryson, who wrote in his *Itinerary* (p. 476), published in 1617, that

The Citty of London alone hath foure or five Companyes of players with their peculiar Theaters Capable of many thousands, wherein they all play every day in the weeke but Sunday, with most strang concourse of people, besydes many strange toyes and fances exposed by signes to be seene in private houses, to which and to many musterings and other frequent spectacles, the people flocke in great nombers, being naturally more newe-fangled then the Athenians to heare newes and gaze upon every toye, as there be, in my opinion, more Playes in London then in all the partes of the worlde I have seene, so doe these players or Comedians excell all other in the worlde. Whereof I have seene some stragling broken Companyes that passed into Netherland and Germany, followed by the people from one towne to another, though they understoode not their wordes, only to see theire action, yea marchants at Fayres bragged more to have seene them, then of the good marketts they made.

In the sixteenth century life for the playing companies was a constant battle to keep a foot-hold in London in the teeth of the City Fathers and the Puritan preachers. According to the preachers, apprentices were seduced away into idleness by the temptations of the players, and the Devil finds work for idle hands. The City Fathers, most of whom employed apprentices, understandably felt themselves to be better employers than the Devil. The Court, however, lacking the interest in the matter that the City Fathers had, held no similar objections to playing. In 1572 and 1574 it more or less openly took the leading companies of players under its wing. Only with such protection could the players afford to invest in permanent playhouses. In 1576 and 1577 two public amphitheatres and one indoor theatre opened as commercial venues for playing, all of them for safety just outside the City's jurisdiction. This gave them an immunity the innyards could not have, and with royal help they proved sound and lasting investments. Not until the political balance of power was reversed, nearly seventy years later, did the City finally get its way over the Court and the players. In the early seventeenth century, when the leading London companies all basked in the warmth of royal patronage, the City's hostility was necessarily quiescent. For nearly forty years London never had less than six playhouses, and four regular companies performing daily except on Sundays and for most of Lent, and when the plague set every man apart from his fellows. Only in 1642, when the King's impoverishment forced him to put himself at Parliament's mercy, did the City and the Puritans gain the power to close the haunts of idleness.

The players performed their own small part in the downfall. By the end of the period the leading companies had their eyes more on the rewards of playing for the Court than for idle apprentices, and they readily assisted in the lavish expenditure of the royal bounty on entertainment. The aims and objects of the players changed drastically through the period, reflecting the shifts in the social structure which brought about the revolution in society at large. Under Elizabeth the players might be summoned to Court to make a contribution to the Christmas festivities, and they might more often be called on to entertain a noble or gentleman's friends at his private house. But the plays that were performed on such occasions were not different from the fare the players gave to the citizenry who could not afford such expensive exclusiveness. The idle artisan's admission fee was a minimal penny. For this he had equally the choice of Shakespeare or the baiting of bulls and bears, the same choice as the Queen. The Queen sent for the players or her bear-warden, the players enticed the apprentices with hand-written playbills posted up around the town, on which they might read where plays were available (we don't really know whether they were told *what* plays were being performed). One of the few handbills which have survived shows what the rival kind of entertainment for the apprentices was. It is an undated advertisement for an afternoon at the Beargarden, probably from early in the reign of James (*Henslowe Papers*, p. 106). Written in a large, plain hand, it says

Tomorrowe beinge Thursdaie shalbe seen at the Beargardin on the banckside a great Mach plaid by the gamstirs of Essex who hath chalenged all comers what soever to plaie v dogges at the single beare for v pounds and also to wearie a bull dead at the stake and for your better content shall have plasant sport with the horse and ape and whiping of the blind beare

Vivat Rex

This kind of show, and its theatrical equivalents, was available to high and low alike in the sixteenth century. Except for what the intermittently active boy companies provided, it could be said that the basic penny fee bought the apprentice as much as Elizabeth herself could buy, and entertainment moreover of exactly the same kind.

In the seventeenth century, under the Stuarts, the picture was modified. The public amphitheatres continued to offer a pennyworth of playgoing or bear-baiting throughout the period, but the Court's taste changed, and with that change went an increase in admission prices which necessarily introduced class distinctions into the theatre repertories. The companies performing at the indoor halls used by the boys from 1599 and by the adult players from 1609 charged prices ranging from a minimal sixpence to two shillings and sixpence or more, compared with the penny to shilling price range of the amphitheatres. This was through a time when artisan wages were constant and the cost of living rising. It created something like a social and financial hierarchy in the theatre world.

The industrious artisan throughout the period earned about six shillings a week (6s. 5¾d. for masons, 6s. 2¾d. for carpenters).[6] Apprentices earned very considerably less than that, though board and lodging were provided in the terms of their indentures. To such artisans a good food diet cost as much as half the weekly wage, in Tudor times. The Tudor soldier's daily food allowance was twenty-four ounces of wheat bread and two-thirds of a gallon of beer, each costing a penny; two pounds of beef or mutton (cod or herring on fish days), at a cost of twopence; half a pound of butter, and a pound of cheese. The cost of this diet under Elizabeth was about sixpence, but food prices never recovered from the seven successive bad harvests at the end of the century, and rose by about twenty-five per cent in the early seventeenth

Fig. 1. Hollar's 'Long View' of the Bankside. Etching from Wenceslas Hollar's *Long View of London*. The captions for the two theatres are thought to have been accidentally reversed.

8

century. By the mid-century beef was as much as fivepence a pound. Bread and circuses went together in price throughout the period, but the quantity of bread that could be bought for the price of admission to the playhouse steadily declined.

The price of manufactured articles, as always in a predominantly subsistence economy, was markedly higher than the cost of food. It is difficult to be specific about prices, because they were likely to fluctuate more according to quality than by the type of commodity, and because prices also varied according to the social status of the purchaser. A pair of silk stockings might cost £2 or £4, depending on quality and purchaser. A woman's gown might cost anything from £7 to £20 or more. The Earl of Leicester paid £543 for seven doublets and two cloaks, at an average cost for each item rather higher than the price Shakespeare paid for a house in Stratford. The same Earl's funeral cost £3,000, five times what it cost to construct the second Blackfriars playhouse. The tendency of the better playing companies to cater for the higher income brackets is understandable.

It is difficult to generalise about the distribution of income through the country, and the social patterns to which it relates, and even more difficult to locate the playhouse audiences amongst those social patterns. Statistics are inadequate and potentially misleading. None the less, a broad picture does appear, suggesting that while the poor, and particularly the London artisan poor, grew poorer, the number of the rich grew markedly, and especially in London. The famous rise of the seventeenth-century gentry drew wealth both from the relatively few very rich noblemen of the sixteenth century, and from the poor through the inflation of prices and the stability of wages. Trade especially prospered the London merchant. The East India Company, floated in 1600 with a capital of £72,000, brought its investors a minimum return of 121 per cent on each voyage.[7] In that year, 1600, there were estimated to be in the country as a whole sixty thousand yeomen and others with incomes of £40 to £100, well above the artisan and schoolmaster level of £15. Ten thousand had incomes of £300 to £500. The average income of nobles was £2,000 to £3,000, which was about what a prosperous merchant could rise to.[8] A good deal of the wealth from about that date turned up in the form of money, not land, which was the traditional form that wealth took until the sixteenth century. Drake's bullion ships indirectly helped the players, because the more that wealth came to hand in the readily exchangeable form of money, the more idle gallants, hangers-on at Court and Inns of Court lawyers were created to seek the entertainment the players were selling. Inevitably, the moneyed audience came to over-ride the penny-paying apprentices in the eyes of the players in the course of the seventeenth century.

The different repertories performed at the various seventeenth-century playhouses confirm the evidence of the economic changes.

The 'citizen playhouses', the amphitheatres in the suburbs, notably the Fortune and the Red Bull to the north of the city, generally went on with the repertories established in the previous century. Marlowe's plays survived through at these playhouses until the closure. Heywood was the leading dramatist at the Red Bull, and his lavishly staged plays, or displays, of the Four Ages mark the high point of achievement for the companies who catered to the citizen audiences. On the whole the plays were heroic and spectacular rather than romantic, and the comedy was broad rather than high or witty. Dekker's *Shoemaker's Holiday* might be taken as reasonably typical of one kind of play in this repertory. It glorifies the 'gentle craft' of shoemaking, has journeymen and a master-shoemaker as its heroes, the latter ending in triumph with his election as Lord Mayor of London. The whole play is an enormously cheerful celebration of the citizen virtues of goodwill and hard work. The romantic interest significantly crosses social barriers, with a young noble disguising himself as a shoemaker in order to woo, successfully, the daughter of the Lord Mayor. In this it follows the tradition of such plays as *Friar Bacon and Friar Bungay*, or *Fair Em the Miller's Daughter of Manchester, with the Love of William the Conqueror*, and was imitated in plays like *The Fair Maid of Bristow*.

The implicit acceptance of social mobility in these plays was sharply denied in terms as explicit as they well could be, in Massinger's *A New Way to Pay Old Debts*. This was a play written for an indoor playhouse and a different kind of audience, early in Caroline times. The villain of the piece, the grasping middle-class mercantilist Overreach, tries to persuade the noble Lord Lovell to marry his beautiful (and virtuous) daughter, Margaret. For the sake of the plot Lord Lovell seems to concur, but afterwards he says emphatically (IV.i):

> Were *Overreach*'s stat's thrice centupl'd; his daughter
> Millions of degrees, much fairer than she is,
> (Howe're I might urge presidents to excuse me)
> I would not so adulterate my blood
> By marrying *Margaret*, and so leave my issue
> Made up of several pieces, one part skarlet,
> And the other *London* blew. In my owne tombe
> I will interre my name first.

Scarlet was the colour worn by nobles and Court officials, blue the merchant's colour. Lovell is applauded for his statement.

Other types of play popular in the citizen repertory included the wide-ranging heroics of adventure plays like Heywood's *Four Prentices of London*, which depicts four apprentices, all of whom are nobles in disguise ('all high borne, / Yet of the Citty-trades they have no scorne'). They march across Europe and Asia performing the feats of knight-errantry which had already been long popular in the chivalric romances produced for the sixteenth-century reading public.[9] The citizen taste for this kind of romantic heroics was burlesqued by Beaumont in *The Knight of the Burning Pestle*, written for the private theatre repertory in 1607. Beaumont's burlesque is very much in the manner of *Don Quixote*, which was almost contemporary with it. The play shows a citizen and his wife being fooled by a sophisticated boy company at the Blackfriars into exposing their taste for *Don Quixote*-like feats of improbable valour. At each pause in the play the citizens lay new demands on the players for feats of arms from their apprentice, whom they have thrust on the players to take the leading part. At the beginning of Act IV, for instance, they confer on what they would like to follow:

CITIZEN. What shall we have *Rafe* do now boy?

BOY. You shall have what you will sir.

CITIZEN. Why so sir, go and fetch me him then, and let the Sophy of *Persia* come and christen him a childe.

BOY. Beleeve me sir, that will not doe so well, 'tis stale, it has beene had before at the red Bull.

WIFE. *George* let *Rafe* travell over great hils, and let him be very weary, and come to the King of *Cracovia's* house, covered with blacke velvet, and there let the Kings daughter stand in her window all in beaten gold, combing her golden locks with a combe of Ivory, and let her spy *Rafe*, and fall in love with him, and come downe to him, and carry him into her fathers house, and then let *Rafe* talke with her.

CITIZEN. Well said *Nell*, it shal be so: boy let's ha't done quickly.

BOY. Sir, if you will imagine all this to be done already, you shall heare them talke together: but wee cannot present a house covered with blacke velvet, and a Lady in beaten gold.

CITIZEN. Sir boy, lets ha't as you can then.

BOY. Besides it will shew ill-favouredly to have a Grocers prentice to court a kings daughter.

CITIZEN. Will it so sir? you are well read in Histories: I pray you what was sir *Dagonet*? was not he prentice to a Grocer in London? read the play of the *Foure Prentices of London*, where they tosse their pikes so: I pray you fetch him in sir, fetch him in.

BOY. It shall be done, it is not our fault gentlemen.

The incident with the Sophy of Persia was in *The Travels of the Three English Brothers*, by Day and Wilkins, performed at the Red Bull in 1607. Sir Dagonet was actually King Arthur's jester.

Along with the satire on the citizen taste for improbable heroics in Beaumont's play went a more substantial satire on citizen commercialism. The main plot is a play called *The London Merchant*, and is a comic inversion of the Prodigal Son theme popular with citizens. Plays on this theme in the sixteenth century perverted the biblical parable of forgiveness for transgression into moral tales stressing the virtue of financial prudence. The emphasis was laid not on the father's forgiving his son, but on the son's realisation of his error, and his conversion into the ways of financial prudence.[10] Beaumont's burlesque of this theme gives the victory to a prodigal father, who wins all the commercially-minded characters over to his view, which is expressed in a song Beaumont wrote for the prodigal father to sing (II.ix):

> 'Tis mirth that fils the veines with bloud,
> More then wine, or sleepe, or food.
> Let each man keepe his heart at ease,
> No man dies of that disease.
> He that would his body keepe
> From diseases, must not weepe,
> But whoever laughes and sings,
> . . . contented lives for aye,
> The more he laughes, the more he may.

Beaumont denies as explicitly as he can the merchant's virtues of hard work and care for money. His assumption that such values will be mocked by the 'gentlemen' of the audience points to the social gap that was yawning in the early years of the century.

In the first decade of the century several of the indoor-theatre plays had what Beaumont called 'girds at citizens'. Two or three years after Beaumont's play Nathaniel Field, who probably acted in it, wrote a play of his own for the company, *A Woman is a Weathercock*, in which one player says to another (II.i):

> Ile thinke
> As abjectly of thee, as any Mongrill
> Bred in the Citty; Such a Cittizen
> As the Playes flout still.

The boy companies at the indoor playhouses provided largely witty and satirical comedies for their 'gentlemen' audiences. When they disappeared from the forefront of the scene after 1609 there seems to have followed a period of uncertainty in which girds at citizens were muted. Shakespeare's company had taken over the leading indoor play-house, and their repertory had never been anti-citizen (*The Merry Wives of Windsor* is a beautiful example of a citizen play, ending as it does with a gentleman marrying a wealthy merchant's daughter). *Henry VIII* was produced by Shakespeare's company at both its indoor and its public playhouse: the Blackfriars (where *The Knight of the Burning Pestle* appeared) in winter, and the Globe in summer. Its Epilogue had this to say:

> 'Tis ten to one this play can never please
> All that are here. Some come to take their ease,
> And sleep an act or two; but those, we fear,
> We've frighted with our trumpets; so, 'tis clear,
> They'll say 'tis naught; others, to hear the city
> Abused extremely and to cry 'That's witty!'
> Which we have not done neither.

Later on, however, the taste of the indoor theatre audiences for wit and satire reasserted itself, and by Caroline times the distance between the repertories favoured by the citizens at the northern public playhouses, and the gallants and Inns-of-Court men at the private playhouses in the city was fairly distinct. The wealthier taste was for wit, salacity ('sallets'), a closer fidelity to the unities of time and place, and more complex emotional patterns in romance and tragedy alike. In tragedy the world frequently appears as pervasively corrupt and corrupting, where all motives are expedient and evil brings about the downfall of everyone, as in Middleton's *Women Beware Women*, or Massinger's *The Roman Actor*. In romances the milieu has a pastoral element, the golden world of Sidney's *Arcadia*, especially in the Beaumont and Fletcher plays. Fashions changed in the more aristocratic repertories, however, and it is the changeability more than the principles embodied in the plays which marks the difference from citizen repertories.[11]

On the repertories and the social divisions they reflect, as everywhere else in the picture, we must beware of oversimplification. Satire on contemporary life was not a feature only of the more aristocratic repertories. A letter of 1601 from the Privy Council rapped the players at the Curtain on the knuckles for just that. 'We do understand', they wrote,

that certaine players that use to recyte their playes at the Curtaine in Moore-feildes do represent upon the stage in their interludes the persons of some gentlemen of good desert and quallity that are yet alive under obscure manner, but yet in such sorte as all the hearers may take notice both of the matter and the persons that are meant thereby.[12]

The Curtain players shortly after this became the Red Bull players. It was not only gentlemen of good desert who were their targets, either. In 1638 the Red Bull company found itself in trouble for a play which lampooned one of the most notorious of the monopolist merchants, Sir William Abell, a City Alderman.[13] Clearly, the identification of 'citizen' playhouses does not also imply an identification with City interests. Nor can one even identify the interests of the citizen playhouses simply with the apprentices against their masters the City Fathers. A traditional festive activity for apprentice mobs was to wreck the bawdy-houses, in the interests of rough morality if not of rough justice. On occasions they turned their reforming zeal on the neighbouring playhouses. In 1617 the new indoor playhouse to which a Red Bull company had just moved was wrecked by such a mob. In the words of a contemporary account,

The Prentizes on Shrove Tewsday last, to the nomber of 3. or 4000 comitted extreame insolencies; part of this nomber, taking their course for Wapping, did there pull downe to the grownd 4 houses, spoiled all the goods therein, defaced many others, & a Justice of the Peace coming to appease them, while he was reading a Proclamacion, had his head broken with a brick batt. Th' other part, making for Drury Lane, where lately a newe playhouse is erected, they besett the house round, broke in, wounded divers of the players, broke open their trunckes, & whatt apparrell, bookes, or other things they found, they burnt & cutt in peeces; & not content herewith, gott on the top of the house, & untiled it, & had not the Justices of Peace & Sherife levied an aide, & hindred their purpose, they would have laid that house likewise even with the grownd. In this skyrmishe one prentise was slaine, being shott throughe the head with a pistoll, & many other of their fellowes were sore hurt, & such of them as are taken his Majestie hath commaunded shal be executed for example sake.[14]

No particular motive for the attack has been found. As a sign of hostility by a group of apprentices to the new house of a company which played a citizen repertory, it may serve as a warning against oversimplifying the social background.

The social divisions and allegiances were complex, and in numerous respects obscure. On the citizen side the union of Puritans and City Fathers in opposition to playing was counterbalanced by the continued patronage of the northern playhouses by citizens and apprentices, and made complex by the ambiguities of apprentice behaviour. On the wealthy side, the satires against citizens and the attachment to the pleasures of the Court are part of a more consistent picture. There were sharp comments about the foolishness of the royal taste for masques and similar shows of make-believe golden worlds, of gorgeous costumes and trompe-l'oeil scenery. The Mannerist artificialities of masques were by no means a universally popular fashion even in Court circles. There were stern warnings from the chief author of the Court masques, Ben Jonson, that the pleasures they gave should not be purely pleasure. As he wrote in the prefatory note to his masque *Love's Triumph*,

all Repraesentations, especially those of this nature in court, publique Spectacles, eyther have bene, or ought to be the mirrors of mans life, whose ends, for the excellence of their exhibiters (as being the donatives, of great Princes, to their people) ought always to carry a mixture of profit, with them, no lesse then delight.[15]

On the whole the divisions within the Court party were rather those of rival playgoing factions than of friends and enemies of the theatre.

Even in the Court, however, some curious allegiances came to light during the Civil War. The fourth Earl of Pembroke was Lord Chamberlain from 1625 to 1641, the member of the Privy Council to whom the general overseeing of royal entertainment and the London theatres was given. He was one of the 'incomparable pair' to whom Shakespeare's First Folio was dedicated in 1623. His own household provided some of the very expensive play-acting shows at Court while he was Lord Chamberlain. And yet in the Civil War he joined the Parliamentary Party against the King, the party which closed the play-houses. Political allegiance was not to be decided on any such minor matter as the availability of light entertainment, of course. The Earl's private sympathy with theatre affairs had nothing to do with his responsibilities as a man of affairs. But he does make the business of drawing a clear picture of the social basis to the theatre world a little more difficult.

In describing the general outlines of a picture of the period, it remains now to take some notice of the suppliers to the playing companies, the playwrights themselves. Much the largest body of play-writing in the Shakespearean period was hack-work. In the commercial conditions of the time, when all that was asked of the playwrights was to supply an entertainment industry, it could hardly have been anything else. What has survived into this century is probably not a large proportion of the total output, though it is likely to include most of the cream. Certainly what is read today is only the cream, and being so it can mislead us about the rest.

The grammar schools set up in the sixteenth century were producing scholars for whom there was no work. The theatre's appetite for plays was the most obvious source of income for such men, talented drama-tists or not. And although the demand for plays was great, the number of hack-writers able to supply them was greater still. So it was a buyer's market for plays. Playwrights were the servants of the players, in economic servitude to them. The Cambridge scholars who wrote the Parnassus plays said so from the safety of their university (2 *Return from Parnassus*):

> And must the basest trade yeeld us reliefe?
> Must we be practis'd to those leaden spouts,
> That nought downe vent but what they do receive? [IV. iv.]

There was more money in playing than in play-writing:

> With mouthing words that better wits have framed,
> They purchase lands, and now Esquiers are made.   [V. i.]

That Shakespeare died better off than many of his fellow-dramatists is probably because he had a share in a company of players and in their property to finance him.

Of Shakespeare we really know almost nothing substantial, except that besides being a faithful playwright to his company he was an exceptionally good businessman. In his early years, before 1594 when he joined the Chamberlain's Men and made his fortune with them, he dallied with aristocratic patronage as well as playing, and no doubt received good money for it. But the survival of plays dating from 1594 and earlier is significant. When they were incorporated in the First Folio in 1623 they were the property of the Chamberlain's Men's successors, the King's Men. Plays were then the property of the company which bought them from the playwright. That the King's Men should own the pre-1594 plays suggests that Shakespeare somehow kept the ownership of the early plays from the companies he then belonged to. Through the early years when fortune's wheel was spinning with uncomfortable speed for the companies it was obviously wise to keep playbooks as financial assets, and take them from company to company. Presumably this is how they ended up with the Chamberlain's Men. They may well have been the capital with which Shakespeare bought himself a share in the company. The profit which that brought him, and his later investments as a Stratford property-owner, are well known.

Shakespeare became in effect the Chamberlain's Men's resident playwright. The plays surviving in the First Folio and such accurate dating as can be made for them suggest that he wrote one serious play and one light play a year, more or less, throughout his active writing career. Another player-playwright, Heywood, worked with Queen Anne's Men, the Red Bull company of 1605–19. In 1633 he claimed to have had 'either an entire hand, or at the least a maine finger' in the writing of two hundred and twenty plays.[16]

The appetite for plays and the evident commercial incentive to produce in quantity led to a good deal of collaborative writing. As many as four or five authors might contribute to the text of a single play. Phillip Henslowe, one of the best-known and most prosperous theatre impresarios, kept in close touch with several hack-writers. He frequently employed them to patch on additions or alterations to plays he had bought for his companies, or to old plays which needed freshening up. He paid Ben Jonson to write additions to Thomas Kyd's *Spanish Tragedy* (*Henslowe's Diary*, pp. 182, 203). Some authors shopped around with their services, others stayed more or less literally indebted to one impresario. Jonson was incapable of maintaining good relations with any one employer for long. He moved from Henslowe to the Chamberlain's Men, from them to the boys of Blackfriars, then to and fro between Shakespeare's Men and the boys for a decade, and to other companies thereafter.

Drummond of Hawthornden's pen-portrait of Jonson is the most vivid description of the personality of a playwright in that turbulent age. At the tail of a set of notes he made recording Jonson's outpourings to him on a visit to Scotland in 1618, Drummond wrote

He is a great lover and praiser of himself, a contemner and Scorner of others, given rather to losse a friend, than a jest, jealous of every word and action of those about him (especiallie after drink) which is one of the Elements in which he liveth, a dissembler of ill parts which raigne in him, a bragger of some good that he wanteth, thinketh nothing well bot what either he himself, or some of his friends and Countrymen hath said or done. he is passionately kynde and angry, carelesse either to gaine or keep, vindicative, but if he be well answered, at himself.[17]

The 'tribe' of convivial souls who drank with him and talked about their plays with him included Beaumont and Fletcher. They stood for poetry before money, and wit before all else.

Jonson was a more markedly opiniated poet than most of his fellow-writers. His *Catiline* of 1611 is almost certainly a fictitious presentation of the Gunpowder Plot, and a defence of his own dubious part in it (like Marlowe before him, he seems to have found one source of finance in spying for the government).[18] He was a violent controversialist against several of his fellow-poets in his contributions to the so-called Poetomachia, or War of the Theatres, in 1601–2.[19] With all this, however, he was also and always a passionate moralist, a running commentary on the follies of his times. Whatever the players made out of what he sold them, his entertainments were also statements of opinion, moral and political. The man who could write under a Stuart that 'A *good King* is a publike Servant'[20] was brave as well as outspoken, and no acquiescent royalist. Jonson was imprisoned in 1597 for a seditious play, in 1598 for killing a man (a player) in a duel, and in 1605 for another play, *Eastward Ho!*, which he wrote along with Chapman and Marston for the boys of Blackfriars, and in which he satirised the King and his Scottish entourage.

Other playwrights were less loudly opiniated than Jonson, but not much less forthright. Phillip Massinger, who wrote for several companies, including the King's Men, between 1613 and 1639, on the whole wrote plays like his *The City Madam* (for the King's Men at Blackfriars in about 1632). It has a curiously ambivalent attitude to its citizen characters. It begins with a situation like those of the satires, showing up citizen greed and folly, but it ends with citizen values triumphant. The same author's *The Roman Actor*, however, written in 1625–6 at the beginning of the second Stuart's reign, is a veritable mirror for magistrates, a trenchant sermon to the new ruler and a playwright's manifesto. On the political front it sets out the dangers of wrong rule, displayed in the conveniently distant setting of ancient Rome, where the chronic problem of the divine right of Kings was irrelevant. And defending its author's own interests it puts up a spirited case for players and playing. Players are necessary members of the commonwealth, says the title character at the beginning of the play,

> That with delight joyne profit and endeavour
> To build their mindes up faire, and on the Stage
> Decipher to the life what honours waite
> On good, and glorious actions, and the shame
> That treads upon the heeles of vice.

The profit was of course moral and educational, not financial.

The chapters which follow in this book present the backdrop to the plays in the fullest practicable detail. The history of the playing companies provides the essential story of what happened through the seventy years between the granting of the first royal patent in 1574 and the closure in 1642. The next chapter describes the players themselves, their social backgrounds and their playing. The playhouses which they built for themselves once they had royal protection, and the staging of plays in the playhouses are described next; and finally a look at the audiences for the plays fills in some details of the general picture set out in the Introduction.

2. The Companies

The 'Acte for the punishment of Vacabondes' of 1572 served the companies of players much as it was designed to serve the commonwealth of England as a whole. It authorised the better members of the profession to pursue their trade and turned the idle and poor members to higher things. It was an early step in the progress of the professional players from strolling entertainers, who never performed in the same place twice running, to permanently established repertory companies, with enormous financial investments backing them and a position in London guaranteed by the King himself. The statute of 1572 required each company to be authorised by one noble or two judicial dignitaries of the realm:

All and everye persone and persones beynge whole and mightye in Body and able to labour, havinge not Land or Maister, nor using any lawfull Marchaundize Crafte or Mysterye whereby hee or shee might get his or her Lyvinge, and can gyve no reckninge howe he or shee dothe lawfully get his or her Lyvinge; & all Fencers Bearewardes Comon Players in Enterludes & Minstrels, not belonging to any Baron of this Realme or towardes any other honorable Personage of greater Degree; all Juglers Pedlars Tynkers and Petye Chapmen; whiche seid Fencers Bearewardes Comon Players in Enterludes Mynstrels Juglers Pedlers Tynkers & Petye Chapmen, shall wander abroade and have not Lycense of two Justices of the Peace at the leaste, whereof one to be of the Quorum, when and in what Shier they shall happen to wander...shalbee taken adjudged and deemed Roges Vacaboundes and Sturdy Beggers.[1]

Ordinary gentlemen who wished to support a company of entertainers now ran the risk of losing them as vagabonds. A further statute of 1598 took away the licensing power from the magistrates too, leaving only great nobles with the authority to lend their names to the players. And when James came to the throne in 1603 he took the patronage of the chief London companies into his own family—one for himself, one for the Queen, one for the heir apparent, Prince Henry.[2]

Players were a royal pleasure, and to please royalty was a major aim of the companies. The story of the companies between 1572 and 1642 is one of increasing royal favour and protection, from the first 1572 statute which gave warrant to their quality, through the accolade of direct royal patronage after 1603, to the final period when the royal protection ceased to be meaningful. There is, none the less, despite the royal favours and the origins of the companies in employment as entertainers—adult mummers or boy choristers[3]—no question but that the profit motive was totally predominant. The companies were independent commercial organisations, not doing what pleasure-bent lord or royalty commanded, but going where and doing what brought most money and best audiences. Company organisation was commercial, a core of shareholders and decision-makers, and a periphery of hired hands, backed in many cases by a theatre and property-owning impresario who supplied ready cash in return for a share of the takings. Success meant London, a much larger playing membership than the travelling companies could afford, and the two essentials for continued success, financial backing and a permanent playing-place. The honey was in London, and the bees proved tenacious in clinging to it. Usually what dislodged them was a total prohibition on London playing because of the plague, when they had to resume travelling. In the later years it might be the impresario who broke them up to form new combinations of players more amenable to his financial terms. There were always new combinations ready to swarm in.

As the quality of the common players grew in the course of the sixteenth century, and as they developed from mumming and tumbling to acting, so their recognition by the government increased, and so likewise the hostility to them from the City Fathers. Their status was a matter for hostilities between the Crown and the lord mayor and aldermen for nearly a whole century before 1642. The threat to the common players from the statute of 1572 was a very real one, since the City Fathers had long before given notice of their willingness to enforce it. Primarily it was a renewal of the old series of statutes against retainers, which restricted the number of liveried servants which a noble might employ to those of his immediate household. Technically therefore the companies, if they were to protect themselves against the municipalities, had to enroll themselves in such a household, and carry their patron's livery as his personal retainers; though of course they would not, except for specific services in entertaining him, receive any wage for their position. James Burbage, writing on behalf of his company to the Earl of Leicester in 1572, made this very clear:

To the right honorable Earle of Lecester, their good lord and master.
    Maye yt please your honour to understande that forasmuche as there is a certayne Proclamation out for the revivinge of a Statute as touchinge retayners, as youre Lordshippe knoweth better than we can enforme you thereof: We therfore, your humble Servaunts and daylye Oratours your players, for avoydinge all inconvenients that maye growe by reason of the saide Statute, are bold to trouble your Lordshippe with this our Suite, humblie desiringe your honor that (as you have bene alwayes our good Lord and Master) you will now vouchsaffe to reteyne us at this present as your houshold Servaunts and daylie wayters, not that we meane to crave

any further stipend or benefite at your Lordshippes hands but our lyveries as we have had, and also your honors License to certifye that we are your houshold Servaunts when we shall have occasion to travayle amongst our frendes as we do usuallye once a yere, and as other noble-mens Players do and have done in tyme past, Wherebie we maye enjoye our facultie in your Lordshippes name as we have done hertofore.[4]

The protection of a patron, especially one so powerful and so accommodating as Leicester, was of evident value. Still more so was the explicit royal protection which the same company was offered, unprecedentedly, two years later, in a patent of 10 May 1574. This was the first royal patent for a company of adult players. It specified the permissible scope of the company in unambiguous terms, and came to serve as a model for all patents granted subsequently:

Elizabeth by the grace of God quene of England, &c. To all Justices, Mayors, Sheriffes, Baylyffes, head Constables, under Constables, and all other our officers and mynisters gretinge. Knowe ye that we of oure especiall grace, certen knowledge, and mere mocion have licenced and auctorised, and by these presentes do licence and auctorise, oure lovinge Subjectes, James Burbage, John Perkyn, John Lanham, William Johnson, and Roberte Wilson, servauntes to oure trustie and welbeloved Cosen and Counseyllor the Earle of Leycester, to use, exercise, and occupie the arte and facultye of playenge Commedies, Tragedies, Enterludes, stage playes, and such other like as they have alredie used and studied, or hereafter shall use and studie, aswell for the recreacion of oure loving subjectes, as for oure solace and pleasure when we shall thincke good to see them, as also to use and occupie all such Instrumentes as they have alredie practised, or hereafter shall practise, for and during our pleasure. And the said Commedies, Tragedies, Enterludes, and stage playes, to gether with their musicke, to shewe, publishe, exercise, and occupie to their best commoditie during all the terme aforesaide, aswell within oure Citie of London and liberties of the same, as also within the liberties and fredomes of anye oure Cities, townes, Bouroughes &c whatsoever as without the same, thoroughte oure Realme of England. Willynge and commaundinge yow and everie of yowe, as ye tender our pleasure, to permytte and suffer them herein withoute anye yowre lettes, hynderaunce, or molestacion duringe the terme aforesaid, anye acte, statute, proclamacion, or commaundement heretofore made, or hereafter to be made, to the contrarie notwithstandinge. Provyded that the said Commedies, Tragedies, enterludes, and stage playes be by the master of oure Revells for the tyme beynge before sene & allowed, and that the same be not published or shewen in the tyme of common prayer, or in the tyme of greate and common plague in oure said Citye of London. In wytnes whereof &c. wytnes oure selfe at Westminster the xth daye of Maye.[5]

The players in all probability gave their thanks to Elizabeth when Leicester laid on his famous entertainment at Kenilworth in the following year, and they performed at Court over Christmas in both 1574 and 1575.

They had other business in London too. With such a warrant in his hands James Burbage had no hesitation in taking the next step towards real security, the establishment of the first permanent, custom-built playing headquarters in London itself. His playhouse called the Theatre was constructed and in regular use by early in 1577, and its neighbour the Curtain soon after. It was not as easy as that, of course. The City Fathers' opposition to the players was very much in evidence between 1572 and 1579, and Burbage was cautious if not discreet in situating his playhouse just outside the City limits. The London foot-hold and the corollary London profits were so much the more protected thereby.

For the next few years Leicester's Men and the other companies able to reach London, Sussex's, Warwick's, Essex's, and Oxford's, continued the pattern of playing in London while they could, and travelling each summer. They played at first only once or twice a week, but the Puritans were soon complaining of a greater frequency.[6] The Puritan preachers and City Fathers alike renewed their attacks in 1582-3, and were given ammunition by an Act of God on 13 January 1583 at Paris Garden when some scaffolding collapsed, killing eight spectators and injuring many more.[7] This was at a bear-baiting, but all forms of entertainment were branded alike in City eyes. It may have been this event and the outcry it caused, as much as the scramble of players around London, which led Sir Francis Walsingham on behalf of the government to depute the Master of the Revels to cream off the current acting talent and form one predominant company with the Queen's own name and patronage. As Edmond Howes later described it,

Comedians and stage-players of former time were very poor and ignorant in respect of these of this time: but being now grown very skilful and exquisite actors for all matters, they were entertained into the service of divers great lords: out of which companies there were twelve of the best chosen, and, at the request of Sir Francis Walsingham, they were sworn the queens servants and were allowed wages and liveries as grooms of the chamber: and until this yeare 1583, the queene had no players. Among these twelve players were two rare men, viz. Thomas [i.e. Robert] Wilson, for a quicke, delicate, refined, extemporall witt, and Richard Tarleton, for a wondrous plentifull pleasant extemporall wit, he was the wonder of his time.[8]

The Queen's Company, possessing as it then did all the most famous players—Wilson, John Laneham, and probably Tarlton from Lei-cester's, John Dutton from Oxford's, John Bentley and John Singer—held its predominance for the next five years. Its existence under the royal protection may well have helped the City Fathers to mollify their attitude to the players, at least in what they wrote to the govern-ment. In 1585 they produced a relatively modest list of requirements for the 'toleration' of players, including restrictions on playing during time of plague and restrictions in the authorisation of companies. They summed up their requests as follows:

That they hold them content with playeing in private houses at weddings etc without publike assemblies.

If more be thought good to be tolerated: that then they be restrained to the orders in the act of common Counsell tempore Hawes.

That they play not openly till the whole [plague] death in London have been by xx daies under 50 a weke, nor longer than it shal so continue.

That no playes be on the sabbat.

That no playeing be on holydaies but after evening prayer: nor any received into the auditorie till after evening prayer.

That no playeing be in the dark, nor continue any such time but as any of the auditorie may returne to their dwellings in London before sonne set, or at least before it be dark.

That the Quenes players only be tolerated, and of them their number and certaine names to be notified in your Lordships lettres to the L. Maior and to the Justices of Middlesex and Surrey. And those her players not to divide themselves into several companies.

That for breaking any of the orders, their toleration cesse.[9]

With this on paper, the situation of the companies in London and the relations of City and Court government remained unaltered for a few years.

The Puritan attacks on the stage were aimed fairly precisely at the purveyors of entertainment such as bull- and bear-baiting, tumbling, fencing displays and plays ('Theaters, Curtines, Heaving houses, Rifling boothes, Bowling alleyes, and such places').[10] Nor did they entirely exclude the boy players attached to the singing schools of St Paul's and the Chapel Royal at Windsor, and at such schools as the Merchant Taylors'. There are records of Puritan attacks specifically aimed at them from as early as 1569.[11] Even in the academic exercise of playing the profit-motive was rearing its head, and in 1573 plays were banned at Merchant Taylors' because of the rowdyism of the audience. They were commercial shows open to the public. Therefore they were on a par with and in competition with the adult companies, not only at Court, where they had traditionally entertained the Crown with plays, but also in London.

The Chapel Children moved into the City to a playhouse in the Blackfriars precinct, which was at that time still free of the City's juris-diction, in 1576, the year that the first adult players' theatre was built. This 'first' Blackfriars playhouse was owned by Richard Farrant, deputy to William Hunnis as Master of the Chapel Children. He appears to have taken over Hunnis's duties in 1576 largely in order to run the Children at the playhouse as a commercial enterprise. He can have taken up the lease of the Blackfriars property in that year for no other reason. His company was listed along with the adults in 1578 in a Privy Council protection order.[12] In 1580 he died, and his company was eventually taken in hand by Henry Evans, a scrivener, and John Lyly, the playwright, presumably for similarly commercial purposes. The

Paul's Children at about the same time, 1582, lost their Master, Sebastian Westcote, under whom the commercial aspects of their playing had not been important. After Westcote's death the boys seem to have joined forces with the Blackfriars company, as they had done for Court performances on occasions in the past.

In the course of 1584 the company was deprived of the Blackfriars playhouse, and consequently disappeared from the commercial stage. The Paul's Children resumed activities under their own identity in the same year, under a new Master, Thomas Giles, with the services of Lyly as their playwright. They performed regularly at Court up to 1590. In that year Lyly's part in the Martin Marprelate religious controversies, and his company who had helped to publicise his contributions, were officially disowned and all the playing companies for a time were suppressed. The adult companies were considerably dampened by the experience, and the boy company did not resurface at all.

The adult companies were still rising and falling with some regularity. The Queen's Men were depressed after the death of their famous clown in 1588, and suffered a number of desertions. Worcester's were their closest rivals through the five years they were on top, and it was from Worcester's rather than the Queen's that the leading actors of the next decade, and in particular one, Edward Alleyn (see pl. I), emerged. From 1588 two years of rapidly changing fortunes reshuffled the company membership until in 1590 two companies amalgamated to take the predominant position on the London scene. This was the joint enterprise of the Admiral's and Strange's Men. It lasted until the last of the major reshuffles in 1594, out of which emerged the most successful company of all, Shakespeare's.

The membership of Shakespeare's company and of the company which shared a monopoly of London playing with it after 1594 seems largely to have been drawn from the amalgamated company of 1590–4, and it is illuminating to trace the comings and goings of company membership through these years. We can pick up the trail at Elsinore, of all places, in June 1586, where three players, Will Kempe the clown, George Bryan and Thomas Pope are recorded as playing for Danish royalty, probably after serving the Earl of Leicester in the Netherlands. In September Kempe returned to England while Bryan and Pope went to play for the Elector of Saxony. In 1590 the latter two reappear in the records of the Strange's–Admiral's amalgamation at the Theatre, probably under the leadership of Edward Alleyn. Their names are among the actors named in the plot of the second part of *The Seven Deadly Sins*, which survives among the Alleyn papers at Dulwich College and which has been attributed to the amalgamation in this year.[13] Of Bryan and Pope's fellow-actors in this play, two (Richard Cowley and Augustine Phillips) stayed with them in the Strange's part of the amalgamated company until the four of them went to form the Chamberlain's Men, Shakespeare's company, in 1594. Will Kempe rejoined his former fellows while the amalgamation still lasted, some time before 1593, since he is recorded on the title-page of *A Knack to Know a Knave* (of 1593 or earlier) as having performed his 'merrimentes' in it along with Alleyn. A warrant from the Privy Council of 6 May 1593 permitting the amalgamated company to travel names Alleyn as the Lord Admiral's Man, with Bryan, Pope, Kempe, Phillips, and John Heminges, as the leading Strange's Men.[14] Nothing of Heminges's earlier history is known except that he might have been a Queen's Man; he could have been a long-term member of the amalgamation, his name not appearing in the *Seven Deadly Sins* plot because he played one of the roles for which no player is named. A letter of Alleyn's written from Bristol to his wife in London during the tour mentions Richard Cowley as another member. All of these except Alleyn moved into Shakespeare's company, the Chamberlain's Men, when it was formed in 1594.

The amalgamation was a curious kind of company organisation even for a period of such sharply fluctuating fortunes as the companies suffered over these years. Alleyn had been a Worcester's Man for six or more years up to 1589, when he seems to have joined a new grouping calling itself the Admiral's. The group was suppressed in 1590, possibly because of the players' involvement in the Marprelate troubles, and yet Alleyn retained his personal status as the Lord Admiral's servant, and some of his fellows seem to have retained their separate identity as Admiral's Men with him in the amalgamation. A Strange's company had performed at Court in the winter of 1588–9, and may have suffered with the Admiral's in the cold official winds of the Marprelate displeasure. A combined company would strengthen numbers for London playing while retaining the two patrons' warrants for separate touring with smaller numbers.

The amalgamated group played at James Burbage's playhouse, the Theatre, in 1590–1. The plot of 2 *Seven Deadly Sins* is usually thought to date from this period because in addition to naming all the major players of the amalgamation with the single exception of Alleyn himself, it included among the lesser parts the name of James's son Richard Burbage. The plot of *The Dead Man's Fortune*, another Dulwich manuscript, also has Burbage's name in it, and probably dates from the same time for the same reason.[15] In May 1591, however, there was a quarrel of some sort between the amalgamated company and old Burbage, over his retention of some of the playhouse receipts. John Alleyn, Edward's brother, subsequently testified in a lawsuit brought by the widow of a former gatherer against Burbage for a similar reason that in May 1591, shortly after a fracas with the widow's relatives,

when [Alleyn]...came to [Burbage] for certen money which he deteyned from [Alleyn] and his fellowes, of some of the dyvydent money betwene him & them, growinge also by the use of the said Theater, he denyed to pay the same. [Alleyn] told him that belike he ment to deale with them, as he did with the poore wydowe...wishing him he wold not do so, for yf he did, they wold compleyne to ther lorde & M^r the lord Admyrall, and then he in a rage, litle reverencing his honour & estate, sayd by a great othe, that he cared not for iii of the best lordes of them all.[16]

The players consequently abandoned the Theatre, moving eventually to Phillip Henslowe's playhouse. This was the beginning of Edward Alleyn's long and profitable association with the Henslowe enterprises. In 1592 he married into the family and began to take a share in the financing of the company as well as its acting and organisation. Henslowe's records show the Admiral's–Strange's performing for him regularly from this date until 1594, except when the plague prohibitions forced the company back to its travels.

Not all the amalgamated company seem to have followed Alleyn to Henslowe. Pope, Bryan, Heminges (if he was in the company by 1591), Phillips and Cowley evidently did, since they were travelling with Alleyn as Strange's Men in 1593. But others who appear on the list for the *Seven Deadly Sins* are not mentioned, and their names turn up instead among the debris of the Pembroke's company which is in the records as travelling through Leicester near the end of 1592, at Court that Christmas, and in the country again at York, Rye, Ludlow (their patron's territory), Shrewsbury, Coventry, Bath and Ipswich through the summer of 1593. Henslowe wrote to Alleyn during the Admiral's –Strange's tour in September 1593 that Pembroke's were in difficulties and had been forced to sell their costumes (*Henslowe Papers*, p. 40). They also evidently sold their playbooks, for Marlowe's *Edward II* was entered on the Stationers' Register in July as a Pembroke's play, and *The Taming of a Shrew* a little later. *Edward I*, published in 1594, was probably another of their texts, and the pirated texts of 2 and 3 *Henry VI* were certainly theirs, evidently made up by some of the members of the company once it was broken, from their memories of what they had been used to perform. The text of 2 *Henry VI* as printed in the Shakespeare First Folio names John Holland as an actor at IV.ii.1, and John Sincler is named both in 3 *Henry VI* (at III.i.1) and in *The Taming of the Shrew* (Induction 1.88). He was later to be named in 2 *Henry IV* as a Chamberlain's man. Both Holland and Sincler appear in the *Seven Deadly Sins* list. There is also a 'Nicke' in that list who may be the same as the 'Nicke' named in the Cade scene in the pirated text of 2 *Henry VI* and in *The Taming of the Shrew* (III.i.82). It would perhaps be stretching coincidence too far to identify these Nickes with Nicholas Tooley, who was to become a sharer in Shakespeare's company and who was once Richard Burbage's boy,[17] but it is at least possible that the Nickes were the same person and that he moved with Sincler and Holland from the amalgamated company in 1590 to Pem-

26

broke's in 1592-3, and thence to Shakespeare's company, along with the plays in which all their names appear. The possibility that it was Tooley is strengthened by the probability that his master Burbage did the same. Burbage's break with the amalgamated company must have come when they quarrelled with his father; he is noted in the lawsuit which describes the quarrel as vigorously defending his father's property and profits.[18] He may have formed a new company to play at his father's abandoned Theatre, along with Sincler and Holland, perhaps Tooley, and others from the amalgamation, and taken up with the Earl of Pembroke as a new master. The Earl described the player as his 'old acquaintance' in 1619 when Burbage died. Shakespeare may have been another Pembroke's man, if their possession of his plays is any indication of where his allegiance lay.[19]

Travelling seems to have been the great disintegrator. The size of company which could thrive in London was impossibly cumbersome on the road, and most of the changes in personnel seem to have happened when a company 'broke and went into the country' as Henslowe put it of the Queen's, or when they returned to a foot-hold in London. Pay in the provinces was markedly less than in London— Henslowe paid hired men five shillings weekly when they were travelling as against ten in London—and any player who could join a well-placed London company when his own was forced out of town would presumably have done so. The amalgamation of Strange's and the Admiral's seems to have related to these circumstances, as we learn from their plea to the Privy Council of 1591 or 1592,[20] which pointed out that 'oure Companie is greate, and thearbie our chardge intollerable, in travellinge the Countrie, and the Contynuaunce thereof wilbe a meane to bringe us to division and seperacion'. When the amalgamated company went on its travels it does seem sometimes to have divided into its constituent parts—the records show a joint tour in the summer of 1593 and separate tours in 1592 and the spring of 1594.[21]

We can see, then, a shifting population amongst the companies, players moving from group to group as their financial circumstances pushed them. If the *Seven Deadly Sins* dating of 1590 is to be trusted, we can recognise among the Admiral's–Strange's combination at that time the following players: Edward and John Alleyn, George Attewell, James Tunstall, Pope, Bryan, Phillips, Cowley, Burbage, Sincler, Holland, Will Sly, John Duke, the boy Robert Gough, and a 'Harry', 'Nicke', 'Kit' and 'Sander' who may or may not have been Henry Condell, Nicholas Tooley, Christopher Beeston and Alexander Cooke respectively, all of whom turn up later in the Chamberlain's company. Kempe and Heminges had joined by 1593, and were leading members along with Alleyn, Pope, Bryan, and Phillips. Cowley and Thomas Downton were also in the amalgamation in 1593,[22] and Attewell and Tunstall, who reappear in the Admiral's in 1595, were probably members throughout the period too. We have no record of John Alleyn playing after 1591, but there is no reason for him to have left his brother's company for any other. Of Burbage, Holland, Sincler, Sly, Duke, Gough, Condell, Tooley and Beeston there is no positive record until they reappear in the Chamberlain's Men after the reshuffle of 1594. They may have gone to Pembroke's when the amalgamated company quarrelled with old Burbage. The 'Bevis' who appears in 2 *Henry VI* with John Holland, was certainly a member of the Pembroke's which pirated the play (the pirated version has a gratuitous reference to 'Bevys of South-hampton'), and two other players named by Shakespeare, 'Humfrey' (along with Sincler in 3 *Henry VI*, III.i.1) and 'Gabriel' (3 *Henry VI*, I.ii.48, and *Taming of the Shrew* with 'Nicke' at III.i.82), are likely to have been the Humphrey Jeffes and Gabriel Spencer who turn up in the later Pembroke's of 1595–7. The presence of Shakespeare's histories with *The Taming of the Shrew* and others of his plays in the repertory of the Pembroke's pirates would strongly suggest that either Shakespeare himself or a player such as Burbage, able to afford his playbooks, or both, were in the company in 1593 when they broke.[23] Eventually either or both moved to the Chamberlain's Men, who were the later owners of the plays. Strange's had none of Shakespeare's plays in 1593, so far as we can tell from Henslowe's records of their repertory.[24]

The only Shakespeare play which can be positively identified in Henslowe's lists is *Titus Andronicus*, which is noted as performed by Sussex's Men for the first time on 23 January 1594. This was after Pembroke's had broken. If the sequence of companies performing the play which is listed on the title-page of the 1594 quarto is correct, then it went from Derby's (i.e. Strange's), to Pembroke's and thence to Sussex's. This may indeed reflect the changing allegiances of either Shakespeare himself, or of Burbage if he bought the play from its author, and probably some others of their fellows, between the play's composition in about 1590, and 1594 when it was printed. Sussex's were travelling in the summer of 1593 but came to London for the winter, including a six-week season with Henslowe for which they may well have needed reinforcement from the better remnants of the broken Pembroke's.

What may have caused the next reshuffle and the break-up of the amalgamation in the middle of 1594 we cannot tell. The Queen's Men broke in May 1594, and mergers were obviously then desirable, but none of the Queen's Men except the clown John Singer, who joined the new Admiral's, seems to have been involved in this last reshuffle. The membership of the Admiral's and Chamberlain's Men, the two companies which from this date came to bestride the London scene like the monopolistic colossi they were, is known in reasonable detail. They appeared together for Henslowe between 5 and 15 June 1594, probably playing on alternate days, and after that parted company forever. Alleyn's new Admiral's stayed on with father-in-law Henslowe at the Rose, and Burbage's new Chamberlain's went to father Burbage at the Theatre.[25] Alleyn, Attewell, Tunstall, and Downton of the old Admiral's in the amalgamation were joined by Richard Jones, who had been a fellow of Alleyn and Tunstall in Worcester's in 1583–9, and who had spent 1592–3 travelling on the continent, Singer from the Queen's, and Thomas Towne, Martin Slater and Edward Juby, whose names are all recorded in a list in Henslowe's *Diary* amongst memoranda for 1594–6 (pp. 87, 136). Other entries made by Henslowe and additional evidence such as the 1597 plot of *Frederick and Basilea* identify the new names of Edward Dutton, Richard Alleyn, Thomas Hunt, Robert Ledbetter and a number of boys, some of whom ('Sam', 'Pyk', and 'Will') can perhaps be traced back to the earlier Admiral's.

The Chamberlain's Men consisted of Pope, Bryan, Kempe, Phillips, Heminges and Cowley from Strange's, together with Sincler, Holland and 'Nicke' (if it was Tooley) whose names are preserved in Shakespeare's early plays and who probably came through Pembroke's; plus Burbage, Sly, Duke and Gough, who like most of the others had been in the *Seven Deadly Sins* company some years before and after that probably in Pembroke's; and Condell, Cooke, and Beeston, who may have been too. Shakespeare, whose name is not in the *Seven Deadly Sins* list, had probably been a fellow of at least some of the new company in Pembroke's.

The years which followed for the reborn companies were exceptionally stable in comparison with the flux caused by the frequent prohibitions of the previous five years. The Admiral's, for instance, according to Henslowe's records, were able to play through six days a week for forty-nine weeks, breaking only for thirty-seven days of Lent, during which the Rose was renovated. A summer tour of eight weeks or so in 1595 was again followed by forty-two weeks of playing broken only by Lent (*Henslowe's Diary*, pp. 21–37). Such an unprecedentedly trouble-free run in London, shared as it was by only the two companies, provided a stability of conditions in which they laid the basis of their mutual prosperity and predominance for the rest of the reign. Their joint predominance, affirmed by a Privy Council decree of 1598 which limited the number of London companies to the two of them, was hardly challenged for the next forty years.

One slight challenge which they did face just before their monopoly was sealed with official approval in 1598 is worth noting for the light it throws on the financial organisation and problems, as well as the profitability, of the companies at this time. A new Pembroke's company had appeared in the country in 1595–6, and near the end of February 1597 Francis Langley, owner of the new Swan playhouse, made an agreement with a company calling themselves Pembroke's Servants to play for twelve months at the Swan. They included Gabriel Spencer (probably the 'Gabriel' of 2 *Henry VI*), probably Humphrey Jeffes (the 'Humfrey' of 3 *Henry VI*), Robert Shaw and William Bird, together with Jones and Downton who up to then had been with the Admiral's. The Rose was left unoccupied by the Admiral's for three weeks from 12 February, an occurrence which may be connected with the departure of Jones and Downton, either as cause or effect. Each of the named Pembroke's Men gave Langley a surety of £100 to guarantee their staying the stipulated length of time. In July, however their performance of the lost play *The Isle of Dogs* brought down a curb on all London playing, and one of the play's authors, Ben Jonson (who probably also acted in it), was imprisoned along with Spencer and Shaw. One result was that in August Jones fled back to Henslowe, followed by Shaw and Spencer on their release, then Bird, and in October Downton. Humphrey Jeffes and an Anthony Jeffes also turn up in Henslowe's books for the first time after this date. The refugees seem to have taken their playbooks with them to Henslowe, though a renewed or more likely a residual Pembroke's did start touring again at the end of 1597. Langley was subsequently unable to get a licence for playing at the Swan, and so began to sue the departed players for their £100 bonds. Henslowe records loans made to Bird to reach a settlement with Langley (*Diary*, p. 76).

What is illuminating about these varied fortunes is the relationship it reveals between Langley, as theatre impresario, and his tenants. Length of tenure was as important a financial matter to the owner as to the players, and was valued by Langley for insurance purposes at 5 × £100 for a three-year contract. The agreement specifically laid it down that the company was only to perform at the Swan if within five miles of London, except for performances 'in private places'. Langley claimed during the litigation to have spent £300 on apparel for the players and on preparing the playhouse, and in return was to receive half of the gallery takings and to be repaid for his expenditure on apparel out of the players' half. Langley's expenditure was considerable, though of course he expected his returns would be, too. All these arrangements are very like Henslowe's dealings with his companies, and on the evidence of the 1591 lawsuit also like James Burbage's with his (*Henslowe's Diary*, p. xxxii), except that Henslowe seems to have been involved to the extent of owning a number of playbooks himself. Some plays, such as *Friar Bacon* and *The Jew of Malta*, keep on appearing in his lists whatever the company performing on his premises. Henslowe also took out individual bonds with his players to guarantee their continued service. Richard Jones, for instance, was bound on these terms:

Memorandom that the 6 of Aguste 1597 I bownd Richard Jones by & a sumsett of ii^d to contenew & playe with the companye of my lord Admeralles players frome Mihelmase next after the daye a bowe written untell the eand

& tearme of iii yeares emediatly followinge & to playe in my howsse only known by the name of the Rosse & in no other howse a bowt London publicke & yf restraynte be granted then to go for the tyme into the cφntrey & after to retorne agayne to London yf he breacke this a sumsett then to forfett unto me for the same a hundreth markes of lafull money of Ingland wittnes to this E Alleyn & John Midelton.[26]

In return for such bonds Henslowe offered security and such side-benefits as his moneylending business—which helped Bird extricate himself from Langley, for instance. There seems to have been a rather blurred line drawn between loans made to the company, for which Henslowe repaid himself out of the players' half of the gallery takings, and loans to individuals. With the personnel of the company likely to fluctuate as it did, this is understandable.

On the company side, the distinction between sharers, those players with a direct financial interest in the company, sharing profits and expenses alike, and hired men, paid on a weekly basis, seems to have been clear-cut. It is usually assumed that a prefatory 'mr' in Henslowe's accounts denotes a sharer as distinct from a hireling.[27] There were probably ten or so sharers in the full-size London companies through the 1590s; those of the Admiral's after 1597 were Jones, Downton, Singer, Juby, Towne, Shaw, Bird, Spencer, and the two Jeffes.[28] Alleyn, who retired from acting late in 1597, after the Pembroke refugees had been re-enlisted, lived more or less as Henslowe's partner in his theatrical and bull- and bear-baiting affairs. His taking a share in the financial side probably explains why Henslowe's own records are so much more sparse for this period than they are before 1597 or in 1600–2, when Alleyn briefly returned to the stage.

The sharers of the Chamberlain's Men by 1596 seem to have been eight in number: Burbage, Shakespeare, Kempe, Pope, Bryan, Phillips, Sly and Heminges. Bryan dropped out soon after 1596, and Pope was dying by 1603; they were replaced by Condell and Cowley. Kempe left in 1599 to dance his famous morris to Norwich, and was replaced by Robert Armin from Lord Chandos's Men. In 1603, once they had become the King's Men, the number was increased to twelve with the elevation of Alexander Cooke and Nicholas Tooley, the addition of John Lowin from Worcester's, and Laurence Fletcher, who had been favoured by James when he took a company touring in Scotland, and whose addition to the King's Men in 1603 may have been a further mark of royal favour. His name does not recur in the company's actor-lists, and it is not clear who may have replaced him. The number of sharers remained at twelve for the rest of the company's long life.[29]

The Chamberlain's Men's relationship with the owner of their play-houses was probably at first similar to that of the Admiral's with Henslowe, and Pembroke's with Langley. In February 1597 James Burbage died and his property passed on to his son Cuthbert, who probably for a time kept to his father's system. But the ground-lease of the Theatre in 1599 was ending, and the playhouse needed replacing, a costly business. Cuthbert felt he had to cover his new investment, so the company was brought in to a direct financial interest in the playhouse. Cuthbert and Richard took between them a half-interest, or moiety, in the new building, the Globe, and drew the company in with them by allowing five of the sharers the other half-interest between them. The five who came in were Shakespeare, Phillips, Heminges, Pope, and Kempe, the last of whom soon sold his interest to the other four. They thus became not only 'sharers' in the company's finances but 'housekeepers' in the playhouse, entitled to a proportionate share of the owners' traditional half of the gallery takings.

1600 was an important year for Henslowe and his company. Not only did their new playhouse, the Fortune, enable them to move from the Bankside to the northwestern boundary of the city, but also Alleyn returned to the fellowship, at the wish, so it was claimed, of the Queen herself.[30] The times were still favourable to playing, and there does not seem to have been any more travelling until after the Queen's death in 1603. Henslowe's accounts over these years reveal mainly such minor matters as ten shillings paid in May 1601 'to geatte the boye into the ospetalle which was hurt at the fortewne', twenty-four shillings in July to buy eight pounds of copper lace, 6s. 7d. to mend a tawny coat 'which was eatten with the Rattes' in November, and on Christmas Day hose for a boy 'to tumbell in be fore the quen' (Diary, pp. 169, 177, 184, 186). The repertory gained thirty-one new plays between 1600 and 1603, a lower number than in the three years up to 1597, partly because of the extremely large number of new plays bought immediately before 1600, and partly (one would assume) because Alleyn, back in the company, was content to revive his old favourites.

Meanwhile another company, Worcester's, came under Henslowe's spreading wing. He built the Fortune in 1600 to rival the new Globe, and so his old playhouse, the Rose, was going vacant. Worcester's Men can be traced around the country throughout the decade or so after 1589 when Alleyn, Tunstall and Jones left them to become Admiral's Men. They appeared at Court in January 1602, and in March were admitted by the Privy Council as a third London company together with Oxford's, 'being joyned by agrement togeather in on companie'.[31] They appear in Henslowe's Diary in August, receiving advances for playbooks and apparel. Henslowe, who often did business over food (there are frequent entries in the summer the Fortune was being built for meals with the builder), records that the supper at the famous Mermaid Tavern when he reached his agreement with Worcester's cost him nine shillings, a sum he characteristically debited to the company (Diary, p. 214). The Admiral's were now permanently at the Fortune, and Worcester's moved into the Rose.

The Worcester's company may have been new to London, but its membership was not. Among the players who authorised payments for Henslowe are Kempe, John Duke and Christopher Beeston, all former Chamberlain's Men, Robert Pallant, once of the amalgamated Admiral's–Strange's and probably subsequently of the Admiral's, John Lowin, who was soon to join the Chamberlain's Men, and Thomas Heywood, an Admiral's Man as actor and playwright in 1598. Richard Perkins (see pl. III) had joined by the time Elizabeth died, and Heywood and Perkins together formed the core of the company, as leading playwright and player, from the time they became Queen Anne's Men early in James's reign. They were occupying the new Red Bull playhouse by the middle of the decade. In 1609 their licence to play was drafted, on the familiar Leicester's model with the now-standard addition of the customary playing-place, as follows:

Knowe yee that wee of our especiall grace certayne knowledge and meere mocion have lycenced and aucthorised and by these presentes doe lycence and aucthorize Thomas Greene, Christofer Beeston, Thomas Haywood, Richard Pirkyns, Richard Pallant, Thomas Swinnerton, John Duke, Robert Lee, James Haulte, and Roberte Beeston, Servantes to our moste deerely beloved wiefe Queene Anne, and the reste of theire Associates, to use and exercise the arte and faculty of playinge Comedies, Tragedies, historyes, Enterludes, Moralles, Pastoralles, Stageplayes and suche other like, as they have already studied or heareafter shall use or studye, aswell for the recreacion of our loving Subjectes as for our solace and pleasure when wee shall thinke good to see them, during our pleasure. And the said Comedies, Tragedies, histories, Enterludes, Moralles, Pastoralles, Stageplayes and suche like to shewe and exercise publiquely and openly to theire beste commoditye, aswell within theire nowe usuall houses called the Redd Bull in Clarkenwell and the Curtayne in Hallowell, as alsoe within anye Towne halles, Mouthalles and other convenient places within the libertye and freedome of any other Citty, universitye, Towne or Boroughe whatsoever within our Realmes and Domynions.[32]

The position which the Privy Council had spasmodically struggled to maintain after 1598, of simply two pre-eminent adult companies, was complicated in the new decade not only by the arrival of the third adult company, and a fourth, the Duke of York's, at the end of the decade, but also by the return of the two boy companies. Edward Pearce set up a new company of Paul's Boys in 1599, and Henry Evans the scrivener once again established a company in Blackfriars in 1600. To some extent the size of the part which the boy companies played in this decade has been exaggerated, at least so far as the history of the companies is concerned. Rosencrantz's claim that the 'little eyases' were carrying it away, even 'Hercules and his load', that is, the Globe's patronage, has helped this. Also relatively more of their repertory is extant than there is of the adults'. As a theatrical fashion, the one company lasted only six years, the other eight years before

James decided, as Elizabeth had before him, that their services could be dispensed with. They really carried it away only in the first of the three phases of their career, up to the death of Elizabeth, at which point Henry Evans for one was on the point of giving up his venture altogether. By 1608 there was only one company, no longer boys but young adult players, their leaders aged about twenty. Boy companies as such never reappeared. Their chief mark of distinction was that they secured the services of the three most ambitious and opiniated play-wrights of the day—Jonson, Chapman, and Marston—and that they were well-placed to carry out the tasks these three laid on them. Middleton and Dekker also wrote for them.

Paul's were the first to return to the surface, as they had been the last to sink beneath it. By 1599 Marston was writing for them, and in 1600 Jonson was writing for a second company which was located in the Blackfriars, and reminding Londoners of old history by calling itself the Chapel Children. The nature of the enterprise of reviving the boy-actors is shown by the membership of the backers of this second company. The manager was Evans, the former associate of Lyly with the old Blackfriars company. He enlisted to help him two men, Nathaniel Giles, who had been appointed Master of the Chapel Children at Windsor three years before, and Edward Kirkham, the Yeoman of the Revels. Giles had the authority necessary for getting the acting personnel, the power to 'take up' children for service in his choir school, and Kirkham, as officer in charge of the Revels wardrobe, had the necessary materials for acting at his disposal. A fourth associate was Evans's son-in-law Alexander Hawkins. Evans clearly believed in the familiar Elizabethan practice of keeping business affairs in family hands, and the subsequent wrangles over the company's finances give point to his faith in family loyalties.

Of the original four associates, Giles seems to have dropped out with some haste. His authority was to take up boys for singing, not acting, and was clearly going to be abused. A complaint brought against him by one Henry Clifton shows that it was. Clifton alleged that his son had been abducted while on his way to school and forced to 'exercyse the base trade of a mercynary enterlude player, to his utter losse of tyme, ruyne and disparagment'. When the case was heard in 1602 Giles was not summoned and may already have made his peace with the authorities. His powers of taking up boys were renewed with all the other renewals of the new reign in 1604, but somebody had evidently remembered the Clifton case by 1606, for in that year he lost the powers for good.[33] He remained as Master of the Chapel Children at Windsor until his death at the rare age of 75 in 1634, but seems never again to have meddled with playing.

The brunt of the censure over the Clifton abduction fell on Evans, who temporarily dropped out of the company's management in 1602, after making over his lease of the Blackfriars to his son-in-law. According to a later lawsuit, he subsequently enlisted two more backers, William Rastell and Thomas Kendall, to join Kirkham, who between them apparently paid out £200 for apparel and other playing materials, and £400 on the premises. Evans in return made a verbal promise to transfer half the lease to them, but of course did not do so; it was already in Hawkins's name. The associates drew up articles on 20 April 1602 whereby the three financiers gave Hawkins, as front man for Evans, a bond of £200 to guarantee their payment of half the rent and repairs to the premises, in return for which they would get half the profits of the company. It does seem a little odd that, as Kirkham testified in 1612, the financiers were satisfied with a verbal understanding over the lease when they were drawing up articles for the company's finances, especially since they seem to have been already on difficult terms with Evans. At the same time as they drew up the company articles they agreed to pay Evans eight shillings for every week the company performed, apparently to stay out of the way. Perhaps they thought that would be enough to leave them in charge.

Evans did not stay out of the way, for during the prohibition on playing in 1603 he took the pessimistic initiative of discussing with the Burbages, from whom he had leased his playhouse, whether he should give up the lease. In December 1604 he was in the way enough to lock up the 'Chamber called the Schoolhouse' on the premises in order to keep Kirkham and the others out, because they had not paid their share of a £10 repair bill.

The company was renewed after the distractions of 1603, and in February 1604 James gave them a new patent as the Children of the Queen's Revels, naming Kirkham, Hawkins, and Kendall, with a new man, Robert Payne, in place of Rastell. Samuel Daniel the poet was given the unique distinction in the same patent of serving as licenser to them, taking over the duties of the Master of the Revels for this one company. It did not stop him, in this middle period of the company's existence, from getting into trouble over his own *Philotas*, which the boys performed in 1604. A little later another of their plays, *Eastward Ho!*, got two of its authors, Jonson and Chapman, into prison, and the third, Marston, who had a financial interest in the company, had to flee for safety. The company does not seem to have been troubled directly by this incident—the imprisonment may have been occasioned by a complaint on publication rather than performance—but a third play, John Day's *Isle of Gulls*, certainly got them into trouble in February 1606, and over the same thing, satire against James and his tail of Scotsmen. The company lost Queen Anne's patronage and had to drop her name from their title. Some of the responsible members of the company, presumably the leading 'boys', were imprisoned, and a reconstruction of the management took place. Evans was still in the background, and Robert Keysar, a goldsmith, moved in to take control; in part, one presumes, to safeguard his investment. Under Keysar the name became the Children of the Blackfriars, and the system of impressment, originally employed on Giles's authority, seems to have been replaced with an indenture system rather like that the adult companies used to hold their boys.[34] The Paul's company found it expedient to retire from the scene in 1606, and the Blackfriars company may have adjusted its membership to accommodate some of the fallen company.

It was not long, however, before there was a repetition of the troubles of 1606. In March 1608 the French Ambassador took offence over one or both of Chapman's *Byron* plays.[35] Not only did they depict scandalous scenes in the contemporary French Court, but even, according to the same complainant, they satirised

their king, his Scottish mien, and all his favourites astonishingly; for after having made him curse heaven because of the flight of a bird, and having had him strike a gentleman for having beaten his dogs, they depicted him drunk at least once a day.[36]

The result was that the King 'vowed they should never play more, but should first begg their bred...' and gave orders 'to dissolve them, and to punish the maker besides'.[37] Chapman was pursued, and Marston, involved over a related offence, imprisoned along with several members of the now almost adult company. Evans then surrendered the residue of his twenty-one-year lease to the Burbages, apparently without consulting Keysar.

The company was not entirely destroyed. It performed at Court the next Christmas, for the first time in four years, a striking mark of royal forgiveness, or forgetfulness, and soon found a new playhouse just outside the city walls in Whitefriars. In 1610 Keysar allied himself with Phillip Rosseter the lutenist and several adult players, including Richard Jones of the Admiral's, to organise a new company, which he was allowed once again to call the Children of the Queen's Revels. By this time of course many of the 'boys' were not even youths. Nathan Field, who had been the leading actor since 1600, was 22. Two others of the original company, William Ostler and John Underwood, left after 1608 for the King's Men where they had full adult status. In the very earliest days the boys had performed only weekly, as against the daily performances of the adults; after 1610 their practices in this as in all other respects cannot be distinguished from the adults. The King's Men even had the same kind of indoor playhouse, because they moved into the Blackfriars once the children had relinquished it. As a 'Children's' company the Queen's Revels may have had a larger proportion of boys than usual, but there were at least six full adults, some of them with decades of acting behind them.

Apart from the age of the players, and their use of indoor playhouses located inside the city walls, the chief distinctions the boy companies enjoyed came from their repertory. Nearly all the plays they gave, after a few unsuccessful attempts to revive their pre-1590 repertory, were satirical comedies of a kind likely to give enjoyment to the Court gallants by their mockery not only of citizen values but also of the King and his Scottish followers. Scandal purveyed from the theoretical safety of 'their juniority', as the offended Heywood put it, was the staple diet from early on, when the so-called War of the Theatres was fought out between their playwrights.[38] The playwrights had, in all probability, a much larger say in the company's repertory and a freer hand than the playwrights of the adult companies enjoyed.

Once the Burbages had reclaimed their Blackfriars playhouse for their own adult company, all the boys turned out to have accomplished was the entry of adult players into the City itself, the restoration of the right to play in the City which had been lost when the innyards were closed to them. The inhabitants of the Blackfriars precinct stopped the Burbages in 1596 by petitioning the Privy Council, but no protest was raised when they and their adult company took over from the boys twelve years later. In 1608, too, the whole Blackfriars precinct, which had for centuries been exempt from city jurisdiction although inside the city walls, now came into the scope of city government, and yet nothing was done to prevent the adults from playing there.

It was an unparalleled stroke of good fortune for the King's Men. They could revive their old practice of separate winter and summer venues, this time with not an innyard for the bad-weather season but an already well-patronised indoor theatre. The King's Men's predominant position was never again to be seriously challenged so long as the theatres lasted, even when the indoor Cockpit and Salisbury Court were used by other adult companies with a similar object. From 1610 the picture becomes one of a pyramidal structure, with the King's Men (at the Globe for four months of the summer and Blackfriars the rest of the year) as the apex, more or less co-extensively with the other, social, pyramid, and the companies of the Fortune and Red Bull maintaining a fairly constant position along the base line. The Cockpit companies rivalled the King's Men in later years, but generally floated somewhere between the apex and the base line occupied by the Red Bull companies.

The story of the London companies of the last thirty years of playing is basically one of consistent tenure and prosperity, though the prosperity came more to the managers than the companies themselves, and with the exception of the King's Men, the only company to last unaltered throughout, there was a fairly regular turnover of companies. Apart from the two disastrous fires, at the Globe in 1614, which the King's Men were able to survive, and at the Fortune in

1621, which the Palsgrave's, descendants of the Admiral's, were not,[39] the chief disturbances were in litigation over company finances, and in the relations of companies with their theatre-owners and impresario-backers.

The Red Bull company's is a characteristic story of the decade after 1610. The last eleven years of their existence, 1612–23, began with the death of one of the sharers, Thomas Greene, who left his widow his share in the company, valued at £80, and a credit of £37 owed to him by the company. After some argument, the widow and her next husband, James Baskervile, agreed with the company in 1615 to give them an investment of a further £57. 10s. 0d. in return for a pension of 1s. 8d. every playing day for the couple's lifetime. A year later the company, not having honoured its agreement and still short of ready money, managed to get another £38 from Mrs Baskervile for a further pension of 2s. for her and her son's lifetime. The agreement was revised again a year later, for the widow and another of her sons, who was a player with the company and had not been paid his wages. At length, in 1623, Mrs Baskervile took the three players who still survived in the company from the time of the original agreements to Chancery for their bonds to pay her, and the company broke.

The Chancery records contain a number of revealing depositions about the company's affairs at the time the bonds were made. In the first place they show that the original £80 which the company admitted they owed the widow of their former fellow was the value of a current share, and their payment to her was to cover the value, not to buy back the share. This automatically remained with the company. The value of a share of course depended entirely on the state of the company's health, and their difficulties grew largely because they were committed to repay a healthy value in time of sickness. As C. J. Sisson has described it,

The accepted and agreed value of a share was a safeguard of the interests of the individual sharer and of his family, being part of a body of assets, including goodwill as well as properties, playbooks and costumes, to which he had contributed either in money or by his skill, or both. But it was also a pawn or hostage by which the whole body of sharers safeguarded the general interests of the company. The actual and real value of a share depended upon the condition of the company and of the trade in which it was engaged. It seems pretty clear that it was not an asset likely to justify itself in a Court of Law. It was very different, of course, with a share by lease in a playhouse building or ground.[40]

The villain of this particular piece, and the only player to come out of it with any profit, was Christopher Beeston, former King's and Queen's man, who had been a member of the company since its arrival on the London scene and increasingly through the second decade of the century its financier. He rose to power as James Burbage and Alleyn had done before him, by supplying his fellows with money for playbooks and properties, and by renting other properties to them. At times, judging by the depositions in the Baskervile case, it looks as if he rented them properties which he had in fact bought with company funds; considering the fluctuating condition of company membership, the verbal nature of many of the agreements and the secretive nature of the accounting, this is not unlikely. One might attribute some of the success of the King's Men to the patent honesty of the man who did their paperwork, John Heminges. It seems to have been Beeston who was instrumental in milking Mrs Baskervile, and his adroitness in departing from the company without himself being bound to answer for repaying her is of a piece with the other indications of his character. The depositions of the players in 1623 actually allege that Beeston, upon whom the players 'at that tyme and long before and since did put the managing of their whole businesses and affaires belonging unto them joyntly as they were players in trust',[41] had been bribed by Mrs Baskervile to commit the company in her favour.

In 1619 Queen Anne died, and the company was divided. Perkins and others remained at the Red Bull and Beeston went to Prince Charles's Men as manager. An otherwise unknown mercer by the name of John Smith promptly took them all to court to get payment for 'tinsell stuffes and other stuffe' delivered on Beeston's instructions to the company between 1612 and 1617. The other players charged Beeston in this lawsuit with consistently looking after himself before he served the company, while he 'much enritched himself', and falsely billed the company for £400. Furthermore he had taken all the company's property with him when he left the Red Bull. He may even have taken a whole playhouse with him, for the recently constructed Cockpit, at which the Red Bull company played for a while in 1617, remained at Beeston's disposal. But of the financing of the Cockpit we know nothing except that the lease taken out in 1616 was in Beeston's name. In this case, as with the 1623 suit, the players were all too anxious to rid themselves of the burden of bills which they felt Beeston had unfairly left with them, and were certainly interested in shifting the onus on to him.

We need not feel that Beeston was the only mismanager of company finance at the time. The Dulwich records left by Alleyn once had a splendidly itemising document, dating from 1615, drawn up by the Lady Elizabeth's Men as 'Articles of Grievance and of Oppression against Phillip Henslowe'. The Lady Elizabeth's Men had come to London in the Christmas season 1612–13 and had been reconstituted by amalgamation with Phillip Rosseter's Queen's Revels, the old Blackfriars Children, with Nathan Field, Joseph Taylor and William Ecclestone, all later to become King's Men. The articles of complaint speak for themselves as a compendium of all that could be said against

Henslowe, and as a comment on his increasingly casual and autocratic dealings after twenty-five years as an impresario (*Henslowe Papers*, pp. 86–90):

Imprimis in March 1612 uppon m^r: Hynchlowes Joyninge Companes with m^r: Rosseter ye Companie borrowed £80 of one m^r: Griffin and the same was put into m^r: Hinchlowes debt; which made itt sixteene score poundes whoe [a]fter the receipt of the same or most parte thereof in March 1613 hee broke the saide Comp[any a]gaine and Ceazed all the stocke; under Culler to satisfie what remayned due to [him]; yet perswaded M^r: Griffyne afterwardes to arest the Companie for his £80: whoe are still in daunger for the same; Soe nowe there was in equitie due to the Companie £80

Item m^r Hinchlowe having lent one Taylor £30: and £20 to one Baxter fellowes of the Companie Cunninglie put theire said privat debts into the generall accompt by which meanes hee is in Conscience to allowe them £50

Item havinge the stock of Apparell in his handes to secure his debt he sould tenn poundes worth of ould apparrell out of the same with out accomptinge or abatinge for the same; heare growes due to the Companie £10

Also uppon the departure of one Eglestone a ffellowe of the Companie hee recovered of him £14: towardes his debt which is in Conscience likewise to bee allowed to the Companie £14

In March 1613 hee makes upp a Companie and buies apparrell of one Rosseter to the value of £63: and valued the ould stocke that remayned in his handes at £63: likewise they uppon his word acceptinge the same at that rate, which being prized by M^r: Daborne justlie, betweene his partner Meade and him Came but to £40: soe heare growes due to the Companie £23

Item hee agrees with the said Companie that they should enter bond to plaie with him for three yeares att such house and houses as hee shall appointe and to allowe him halfe galleries for the said house and houses; and the other halfe galleries towardes his debt of £126: and other such moneys as hee should laie out for playe apparrell duringe the space of the said 3 yeares, agreeinge with them; in Consideracion theareof to seale each of them a bond of £200: to find them a Convenient house and houses; and to laie out such moneies as fower of the sharers should think fitt for theire use in apparrell which att the 3 yeares, being paid for: to be delivered to the sharers; whoe accordinglie entered the said bondes; but M^r: Henchlowe and M^r: Mead deferred the same; an in Conclusion utterly denied to seale att all.

Item M^r: Hinchlowe havinge promised in Consideracion of the Companies lying still one daie in forteene for his baytinge to give them £50: hee havinge denied to bee bound as aforesaid gave them onlie £40 and for that M^r: ffeild would not Consent thereunto hee gave him soe much as his share out of £50: would have Come unto; by which meanes hee is dulie indebted to ye Companie £10

In June followinge the said agreement, hee brought in M^r: Pallant and shortie after M^r: dawes into the said Companie; promisinge one 12^s a weeke out of his part of the galleries; and the other 6 a weeke out of his parte of the galleries; and because M^r: ffeild was thought not to bee drawne thereunto; hee promised him six shillinges weekelie alsoe; which in one moneth after unwilling to beare soe great a Charge; he Called the Companie together; and told them that this 24^s was to bee Charged uppon them; threatninge those which would not Consent thereunto to breake the Companie and make upp a newe with out the[m] Wheareuppon knowinge hee was not bound; the threequarters sharers advauncinge them selves to whole shares Consented thereunto by which meanes they are out of purse £30 and his parte of the galleries bettred twise as much £30

Item havinge 9 gatherers more then his due itt Comes to this yeare from the Companie £10

Item the Companie paid for [Arra]s and other properties £40 which Mr: Henchlow deteyneth £40

In ffebruarie last 1614 perceav[ing]e the Companie drewe out of his debt and Called uppon him for his accompts hee brooke the Companie againe; by with drawinge the hired men from them; and selles theire stocke (in his hands) for £400 givinge under his owne hand that hee had received towardes his debt £300: Which with the juste and Conscionable allowances before named made to the Companie which Comes to £267: makes £567

Articles of oppression against M^r: Hinchlowe.|

Hee Chargeth the stocke with £600 and odd; towardes which hee hath received as aforesaid £567 of us; yet selles the stocke to strangers for fower hundred poundes; and makes us no satisfacion./

Hee hath taken all boundes of our hired men in his owne name whose wages though wee have truly paid yet att his pleasure hee hath taken them a waye; and turned them over to others to the breaking of our Companie./

ffor lendinge of £6 to p[ay] them theire wages; hee made us enter bond to give him the profitt of a warraunt of tenn poundes due to us att Court./

Alsoe hee hath taken right gould and silver lace of divers garmentes to his owne use with out accompt to us or abatement./

Uppon everie breach of the Companie hee takes newe bondes for his stocke; and our securitie for playinge with him Soe that he hath in his handes, bondes of ours to the value of £5000 and his stocke to; which hee denies to deliver and threatens to oppresse us with.

Alsoe havinge apointed a man to the seeinge of his accomptes in byinge of Clothes (hee beinge to have vi^s. a weeke; hee takes ye meanes away and turnes the man out./

The reason of his often breakinge with us; hee gave in these wordes should these fellowes Come out of my debt, I should have noe rule with them

Alsoe wee have paid him for plaie bookes £200 or thereaboutes and yet hee denies to give us the Coppies of any one of them./

Also with in 3 yeares hee hath broken and dissmembred five Companies./

Henslowe died at the end of the year, probably not of a broken heart, and Alleyn amalgamated various companies into one, Prince Charles's Men. Membership was reshuffled considerably. Field left to take Shakespeare's place as a King's Men's sharer, Taylor and Robert Pallant moved to the new company, which took up third place in eminence behind the always predominant King's and the Fortune company. From about this time there were four companies consistently licensed to play in London, and it seems to have been in the brief of the

Revels Office to maintain that number. In January 1618 the Revels records carry a note of the payment of 44s. by Heminges 'in the name of the four companys, for toleration in the holdy-days'.[42] Further references to 'the four companys' appear in 1623 and 1636, when the Master of the Revels noted that warrants were sent ordering 'the four companys of players' to stop playing because the plague bill had risen to fifty-four. Other companies (including in 1629 and 1635 a celebrated French troupe) might visit, but no more than four were in residence.[43] The four in 1618 were the King's at the Globe and Blackfriars, Palsgrave's at the Fortune, the Queen's at the Red Bull and Cockpit, and the Prince Charles's, who probably followed the Queen's at the Red Bull when they left for the Cockpit, and then succeeded them at the Cockpit, when Beeston left the Queen's to join them.[44]

1619 was the next important year for change. For the King's it was a difficult time: Burbage died in March, and the citizens of Blackfriars renewed their protest about the presence of the theatre and the effect of the carriages which thronged the streets around the playhouse and blocked trade:

there is daylie such resort of people, and such multitudes of Coaches (whereof many are Hackney Coaches, bringinge people of all sortes) That sometymes all our streetes cannott containe them, But that they Clogg upp Ludgate alsoe, in such sort, that both they endanger the one the other breake downe stalles, throwe downe mens goodes from their shopps, And the inhabitantes there cannott come to their howses, nor bringe in their necessary provisions of beere, wood, coale or haye, nor the Tradesmen or shopkeep[er]s utter their wares, nor the passenger goe to the comon water staires without danger of ther lives and lymmes, whereby alsoe many times, quarrelles and effusion of blood hath followed; and what further danger may bee occacioned by the broyles plottes or practises of such an unrulie multitude of people yf they should gett head, yoᵗ wisedomes cann conceave; Theise inconveniences fallinge out almost everie daie in the winter tyme (not forbearinge the tyme of Lent) from one or twoe of the clock till sixe att night, which beinge the tyme alsoe most usuall for Christeninges and burialls and afternoones service, wee cannot have passage to the Church for performance of those necessary duties, the ordinary passage for a great part of the precinct aforesaid beinge close by the play house dore.[45]

Their move was eventually checked by a renewal of the company's patent of 1604, in which the name of the Blackfriars theatre was added to the Globe as the licensed playing place. They sailed on as before.

Burbage's place was filled by the acquisition of Joseph Taylor, once of the Revels children, from Prince Charles's, and this in turn seems to have led the Prince's to welcome Beeston from the flag-fallen Queen Anne's, who were reorganised when their patron died, also in March 1619. Beeston's transfer in the long run proved to be a major event in company history, for Beeston gave the Prince's Men the

Cockpit, the first indoor theatre to offer a chance of rivalling Black-friars as the most popular playhouse with the moneyed section of the London audiences.

The change understandably proved more to Beeston's advantage than his company's. As property-owner and theatre manager Beeston's practice seems to have been to run a company for only so long as it remained amenable to his dealings—usually three years—then deliberately break it, as the Lady Elizabeth's Men accused Henslowe of doing, reforming it later with a few survivors from the old company and a large infusion of new blood. One can only speculate darkly on his motives. The Prince's Men lasted until 1622, when they were supplanted by a new group called the Lady Elizabeth's Men, drawing Andrew Cane, destined to be one of the leading Caroline actors, from Palsgrave's, Joseph Moore from the original Lady Elizabeth's, and William Sherlock and Anthony Turner from unknown groups. The year 1625 brought not only the death of James but the worst visitation of plague in London's history, and an eight-month closure period for all theatres. Beeston reopened with a company patronised by the new Queen, Henrietta. It was headed by Richard Perkins, perhaps the most famous actor of his day, formerly of the Red Bull and since then briefly a King's Man, and others from the Red Bull company, together with Sherlock and Turner from the old company.

The new Cockpit company rose steadily in prosperity and reputation for the next ten years, the only company to stay at Beeston's playhouse for more than three. The Master of the Revels signalled his judgement of their success in the winter season 1629–30 by giving them ten Court performances compared with twelve for the King's Men, who up to then had given as much of the Court entertainment as all the other companies put together. Shirley was the dramatist for Beeston, and more popular than Davenant or the other young wits currently providing for the Blackfriars (see p. 146 below). In the 1630–1 season they gave sixteen plays at Court, and were the only company besides the King's to receive the grant of royal liveries.[46] In 1637 the Lord Chamberlain forbade the printing of any plays without

some Certificate in writeing under the handes of John Lowen & Joseph Taylor for the Kings servantes & of Christopher Bieston for ye Kings & Queenes young Company.[47]

The 'young Company' was Beeston's latest. In 1636 during a nine-month-plagued interruption of playing Beeston deliberately broke the Queen's company and in 1637 reopened with a new group largely made up of young actors. As the Master of the Revels noted:

At the increase of the plague to 4 within the citty and 54 in all—This day the 12 May, 1636, I received a warrant from my Lord Chamberlin for the suppressing of playes and shews, and at the same time delivered my severall

43

warrants to George Wilson for the four companys of players, to be served upon them.

On thursday morning the 23 of February the bill of the plague made the number at forty foure, upon which decrease the king gave the players their liberty, and they began the 24 February 1636 [1637].

The plague encreasinge, the players laye still untill the 2 of October, when they had leave to play.

Mr Beeston was commanded to make a company of boyes, and began to play at the Cockpit with them the same day.

I disposed of Perkins, Sumner, Sherlock and Turner, to Salisbury Court, and joynd them with the best of that company.[48]

The old company was broken, though it later came together again and played at Salisbury Court. As that theatre's manager, Richard Heton, noted,

When her Majesties servants were at the Cockpitt, beinge all at liberty, they disperst themselves to severall Companies, soe that had not my lord of Dorsett taken care to make up a new Company for the Queene, she had not had any at all.[49]

Perkins, Sherlock and Turner went to Salisbury Court with the revived company, five others went to the King's Men, and at least six returned to Beeston. The new company was known to the Revels Office as Beeston's Boys, and seems to have consisted of a much larger than usual ratio of boys to adults,[50] rather like the Queen's Revels Children after 1610. There were enough adults for five to be summoned before the Privy Council in 1637 and three to be committed to Marshalsea prison in 1640. They managed their own affairs in a sufficiently adult way for Beeston to bequeath them two of the six company shares, half his own holding, when he died in 1638. In addition to the adults retained from the old Queen Henrietta's Men, two came from the King's Revels, and two had been in Prince Charles's as early as 1631–2. Of the other recruits, two had been boys with the King's.

When Beeston died in 1638 his son William took over management of the company's affairs. William was a less adroit diplomat than his father, who is recorded by Herbert, the opiniated and self-satisfied Master of the Revels, as on one occasion giving 'my wife a payre of gloves, that cost him at least twenty shillings'.[51] Beeston no doubt found it money well spent. In the spring of 1640 William became involved, as his father had more than once before him, in trouble with Herbert for failing to consult him over a play which contained political matters. The play was almost certainly Richard Brome's *The Court Beggar*, which satirised the courtier and wit of the Queen's circle John Suckling, his friend Davenant, and several other members of the circle. The times were getting warmer as they moved nearer the explosion, and William was unable to mollify Herbert for his audacity as his father had done. He was visited with a total prohibition:

44

Wheras William Bieston and the Company of Players of the Cockpitt in Drury Lane have lately Acted a new play without any Licence from the M^r of his Ma^{tes} Revells & beeing commaunded to forbeare playing or Acting of the same play by the sayd M^r of the Revells & commaunded likewise to forbeare all manner of playing have notwithstanding...Acted the sayd Play & others...Theis are therfore in his Ma^{tes} name, & signification of his royall pleasure to commaund the sayd William Bieston & the rest of that Company of the Cockpitt Players from henceforth & upon sight heerof to forbeare to Act any Playes whatsoever untill they shall bee restored by the sayd M^r of the Revells unto their former Liberty. Wherof all partyes concernable are to take notice & to conforme accordingly as they and every of them will answere it.[52]

Furthermore William lost his position as 'Governor & Instructer' to the company, and with two of his company was put in the Marshalsea. Ironically, he was replaced by Davenant himself, the putative son of Shakespeare, former King's playwright, current Court masque-writer and Poet Laureate, and founder of the most ambitious theatre project to date, one which had been squashed (ironically again with Herbert's connivance) only a year or so before. Davenant had little time to work as manager, for he was soon away at the so-called Bishops' Wars against the Scots, and after the collapse of the second campaign it was obvious that he along with all he stood for were on the losing side in a conflict which was more and more quickly coming into the open. In May 1641 Suckling was summoned before the House of Lords about a band of soldiers he had gathered together in London, supposedly to rescue the King's strong man, Strafford, from the Tower, where Parliament, with mortal intent, had put him. Suckling gained time by declaring with characteristic smoothness that he was raising a force for service in the Portuguese army, and by the time Parliament had obtained a denial from the Portuguese Ambassador Suckling and his fellow-conspirators in what became known as the Army Plot were on their way out of the country. Four of the five named by Parliament escaped; Davenant, with an ostentation as characteristic as Suckling's smoothness, managed to get himself captured in Kent. His famous 'saddleback' nose perhaps made him easily recognisable. He was held until Parliament realised it could not decide what to do with him and allowed him to depart into exile.[53] Beeston meanwhile seems to have slipped back into his managership—his mother still had the lease of the playhouse and a one-third holding in the company—but in any case the end was too near for either profit or delight, and at the beginning of September 1642 Parliament put a stop to both.

The authority the Master of the Revels had over the theatre impresarios is signalled by Herbert's part in the transfer from Beeston to Davenant. His degree of control, and the extent to which the impresarios had taken over a directly managerial role, is shown in a document drawn up in 1639 by Richard Heton for the Salisbury Court company. According to this document, Heton was to have the sole patent for the company, and he stipulated moreover

That such of the company as will not be ordered and governed by me as of their governor, or shall not by the M^r of his M^{ts} Revells and my selfe bee thought fitt Comedians for her M^{ts} service, I may have power to discharge from the Company, and, with the advice of the M^r of the Revells, to putt new ones in their places; and those who shalbe soe descharged not to have the honor to be her M^{ts} servants, but only those who shall continew at the aforesaid playhouse. And the said Company not to play at any tyme in any other place but the forsaid playhouse without my consent under my hand in wryting, (lest his M^{ts} service might be neglected) except by speciall comand from one of the Lo. Chamberlaines, or the M^r of his M^{ts} Revells, &c.[54]

A recognition of the pattern of change in the history of the London companies is necessary before any meaningful generalisation about their organisation and practices sufficient to apply over the whole seventy years can be set up. Subject to the conditions of perpetual change, some picture can be made of the primary features, that is, the management of company finances and the pattern of governmental regulations by which the companies were bound. Between these tangible matters some filling in of the more human company affairs, the customs, corporate tastes, and traditions might be attempted.

The chief distinction of London companies from travelling companies was their size. This in turn made their financial organisation different from that of the travelling groups, which had no more than eight players, few properties other than costumes, and which were led by a player who was at once leading man, manager, financier and warrant-holder.[55] The London companies after about 1580 consisted of a core of between eight and twelve co-owning players, 'sharers', who shared both profits and costs, such as properties and apparel, rent, and the wages of hired men. Most plays required casts of at least twenty, and the companies had in addition in London the extra costs of stage-keepers, tiremen, gatherers, musicians and other assistants. The Admiral's 1 *Tamar Cam* of 1596 ended with a procession of twelve pairs representing a number of different races, made up from the players not already on the stage.[56] The biggest companies in the seventeenth century had a total personnel of forty or more, of whom thirty were hirelings of one kind or another. Sometimes, as in that peak of stage spectacle, Heywood's *Ages*, two companies might join forces for a particular production. Heywood noted in his preface to *The Iron Age* that the *Ages* were 'often...Publikely Acted by two Companies, uppon one Stage at once'. The cast-list of *The Silver Age* lists forty-one named parts, with additional 'servingmen, swaines, Theban ladies, the seven Planets and the Furies'. But such amalgamations were extremely rare. It was quite costly enough in terms of extras to perform an ordinary play. Even with the maximum doubling of parts a 'normal' London company would need to employ, in addition to the eight, ten or twelve sharers, three or four boys for the women's parts, and six or more hired players, plus stage hands and musicians. To be a shareholder in a London company was to be involved in a commercial enterprise with a substantial turnover in both income and expenditure.

In a normative situation a company sharer would be expected to buy his way into the company, and if the company remained a going concern, could sell his share when he left, providing he left with the agreement of his fellow-sharers.[57] A share in the Admiral's Men, with ten sharers, in 1597 or 1602, was worth £50; in its successor in 1613 with twelve it was worth £70. A Queen Anne's share in 1612 was valued at £80; the Blackfriars company in 1610 had less than an adult company, six shares, but they were valued at £100 each, a total of £600 against the £840 in 1613 of the Palsgrave's. The income on a King's Company share in 1634 was £180 for the year.[58] If a sharer died, the company reimbursed his widow for the value of her husband's share, and resold the share to a new active member of the company. It was an essential feature of the share system that it should operate not only as an investment for the sharer but as a commitment binding the owner to play for the company and to keep its interests his own. If a sharer left without his fellows' consent he was not reimbursed for his share. A begging letter from Charles Massey to Henslowe in 1613 describes the traditional sharers' agreement (*Henslowe Papers*, p. 64):

I know [you] und[er]stande th[at ther] is [the] compositions betwene oure compenye that if [any] one gi[ve] over with consent of his fellowes, he is to r[ece]ve thr[ee] score and ten poundes (antony Jefes hath had so mu[ch]) if any on dye his wi[dow] or frendes whome he appoyntes it tow reseve fyfte poundes (m^{r}es pavie, and m^{r}es roune hath had the lyke) be sides that lytt[ell] moete I have in the play housses, which I would willing[ly] pas over unto you by dede of gifte or any course you [w]ould set doune for your securete, and that you sho[ul]d be sure I dow it not with oute my wiffes consenn[te] she wilbe willinge set her hand to any thinge that myght secure it to to you, Ser fifte poundes would pay my detes, which for on hole twelve month I would take up and pay the intreste, and that I myght the better pay it in at the yeares ende, I would get m^r Jube to reseve my gallery mony, and my qua[r]ter of the house mony for a yeare to pay it in with all, and if in [six] monthes I sawe the gallerye mony would not dow [then in] the other six monthes he should reseve [my whole] share, only reservinge a marke a wekke to furnish my house with all.

In the later years, when verbal agreements were supplemented by written articles, the bonds committed the sharer to stay with the company for a specified number of years, usually three, and gave financial penalties for such unco-operative actions as missing performances or rehearsals or being drunk. This, at least, is what Henslowe got Robert Dawes to agree to when he joined the Henslowe enterprises:

the said Robert Dawes shall and will plaie with such company, as the said Phillipp Henslowe and Jacob Meade shall appoynte, for and during the tyme and space of three yeares from the date hereof for and at the rate of one whole share, accordinge to the custome of players; and that he the said Robert Dawes shall and will at all tymes during the said terme duly attend all suche rehearsall, which shall the night before the rehearsall be given publickly out; and if that he the saide Robert Dawes shall at any tyme faile to come at the hower appoynted, then he shall and will pay to the said Phillipp Henslowe and Jacob Meade, their executors or assignes, Twelve pence; and if he come not before the saide rehearsall is ended, then the said Robert Dawes is contented to pay Twoe shillings; and further that if the said Robert Dawes shall not every daie, whereon any play is or ought to be played, be ready apparrelled and—to begyn the play at the hower of three of the clock in the afternoone, unles by sixe of the same company he shall be lycenced to the contrary, that then he, the saide Robert Dawes, shall and will pay unto the said Phillipp and Jacob or their assignes Three [shillings]; and if that he, the saide Robert Dawes, happen to be overcome with drinck at the tyme when he [ought to] play, by the judgment of ffower of the said company, he shall and will pay Tenne shillings; and if he, [the said Robert Dawes], shall [faile to come] during any plaie, having noe lycence or just excuse of sicknes, he is contented to pay Twenty shillings...And further the said Robert Dawes doth covenant, [promise, and graunt to and with the said Phillip Henslowe and Jacob Meade, that if he, the said Robert Dawes], shall at any time after the play is ended depart or goe out of the [howse] with any [of their] apparell on his body, or if the said Robert Dawes [shall carry away any propertie] belonging to the said company, or shal be consentinge [or privy to any other of the said company going out of the howse with any of their apparell on his or their bodies, he, the said] Robert Dawes, shall and will forfeit and pay unto the said Phillip and Jacob, or their administrators or assignes, the some of ffortie pounds of lawfull [money of England][59]

The sharers had to pay for the rental of their theatre, the purchase of costumes and other playing materials, the wages of all their hirelings, and the various fees exacted by the Revels Office. There was also, at least in the early days, a customary payment to the parish poor. The burlesqued company Sir Oliver Owlet's Men in *Histriomastix* (*c.* 1598) is accosted by the local constable for their 'taxe mony,/To releeve the poore'. The rent was traditionally half of the gallery takings. If the theatre owner was loaning the company money to buy properties he took his repayments from the other half of the gallery takings, the gathering of which was usually his concern rather than the company's. Much of the function of impresarios like old Burbage, Henslowe, Langley and Beeston lay in financing the purchase of such properties. It was an exceptionally stable company which could afford its own; apart from the King's Men not many seem to have done so. They usually began with a loan from the impresario to buy playbooks and apparel, and never got out of his debt. It was in the interests of the Henslowes and Beestons to maintain a turnover of companies since each fresh company needed fresh finance to renew its apparel and repertory.

The system whereby several sharers of a company became theatre owners or housekeepers began when Shakespeare and some of his fellows were called in by the Burbages, who needed a guarantee of tenure and capital for their new Globe in 1599. It was copied by some companies—the Queen's Men at the Red Bull and the Prince's at the Fortune after 1615 are the chief examples[60]—but it was less common than single managerial ownership, and frequently led to difficulties. A share in a playhouse was more durable than a share in a company, and could easily pass out of the company's possession. This when it happened almost always led to trouble and often litigation in order to secure for the householder his proportion of the rent, or for the company or other householders the share of the cost of repairs and maintenance which went with a property share.

It was a litigious age, or course, and the opportunities for human backsliding and inhuman sharp practice were omnipresent. The valuation of a company share was a subjective consideration, depending on the appearance of the company's health and prospects. The proportion of a householder's obligation for payment of a small repair bill was difficult to assess as well as to collect if, as not infrequently happened, a share had been passed on by inheritance and the original holding split into several fractions. The opportunities for a single financier to play on the fallible memories of verbal agreements made by a corporate organisation over several years amongst a changing membership were numerous. Even the gatherers might prove less than reliable, if a reference in 1643 to gatherers who 'seeme to scratch their heads where they itch not, and drop shillings and half crowne-pieces in at their collars'[61] is any guide.

The sums of money involved were enormous by the standards of the time in relation to the social class of those involved. Henslowe is reckoned to have spent £1,317 between 1597 and 1603 directly on the Admiral's Men's properties, of which playbooks took a half.[62] This, on a unit of comparison of a normal working-man's wage as one shilling a day[63] is equivalent to the wages of thirteen or fourteen such men over the whole six years. In 1631 a committee studying the Blackfriars property in an attempt to get the playhouse removed noted that the players had presented an itemised account valuing the property at £21,990. The committee's own valuation, covering loss of rent and interest in the site, was £2,900. 13s. 4d.[64] The householders' price was understandably high and the committee's understandably low, but even the low figure is impressive for simply the estimated rental value of a single playhouse for the fourteen years that remained of the lease.

On the day-to-day level we have detailed records of Henslowe's gallery receipts and more fragmentary records of other enterprises. The Admiral's gallery takings were averaging £20 a week in 1597 (*Diary*, p. xxxv). To build the Fortune in 1600 cost £520; to rebuild the Globe in 1614 about £1,400. Ground-rent was £16 for the Fortune, £14. 10s. 0d. for the Globe. The licensing fee for playhouses rose from ten shillings a week in 1596 to £3 a week in 1600 (for the new Fortune). A King's Company housekeeper in 1615 took £20 for one-fourteenth of the Globe and a similar amount for one-seventh of the Blackfriars, the combined takings from half the galleries of both houses therefore amounting to £420 in the year. By 1635 the Blackfriars was yielding £700–£800 a year and the Globe rather less, though it was still worth twice as much as the Rose in the 1590s.[65] A single performance at Court brought the company £10.

At the lowest level the pay of a player was little different from a journeyman's daily shilling. Henslowe in 1597 contracted to pay William Kendall ten shillings weekly for playing in London, and five 'in ye Cuntrie' (*Diary*, p. 269), while *Ratsey's Ghost* (anon., 1606) claimed that 'the very best' of provincial actors 'have sometimes beene content to go home with fifteene pence share apiece' (A 4r). A reference in 1620 to 'twelvepenny hirelings' at the Fortune suggests that even Kendall was lucky while playing in London (John Melton, *Astrologaster*, E 4r). Richard Jones wrote to Alleyn in 1592 to borrow £3 to get his clothes out of pawn, so that he could join a company about to travel in Germany, complaining that 'some tymes I have a shillinge a day, and some tymes nothing, so that I leve in great poverty' (*Henslowe Papers*, p. 33). Hired men none the less had the promise of shareholding in their future, and were even prepared to furnish bonds of £40 to guarantee their stay with their company (*Henslowe's Diary*, p. 242).

Boys were paid less than hired men. Henslowe charged the company 'a Ratte of iii s A wecke' in 1600 for his boy James Bristow (*Diary*, p. 167). The *Articles of Oppression against Mr Hinchlowe* record six shillings weekly for the man responsible for 'bying of Clothes', which compares with the wages of the hired players. The other hirelings would hardly have been paid more, unless perhaps the 'book-keeper' was felt to be especially responsible. Musicians were more generously rewarded, but in any case often existed as a separate organisation; they had to be licensed separately by the Revels Office. In every case, of course, the wage would have to vary according to the company's takings and general prosperity. Nobody was paid during inhibitions. Roger Clarke joined the Red Bull company for a six-shilling wage, as was 'sett downe in their booke', but in the hard times that followed his income went down to a half-crown or two shillings weekly.[66]

Even the hired men were sharers in a company's misfortunes. The Red Bull appears to have found even cheaper labour on occasions. Pepys records how he heard of

Thos. Killigrew's way of getting to see plays when he was a boy. He would go to the Red Bull, and when the man cried to the boys, 'Who will go and be a devil, and he shall see the play for nothing?' then would he go in, and be a devil upon the stage, and so get to see plays.[67]

One other matter of company finances is of interest. Playwrights were often directly employed by Henslowe, and their products were a regular and major drain on company finances. Thomas Dekker in 1598 had a busy year, during which he shared in the writing of sixteen plays; his total payment from Henslowe was £30, representing a weekly income of a little over twelve shillings. Henslowe at this time was paying about £5 for a play purchased outright. By 1615 his prices had been pushed up to £20. The Court was paying £50 for masques. In later years the Restoration practice of benefit nights seems to have been used in some cases.[68] Companies had a necessary appetite for new plays; the Admiral's absorbed roughly one a fortnight in the years up to 1600; the boys at Blackfriars after their initial period took about four a year. In the last twenty years of playing the incomplete records of the Revels Office suggest a similar rate of consumption by each of the four companies.

Government regulation of the companies grew up as a natural concomitant of both the government's and the companies' interests. The government gained by its power to limit plays, players, and playhouses in what was spoken and by whom, and by the incidental command of the quality of the players who entertained the Court. The players gained above all protection from hostile local authorities. In the later years they profited by the security of the artificially monopolistic situation maintained under the Revels Office, and by such protection as the Master of the Revels could offer in preventing unauthorised performing or printing of the various companies' repertories.

The Crown's interest was exercised through the Privy Council, with the Lord Chamberlain as the Council's officer delegated to watch over plays and playing matters. His executive came to be the Revels Office, originally run intermittently under Henry VIII to organise Court shows, with a Master in the managerial role, one and a half clerks, and a Yeoman, who in the early days was a tailor concerned to maintain the extensive Revels Office wardrobe.[69] Under the Stuarts he seems to have been more of a stage manager. Once the adult theatres were permanently established in London it became expedient to extend the powers of the Office, and in 1581 the Master was granted wide powers, including the censorship of plays. The licensing of plays for performance had been required by proclamations of as early as 1559, when licences were to be issued 'within any Citie or towne corporate, by the Maior or other chiefe officers of the same, and within any shyre, by suche as shalbe Lieuetenauntes for the Quenes Majestie in the same shyre, or by two of the Justices of peax inhabyting within that part of the shire where any shalbe played'.[70] The royal patent to Leicester's Men in 1574, as we have seen, specified that their plays should be 'sene & allowed' only by the Master of the Revels. The 1581 commission to the Master, after specifying his rights to employ 'propertie makers and conninge artificers and laborers' and to buy materials for Court shows, laid it down that he was to take over all licensing authority:

we have and do by these presents authorize and command our said servant, Edmunde Tilney, Master of our said Revels, by himself, or his sufficient deputy or deputies, to warn, command, and appoint in all places within this our realm of England, as well within franchises and liberties as without, all and every player or players, with their playmakers, either belonging to any nobleman, or otherwise, bearing the name or names of using the faculty of playmakers, or players of comedies, tragedies, interludes, or what other showes soever, from time to time, and at all times, to appear before him with all such plays, tragedies, comedies, or shows, as they shall have in readiness, or mean to set forth, and them to present and recite before our said servant, or his sufficient deputy, whom we ordain, appoint, and authorise by these presents, of all such shows, plays, players, and playmakers, together with their playing places, to order and reform, authorise and put down, as shall be thought meet or unmeet unto himself, or his said deputy in that behalf.

And also likewise we have by these presents authorized and commanded the said Edmunde Tilney that in case if any of them, whatsoever they be, will obstinately refuse upon warning unto them given by the said Edmunde, or his sufficient deputy, to accomplish and obey our commandment in this behalf, then it shall be lawful to the said Edmunde, or his sufficient deputy, to attach the party or parties so offending, and him or them to commit to ward, to remain without bail or mainprise until such time as the same Edmunde Tilney, or his sufficient deputy, shall think the time of his or their imprisonment to be punishment sufficient for his or their said offences in that behalf; and that done, to enlarge him or them so being imprisoned at their plain liberty, without any loss, penalty, forfeiture, or other danger in this behalf to be sustained or borne by the said Edmunde Tilney or his deputy, any act, statute, ordinance, or provision heretofore had or made to the contrary hereof in any wise notwithstanding.[71]

The edict of 1598 from the Privy Council which limited the number of London companies to two also strengthened the Master's position. Subsequent commissions, in 1603 and 1622, simply renewed these terms.

Censorship was now centralised, and the censor had close contact with the London companies. Not only did he license all plays but in effect he also licensed the companies. Each royal patent was issued through the Revels Office and specified his control. His exercise of

1   Edward Alleyn as Tamburlaine

11   Richard Burbage

111 Richard Perkins

IV   Nathan Field

v   De Witt's sketch of the Swan

VI Richard Tarlton

VIII   A Daughter of the Niger

his function is indicated in a warrant of 1616 which was evidently sent round the country, and which has survived because the local authorities in Norwich copied it into their records:

Whereas Thomas Swynnerton and Martin Slaughter beinge two of the Queens Ma^ts company of Playors havinge sepated themselves from their said Company, have each of them taken forth a severall exemplification or duplicate of his ma^ts Letters patente graunted to the whole Company and by vertue thereof they severally in two Companies with vagabonds and such like idle psons, have and doe use and exercise the quallitie of playinge in divse places of this Realme to the great abuse and wronge of his Ma^ts Sub^ts in generall and contrary to the true intent and meaninge of his Matie to the said Company And whereas William Perrie haveinge likewise gotten a warrant whereby he and a certaine Company of idle psons with him doe travel and play under the name and title of the Children of his Ma^ts Revels, to the great abuse of his Ma^ts srvice And whereas also Gilberte Reason one of the prince his highnes Playor^s having likewise sepated himselfe from his Company hath also taken forth another exemplification or duplicate of the patent granted to that Company and lives in the same kinde & abuse And likewise one Charles Marshall, Homfry Jeffes and Willm Parr: three of Prince Palatynes Company of Playo^rs haveinge also taken forthe an exemplification or duplicate of the patent graunted to the said Company and by vertue thereof live after the like kinde and abuse Wherefore to the and such idle psons may not be suffered to continewe in this course of life These are therefore to pray, and neatheless in his Ma^ts name to will and require you upon notice given of aine of the said psons by the bearer herof Joseph More whome I have speciallye directed for that purpose that you call the said pties offendo^rs before you and thereupon take the said sev[er]all exemplifications or duplicats or other ther warrants by which they use ther saide quallitie from them, And forthwith to send the same to me.[72]

From the 1590s the Master's powers included the licensing of playhouses, and early in James's reign he began to license plays for printing as well as performing. The main point of licensing companies and playhouses seems to have been not so much the control it established as the revenue it gave the Master. By the time of Henry Herbert, the last and most eager fulfiller of the office, the playhouse fee and the company fee were lumped together in a single annual payment, either from a benefit performance or as a lump sum. The King's Men gave him one day's takings each from the Blackfriars and Globe up to 1633, when they replaced them with a lump sum of £10 every Christmas and Midsummer. Beeston seems to have made a single payment.[73] Herbert's predecessor, Sir George Buc, noted in 1613 a payment of £20 for licensing the new Whitefriars playhouse, but this was a rare windfall, and in contrast we should note at least two occasions when the Master prevented a playhouse going up: Buc stopped Rosseter from building in Blackfriars in 1615; Herbert stopped Davenant in 1639.

The licensing of plays was also profitable for the Master, but in this case the ostensible object, censorship, was also a very real one, and the Master's labours were a serious duty taken seriously. The ordinance of 1559 had specified censorship of 'matters of religion or of the governaunce of the estate of the common weale'.[74] The hand of the censor can be seen descending on such matters in four extant manuscripts, *Sir Thomas More* (1594), *The Second Maiden's Tragedy* (1613), *Sir John Van Olden Barnavelt* (1619), and *Believe as you List* (1628), the last of which was prohibited altogether. The deposition scene in Shakespeare's *Richard II* is missing from the early quartos, evidently for censorship reasons, and the texts of *The Isle of Gulls* and Chapman's *Byron* plays are obviously censored.

In 1606 an Act 'to Restraine Abuses of Players' ordered the censorship of profane oaths: 'if...any person or persons doe or shall in any Stage play, Interlude, Shewe, Maygame, or Pageant jestingly or prophanely speake or use the holy name of God or of Christ Jesus, or of the Holy Ghoste or of the Trinitie...shall forfeite for everie such Offence by him or them committed Tenne pounds.'[75] This is one reason why the pagan gods begin to be called on with more frequency in the drama after this date. Herbert, the censor whose judgements we have most record of, in 1634 clarified the interpretation of the statute of oaths in a tiff with his royal master. As he noted,

This morning, being the 9th of January, 1633, [i.e. 1634], the kinge was pleasd to call mee into his withdrawinge chamber to the windowe, wher he went over all that I had croste in Davenants play-booke, [*The Wits*] and allowing of *faith* and *slight* to bee asseverations only, and no oathes, markt them to stande, and some other few things, but in the greater part allowed of my reformations. This was done upon a complaint of Mr. Endymion Porters in December.

The kinge is pleasd to take *faith*, *death*, *slight*, for asseverations, and no oaths, to which I doe humbly submit as my masters judgment; but, under favour, conceive them to be oaths, and enter them here, to declare my opinion and submission.[76]

Herbert's basic concerns are revealed in a few of the opinions he recorded, such as these:

1623, August 19. 'For the king's players. An olde playe called *Winter's Tale*, formerly allowed of by Sir George Bucke, and likewyse by mee on Mr. Hemmings his worde that there was nothing profane added or reformed, thogh the allowed booke was missinge, and therefore I returned it without a fee, this 19 of August, 1623.'

1624, January 2. 'For the Palsgrave's Company; *The History of the Dutchess of Suffolk*; which being full of dangerous matter was much reformed by me; I had two pounds for my pains: Written by Mr. Drew.'

1632, November 18. '18 Nov. 1632. In the play of *The Ball*, written by Sherley, and acted by the Queens players, ther were divers personated so naturally, both of lords and others of the court, that I took it ill, and would have forbidden the play, but that Biston promiste many things which I found faulte withall should be left out, and that he would not suffer it to be done by the poett any more, who deserves to be punisht; and the first that offends in this kind, of poets or players, shall be sure of publique punishment.[77]

His one detailed note on the reforming of matters of governance of the commonwealth again followed his master's voice:

> Monys? Wee'le rayse supplies what ways we please,
> And force you to subscribe to blanks, in which
> We'le mulct you as wee shall thinke fitt. The Caesars
> In Rome were wise, acknowledginge no lawes
> But what their swords did ratifye, the wives
> And daughters of the senators bowinge to
> Their wills, as deities, &c.

This is a peece taken out of Philip Messingers play, called *The King and the Subject*, and entered here for ever to bee remembered by my son and those that cast their eyes on it, in honour of Kinge Charles, my master, who readinge over the play at Newmarket, set his marke upon the place with his owne hande, and in thes words:

> This is too insolent, and to bee changed.

Note, that the poett makes it the speech of a king, Don Pedro, king of Spayne, and spoken to his subjects.[78]

Don Pedro was only slightly exaggerating the King's practices over money.[79]

The payment for licensing plays was seven shillings under Edmund Tilney, the first regular Master of the Revels. His successor, Buc, who was also his nephew, served as his deputy from 1597 and performed all the duties from 1607, when he started licensing plays for printing as well as performing, and charged £1 for either service. Herbert, who bought the reversion of the office in 1622, charged the same, doubling it for plays needing a lot of correction, and charging £2 regularly after 1632. Herbert paid £150 a year for the privilege of fulfilling the Master's duties, so his total income must have been substantially more than that.

The companies were not obliged to the Revels Office only for the licences which regulated and protected them. The Master also safeguarded public health by enforcing the plague regulations, and safeguarded religion by enforcing the prohibitions on playing through Lent, though in the later years Mammon was worshipped as well, in the form of profitable Lenten dispensations to play issued by Herbert.

Plague regulations so far as the theatres were concerned followed simply from the general requirement that places of public assembly should be closed in time of infection. The City made the point as early as 1569:

Forasmuch as thoroughe the greate resort, accesse and assembles of great multitudes of people unto diverse and severall Innes and other places of this Citie, and the liberties & suburbes of the same, to thentent to here and see certayne stage playes, enterludes, and other disguisinges, on the Saboth dayes and other solempne feastes commaunded by the church to be kept holy, and there being close pestered together in small romes, specially in this tyme of sommer, all not being and voyd of infeccions and diseases, whereby great infeccion with the plague, or some other infeccious diseases, may rise and growe, to the great hynderaunce of the comon wealth of this citty, and perill and daunger of the quenes majesties people, the inhabitantes thereof, and all others repayrying thether, about there necessary affares.[80]

The battles between City and Court in the 1570s and 1580s inevitably included the plague question. The Leicester's patent of 1574 forbade playing 'in the tyme of common prayer, or in the tyme of great and common plague'. The clashes ten years later which produced the Queen's Men and the City's 'Remedyes' over playing concluded that playhouses should not open until the weekly bill of plague victims had been less than fifty for three weeks. In 1604 the Privy Council brought this down to less than thirty a week.[81] The King's Men's patents of 1619 and 1625 specify forty. The limits were not always very exactly enforced, but the visitations of plague none the less were by far the most severely limiting phenomenon the players encountered. The prolonged closures of the really bad years, 1581–2, 1592–3, 1603–4, 1608–9, 1609–10, 1625, 1630, 1636–7, 1640 and 1641 never failed to endanger the companies and usually caused major reshuffles of membership.

The worship of God was less disruptive than the visitations. The Privy Council ordered the closing of theatres through Lent in 1579, and Henslowe's records show an obedient closure in 1595 and 1596. In 1597 however the Admiral's Men played through twelve days of Lent and observed the closure for less than the whole period again in the following year. In 1600, 1601 and 1604 the Privy Council renewed its orders about Lenten playing, yet in 1605, though Lent began on 13 February, the Prince's Men played at Whitehall on the 19th. In 1607 the King's Men played before James nine days after Lent had begun. In 1615 there were substantial violations of the closure order, and there is little evidence in later Revels Office records of any very strict enforcement. There is actually some evidence to suggest that the Master of the Revels took a fee for a 'Lenten dispensation', allowing playing throughout Lent excepting only 'sermon days', that is, Wednesdays and Fridays, and Holy Week. The performances are often noted as being displays of fencing or acrobatics rather than the more directly provocative stage-plays.[82] Dispensations of this kind make it readily understandable that in 1642 the whole business of playing should be taken out of the Privy Council's and its deputy's hands by Parliament's firm pronouncement that

Whereas the distressed Estate of Ireland, steeped in her own Blood, and the distracted Estate of England, threatned with a Cloud of Blood, by a Civill Warre, call for all possible meanes to appease and avert the Wrath of God appearing in these Judgements; amongst which, Fasting and Prayer having bin often tryed to be very effectuall, have bin lately, and are still ejoyned; and whereas publike Sports doe not well agree with publike Calamities, nor publike Stage-plays with the Seasons of Humiliation, this being an Exercise of sad and pious solemnity, and the other being Spectacles of pleasure, too commonly expressing lacivious Mirth and Levitie: It is therefore thought fit, and Ordeined by the Lords and Commons in this Parliament Assembled, that while these sad Causes and set times of Humiliation doe continue, publike Stage-Plays shall cease, and bee forborne.[83]

The single most characteristic feature of the companies throughout the period was their repertory system. Nothing can have shaped the nature of the organisation and playing so much as having to perform a different play every day, and to produce new plays at frequent intervals. The Admiral's in their 1594-5 season, performing six days a week, offered their audiences a total of thirty-eight plays, of which twenty-one were new to the repertory, added at more or less fortnightly intervals. Two of the new plays were performed only once, and only eight survived through to the following season. Even the most popular plays the Admiral's had, those of Marlowe, could be put on stage not more often than once every month or so. The first part of *Tamburlaine* appears in Henslowe's records for this season fourteen times, the second part six, *Faustus* twelve, *The Massacre at Paris* ten and *The Jew of Malta* nine. The repertory in the next season, 1595-6, was again large—thirty-seven plays, of which nineteen were new—and in 1596-7 thirty-four plays were performed of which fourteen were new. The most popular play over the whole three seasons, *The Wise Men of Westchester*, was performed altogether in the three years thirty-two times, or less than once a month even allowing for Lent.

The company's appetite for new plays was at its height at this time, of course, with security, a quasi-monopoly of London playing, and Marlowe's plays as the most famous of the day performed by the leading player of the day, to draw the crowds to them. Their appetite slackened off markedly later on. None the less, the stringent organisation and the feats of memory required from the company as a whole would have involved a number of consistent and traditional practices which must have persisted through the whole period and which we can recognise as characteristic. The most important of these would have been the custom of acting 'lines'. It is a ready presumption that each player was allocated the part in each new play which most closely suited his talents. No player would wish to change his part in a play once he had learnt it—there were enough new parts in new plays without that—so if one player left the company, his successor would have to take over all his abandoned parts, and would therefore be admitted to the company on the understanding that his 'line' matched that of the departed player. Such a system probably explains the insistence of the company agreements on a player being reimbursed for his share in the company only if he left with his fellows' consent. Personnel had duties too specific to allow easy coming and going.

The most tangible testimony for such a custom is to be found in the plays written by a company's resident playwright, most notably in the sequence of plays written first by Shakespeare, then by the authors of the Beaumont and Fletcher canon, for the King's Men. Such plays might reasonably be presumed to have been tailored to the company's personnel and particular talents at the time of writing. A number of cast-lists which survive from the later years of the company (1623–32) corroborate the presumption for at least those years. From these lists it appears that all members of the company were employed in every play; that there were consistently seven or eight major roles, two or three of them for women, who were played by the apprenticed boys; and that hired men did not take major parts.[84] The major roles can be roughly categorised as those of the hero (played by Joseph Taylor), the blunt foil for the hero, a tyrant or a soldier (John Lowin), smooth villain (Eyllaerdt Swanston), dignitary or old king (Robert Benfield), young man or lover (Richard Sharpe), and comic figure (Thomas Pollard). The company's chief clown, John Shank, is not cast prominently in the surviving lists, and may have been left to his own devices.[85] The illness or absence of a single player could not be allowed to stop the company performing, of course, and other players must have been capable of taking over a fellow's 'line' at short notice. But one can understand Henslowe's business interest at work as well as his milk of compassion when he advanced William Bird's wife £3 to get her husband out of prison, where he had been put 'for hurting of a felowe which browght his wiffe a leatter' (*Diary*, p. 83).

By projecting back through the King's Men's repertory a vaguely similar patterning of 'lines' in the earlier plays can be recognised. We can give some credence, for instance, to the view that when Joseph Taylor joined the King's Men, which he had done shortly before May 1619, he was there to replace Burbage, who had died in March.[86] Similarly Benfield joined the company in 1615 in all probability to replace William Ostler, who died in December 1614, and whose part as Antonio in *The Duchess of Malfi* he certainly took over. It is difficult to see how far the lineage can be traced back, or how invariably it can have operated. The company was enlarged from ten to twelve sharers in 1603, after all, and the experiences before that, and especially before 1594, with the shuffling of membership and ready passage of play-ownership from one company to another, could only have been forgotten after several years of steady membership and a secure London tenure. Equally, the writing of the many non-resident playwrights, who did not know the company so well, or who did not know which company would buy their work, would not necessarily fit the established 'lines'. It is not saying very much to note that the categorisations of characters in Elizabethan and Jacobean plays usually admit of half a dozen broad types which recur through most plays. Some plays, perhaps Shakespeare's, perhaps Jonson's for the Blackfriars boys, and possibly Fletcher's and Massinger's, were probably written on the presumption that certain players would take certain parts. This is enough to allow the theory of acting 'lines' as a repertory company's convenient practice, without pursuing the identification of particular parts and particular players of those parts too far.

3. The Players

In an epigram to Robert Armin, a King's player, John Davies of Hereford wrote:

> Wee all (that's Kings and all) but Players are
> Upon this earthly Stage. [*The Scourge of Folly* (1610), Q2v.]

Kings might well be compared to players. Comparing players to Kings, however, was a very different matter. The standard attitude to players was that put by an anonymous author in the mouth of the highwayman Gamaliel Ratsey, whose execution in 1605 was the occasion for the publication of several pamphlets about his life and opinions. One anecdote involved his exploitation of a troupe of travelling players (*Ratsey's Ghost*, A3v–B1v). Ratsey, according to the pamphleteer, came to an inn where

> that night there harbored a company of Players: and Ratsey framing him-
> selfe to an humor of merriment, caused one or two of the chiefest of them
> to be sent for up into his chamber, where hee demanded whose men they
> were, and they answered they served such an honorable Personage. I pray
> you (quoth Ratsey) let me heare your musicke, for I have often gone to
> plaies more for musicke sake, then for action. For some of you not content
> to do well, but striving to over-doe and go beyond your selves, oftentimes
> (by S. George) mar all; yet your Poets take great paines to make your parts
> fit for your mouthes, though you gape never so wide. Othersome I must
> needs confesse, are very wel deserving both for true action and faire deliverie
> of speech, and yet I warrant you the very best have sometimes beene content
> to goe home at night with fifteene pence share apiece.
>
> Others there are whom Fortune hath so wel favored, that what by penny-
> sparing and long practise of playing, are growne so wealthy, that they have
> expected to be knighted, or at least to be conjunct in authority, and to sit
> with men of great worship, on the Bench of Justice.

Evidently for this play-going highwayman it was a deplorable ambition (Ratsey himself was the son of a wealthy Lincolnshire gentleman). Having patronised his guests, Hamlet-fashion, and sympathised with their hard lot, Ratsey rewards them for listening to him and goes his way. A week later, still in his humour of merriment, he meets them again in a different disguise, like the players themselves, who were now masquerading under another name:

> lying as they did before in one Inne together, hee was desirous they should
> play a private play before him, which they did not in the name of the former

Noblemans servants. For like Camelions they had changed that colour; but in the name of another, (whose indeede they were) although afterwardes when he heard of their abuse, hee discharged them, and tooke away his warrant. For being far off, (for their more countenance) they would pretend to be protected by such an honourable man, denying their Lord and Master; and comming within ten or twenty miles of him againe, they would shrowd themselves under their owne Lords favour.

Ratsey heard their Play, and seemed to like that, though he disliked the rest, and verie liberally out with his purse, and gave them fortie shillings, with which they held themselves very richly satisfied, for they scarce had twentie shillings audience at any time for a Play in the Countrey.

Ratsey has other ideas of what they deserved, of course, and they become targets for his Robin Hood-like rough justice. The next day he overtakes them on the road and retrieves his bounty, taking the opportunity to reprove them for their 'idle profession'. The leader he singles out for gratuitous good counsel:

And for you (sirra saies hee to the chiefest of them) thou hast a good presence upon a stage, me thinks thou darkenst thy merite by playing in the country: Get thee to London, for if one man were dead, they will have much neede of such a one as thou art. There would be none in my opinion, fitter then thy selfe to play his parts: my conceipt is such of thee, that I durst venture all the mony in my purse on thy head, to play Hamlet with him for a wager. There thou shalt learne to be frugall (for Players were never so thriftie as they are now about London) & to feed upon all men, to let none feede upon thee; to make thy hand a stranger to thy pocket, thy hart slow to performe thy tongues promise: and when thou feelest thy purse well lined, buy thee some place or Lordship in the Country, that growing weary of playing, thy mony may there bring thee to dignitie and reputation: then thou needest care for no man, nor not for them that before made thee prowd, with speaking their words upon the Stage. Sir, I thanke you (quoth the Player) for this good counsell, I promise you I will make use of it; for I have heard indeede, of some that have gone to London very meanly, and have come in time to be exceeding wealthy. And in this presage and propheticall humor of mine, (says Ratsey) kneele downe, Rise up Sir Simon two shares and a halfe: Thou art now one of my Knights, and the first Knight that ever was Player in England. The next time I meete thee, I must share with thee againe for playing under my warrant, and so for this time adiew.

How ill hee brooked this new knighthood, which hee durst not but accept of, or liked his late counsell, which he lost his coine for, is easie to be imagined. But whether he met with them againe after the senights space, that he charged them to play in his name, I have not heard it reported.

The Ratsey anecdote provides a common view of the common player in his own times and troubles, though there is a special antipathy to players in the pamphleteer, which may be explained by his fellow-feeling with 'them that before made thee prowd, with speaking their words upon the Stage'. The providers knew how generously the players treated them; Heywood's company paid out more for the heroine's dress in *A Woman Killed with Kindness* than for the play itself.[1]

The social standing of players, or rather the range of social attitudes to them, can be seen in a comparison of the Theophrastan characterisation 'A Common Player' of 1615 with its counter 'An Excellent Actor'. The first was written by a law student called John Cocke from Lincoln's Inn. It claimed that

The Statute hath done wisely to acknowledg him a Rogue, for his chiefe essence is, *A daily Counterfeit*: He hath beene familiar so long with out-sides, that he professes himselfe, (being unknowne) to be an apparant Gentleman. But his thinne Felt, and his silke Stockings, or his foule Linnen, and faire Doublet, doe (in him) bodily reveale the Broker: So beeing not sutable, hee proves a *Motley*.[2]

The Player Cocke characterised was not necessarily so common either; he might be a King's Man. But he would be, none the less, a rogue:

howsoever hee pretends to have a royall Master or Mistresse, his wages and dependance prove him to be the servant of the people. The cautions of his judging humor (if hee dares undertake it) be a certaine number of sawcie rude jests against the common lawyer; hansome conceits against the fine Courtiers; delicate quirkes against the rich Cuckold a Cittizen; shadowed glaunces for good innocent Ladies and Gentlewomen; with a nipping scoffe for some honest Justice, who hath imprisoned him: or some thriftie Tradesman, who hath allowed him no credit.

Such an imputation was too much for one company with a royal master, and a reply soon appeared in print, probably written by Webster, whose *Duchess of Malfi* had recently been performed by the King's Men. It describes in conventional terms the qualities of a good actor as Heywood had set them down in his definitive *Apology for Actors*, stressing their educational value:

By his action he fortifies morall precepts with example; for what we see him personate, we thinke truely done before us: a man of a deepe thought might apprehend, the Ghosts of our ancient *Heroes* walk't againe, and take him (at severall times) for many of them. Hee is much affected to painting, and tis a question whether that make him an excellent Plaier, or his playing an exquisite painter.[3]

The last reference is meant to remind us of Richard Burbage, still the leading King's player, who was well enough known as a painter to have been commissioned in 1613 and 1616 to paint escutcheons for the Earl of Rutland[4] (see pl. II). Cocke was being unwarrantably snobbish.

The imitating Characterist was extreame idle in calling them Rogues. His Muse it seemes, with all his loud invocation, could not be wak't to light him a snuffe to read the Statute: for I would let his malicious ignorance understand, that Rogues are not to be imploide as maine ornaments to his Majesties Revels.

Cocke subsequently backpedalled, overlooking his explicit reference to the King's and Queen's companies, and protested that he meant only common players. He was let off a good deal more lightly than a later opponent of the theatre, William Prynne, whose *Histrio-mastix* of 1633 was one of the more trenchant Puritan blasts against plays and players. It attacked such decadences as women appearing in Court presentations. Henrietta Maria herself had recently graced a masque with her participation, so Prynne was taken up by the Star Chamber, who stripped him of his academic degrees, fined him, pilloried him, cropped his ears and sentenced him to the Tower for life. The Court was defending its own, and its own openly included the players.

The descriptions of Cocke and Ratsey were probably not entirely inaccurate with regard to the great majority of professional players who travelled for their living and whose fifteen pence or two shillings were rarely as ready to hand as the craftsman's shilling.[5] It was an exceptional player who could indeed profess himself to be an apparent gentleman and conceal his dyer's hand in a courtier's glove. Shakespeare's own purchase of a coat of arms for his father, with its less than eulogistic motto 'Non Sans Droict', earned him a dig from his fellow-actor and playwright Jonson, whose Sogliardo in *Every Man Out of his Humour* proudly declares the motto of *his* new coat of arms to be '*Not without mustard*'.

Ratsey's gibe at the aspiration of prosperous players to knighthoods or at least to the 'Bench of Justice' would probably have been taken as an allusion to Alleyn, Burbage's peer, and the wealthiest of the famous London players at the turn of the century. The Ratsey reference to Hamlet must apply to Burbage, so it is not unlikely that the other player referred to should be Alleyn. In 1605 he was Master of the Royal Game (or Bear-warden), a post which Henslowe's father had held before him, and he was already laying plans for the foundation of his great benefaction, Dulwich College. Alleyn failed in his ambition for a knighthood,[6] though in 1610 he did become a Churchwarden, a position carrying with it some judicial functions. His past as a player did not prevent him making his third marriage in 1623 to a daughter of the Dean of St Paul's. The fifty-two-year-old Dean, who in his days as Jack Donne had seen *Tamburlaine* and therefore presumably Alleyn on the London stage (In *The Calme*, line 33, he speaks of seeing Bajazeth in his cage), was less than amiable to his sixty-year-old son-in-law, but the quarrels were built on financial grounds rather than social.

Money was a major determinant of status in that decade if not before. In 1630 Charles found a new source of income by fining those subjects with annual incomes of £40 a year who had not taken up knighthoods at the time of the coronation in 1625. One subject reluctant to have honour thrust upon him in such a fashion was a Cuthbert Burbage, almost certainly Richard's brother and still a proprietor of the Black-friars and Globe.[7] A source of income from plays was no barrier to the purchase of gentility.

To locate players fairly precisely in the strata of Elizabethan and Jacobean society we should look first at the relationship of the great players to the great nobles. Phillip Sidney was not ashamed to be god-father to the son of Richard Tarlton the clown, and when Burbage died in 1619 the Earl of Pembroke wrote to the Earl of Carlisle that he had stayed away from a play at Court 'which I being tender-harted could not endure to see so soone after the loss of my old acquaintance Burbadg'.[8] On the other hand one of the signatories to the petition of residents which prevented the Burbages and their company from moving into the Blackfriars playhouse in 1596 was their own patron, Lord Hunsden, the Lord Chamberlain. Some at least of the lords of society were not prepared to tolerate the antics and dispositions of the public players except at a distance from home, and there is no evidence that many common players rose beyond their immediate circumstances in the tiring-houses and taverns of London and the provinces. It is probably not an over-statement to say that to the aristocracy they were befriended parasites.

Something of the history of acting as well as actors can be found in the careers of the famous players. The first great names of the 1580s were the clowns of extempore, Tarlton and Robert Wilson, whose fame far exceeded that of their contemporary straight actors in the Queen's Men, Bentley and Knell. By 1600 the position was reversed, and the reputations as tragedians of Alleyn and Burbage dominated the theatre world; in 1599 Kempe danced his way out of the 'world',[9] and his successor Armin was as renowned for being a playwright as for being a clown. Subsequent fame fell less on Alleyn's and Burbage's successors, those who inherited their famous roles, Perkins or Taylor, as on the actor-managers like Beeston or actor-playwrights like Nathan Field. First the witty entertainers, next the great tragedians, lastly the impresarios. Like honour, fame proved increasingly a commercial consideration.

Tarlton was not only a theatrical clown but a man of many parts, a maker of plays and ballads, a drummer, tumbler and qualified Master of Fencing.[10] He became famous in the 1570s, a byword in the 1580s, and a popular legend for a century after his death for his extemporised jests. Howes's additions to Stowe's *Annales* in 1615 characterise his facility as 'a wondrous plentifull pleasant extemporall wit', as distinct from that of his fellow-member of the Queen's and fellow-playwright Robert Wilson, whose wit was 'quicke delicate refined extemporall' (p. 697). His 1585 play, *The Seven Deadly Sins*, enormously popular though it was, has not survived in print (we have only the 'plot' of the second part), and the bulk of the evidence for his facility appears in the numerous jestbooks published after his death and purporting to record the witticisms of his life. Jestbooks were extremely popular reading fare in the sixteenth century, and if the usual practice of fathering common tales on semi-legendary wits like Skelton was also applied to Tarlton few of the anecdotes could be relied on. Fortunately some of his jokes were distinctive enough to be repeated by more reputable authorities than the jestbook writers. John Manningham noted one he heard, in his *Diary*, 1602:

Tarlton called Burley house gate in the Strand towardes the Savoy, the Lord Treasurers Almes gate, because it was seldom or never opened.[11]

This was very likely heard at second or third hand, if not at a further remove, since it was noted down fourteen years after Tarlton's death. Henry Peacham (*Truth of our Times*, 1638) told one at first hand:

I remember when I was a schoolboy in *London*, *Tarlton* acted a third son's part...His father being a very rich man, and lying upon his death-bed, called his three sonnes about him...To the third, which was *Tarlton* (who came like a rogue in a foule shirt without a band, and in a blew coat with one sleeve, his stockings out at the heeles, and his head full of straw and feathers), as for you, Sirrah, quoth he, you know how often I have fetched you out of *Moorgate* and *Bridwell*, you have beene an ungracious villaine, I have nothing to bequeath to you but the gallowes and a rope. *Tarlton* weeping, and sobbing upon his knees (as his brothers) said, O Father, I doe not desire it, I trust in God you shall live to enjoy it your selfe.[12]

The reply may or may not have been extempore; certainly Tarlton's reputation did not entirely rest on his ability to extemporise. He is described as having a squint eye and a flat nose, and his very appearance, as Peacham also noted, was often funny enough:

> Tarlton when his head was onely seene,
> The Tire-house dore and Tapistrie betweene,
> Set all the multitude in such a laughter,
> They could not hold for scarse an houre after.[13]

As early as 1592 Nashe in *Pierce Penilesse* had described a similar reaction and its consequences when the Queen's company was travelling in the country;

A tale of a wise Justice. Amongst other cholericke wise Justices, he was one, that having a play presented before him and his Towneship by *Tarlton* and the rest of his fellowes, her Majesties servants, and they were now entring into their first merriment (as they call it), the people began exceedingly to laugh, when *Tarlton* first peept out his head. Whereat the Justice, not a little moved, and seeing with his beckes and nods hee could not make them cease, he went with his staffe, and beat them round about unmercifully on the bare pates, in that they, being but Farmers & poore countrey Hyndes, would presume to laugh at the Queenes men, and make no more account of her cloath in his presence.[14]

Tarlton's compeer, Wilson, a more scholarly wit, played in the same company with him.[15] Evidently the value of having extemporising wits and versifiers in the group was sufficient to justify two such performers sharing the same performance. Wilson also spent some time with Leicester's Men, touring the Netherlands with them in 1585–6, when he shared his work with 'my lord of Lesters jesting plaier' as Sidney described him, Will Kempe, the clown who later became the resident extemporising comedian in Shakespeare's company and probably the first actor of Falstaff.[16]

Kempe was the last of the famous Elizabethan clowns. He was better known for harlequinade and jigs than wit, and probably served his turn mainly for the dances and jigging sketches which normally accompanied performances on the public stages. He is rightly or wrongly thought to have been the culprit charged by Hamlet with speaking more than was set down for him, and it has even been suggested that his departure from the Chamberlain's Men in 1599 was because he had a hand in the piracy of the last Falstaff play, *The Merry Wives of Windsor*.[17] What is clear is that the role of the clown in adult company plays had diminished markedly in value as plays began to offer more scope for the tragic actors. Hamlet's reprimand simply reflects a new impatience with extempore. Kempe's duties as clown with a part in almost every play of his company's repertory probably did not decline, but his occupancy of the stage during the performance proper was probably less. His parts we know of include Peter in *Romeo and Juliet* and Dogberry in *Much Ado*, where he was given no more than a couple of scenes in which to indulge himself. His successor had significantly different talents. Robert Armin was a playwright as Tarlton and Wilson had been, but much less an extemporiser. He was known for his singing rather than his wit. Where Shakespeare had written Falstaff and Dogberry with Kempe in mind, for Armin he produced Feste and Lear's Fool.[18] Both Kempe and Armin claimed descent from Tarlton, but between 1580 and 1600 the inheritance had dropped sharply in value. Alleyn's Tamburlaine now bestrode the stage.

Alleyn was born in 1566, the son of a London 'innholder'. Possibly his father's occupation brought him into early contact with the players, for he was already with a leading company, Worcester's, by the time he was sixteen. By 1592 he was the outstanding player of his day. As Henslowe's son-in-law and business partner, both in the theatrical affairs and in the bull- and bear-baiting business, he achieved an unparalleled prosperity, not only for himself but for the reputation of the stage as a whole. He became famous as Tamburlaine, Faustus and Barrabas in Marlowe's plays, as Orlando in *Orlando Furioso*, Muly Mahomet in *The Battle of Alcazar* and Tamar Cam in the play of that name.[19] His 'stalking Tamburlaine' drew similes from several pamphleteers at the end of the century. His own mocking name for himself in a family letter was 'the fustian king'.[20] Fuller remembered him as 'the Roscius of our age, so acting to the life, that he made any part (especially a majestick one) to become him' (*Worthies*, 1662, Fff2v). He took the part of Genius in King James's triumphal pageant through London in 1604; Dekker records that 'his gratulatory speech was delivered with excellent Action, and a well tun'de, audible voyce' (*The Magnificent Entertainment*, 1604, C1r). Early in the new century he gave himself up wholly to his business interests, retaining his shares in the Admiral's Men as manager rather than as player. He began negotiations to purchase the manor of Dulwich in about 1605, when he was thirty-nine, the year of Ratsey's anecdote, and began the school and hospital which have since become Dulwich College as a work of piety in 1613. The property cost £10,000 initially, and subsequent expenditure was about £1,700 a year, all of which derived in the first instance from Alleyn's theatrical interests.[21] He and his College were the age's tidemark for the commercial and pietistic respectability of his first profession.

The name linked with Alleyn's by the early historians of the Elizabethan stage as the greatest of its players was of course Burbage. Baker's *Chronicle* (1674) celebrates '*Richard Bourbidge* and *Edward Allen*, two such Actors as no age must ever look to see the like'.[22] Seven years younger than Alleyn, Burbage was the younger son of the carpenter turned impresario who built the Theatre in 1576, and first appears at the age of seventeen, named in a lawsuit as defending his father's takings. He protected them with 'a broom staff' when the deponents came to collect their share in accordance with a Chancery Court order, and

scornfully and disdainfully playing with this deponent's nose, said that if he dealt in the matter, he would beat him also, and did challenge the field of him at that time.[23]

He was then in the company of Alleyn with the Strange's–Admiral's amalgamation of 1590. He probably left them for Pembroke's after this, as we have seen, and reappeared in the new Chamberlain's Men in 1594, as their leading actor and a major shareholder.[24] His father left the Theatre and his Blackfriars property to Richard and his elder brother Cuthbert in 1597. Burbage seems to have been less commercially minded than Alleyn. He avoided the temptations of managership and remained in acting until his death in 1619, when he left his wife according to contemporary rumour 'better than £300 land',[25] which though considerable in his time hardly compares with Alleyn's holdings or even with those of his fellow-actor Shakespeare in Stratford. He was forty-six when he died, by which time he had made famous such roles as Richard III, Jeronimo, Hamlet, Lear, Othello, and Ferdinand in Webster's *Duchess of Malfi*; his name appears in all the King's Men's plays for which actor-lists survive between

1599 and 1618. He was Ratsey's Hamlet as Alleyn was the one hoping to be knighted.

In the second decade of the seventeenth century Nathan Field came to rival Burbage in fame. Jonson linked the two names in *Bartholomew Fair* in 1613, and Richard Flecknoe in a retrospective comment in 1664 spoke of them as the leading players at the time when Jonson, Shakespeare and Beaumont and Fletcher were the leading playwrights. 'It was the happiness of the Actors of those Times to have such Poets as these to instruct them and write for them; and no less of those Poets, to have such docile and excellent Actors to Act their Playes, as a *Field* and *Burbidge*.'[26] Field was a contemporary of Burbage in the King's Men for the last four years of his life, and died only a few months after him. His fame was not entirely for playing. He died a bachelor with a considerable reputation, of the kind not uncommon among players, for success with women. A story circulating in 1619 reckoned that the Earl of Argyll had paid 'for the nourseing of a childe which the worlde says is a daughter to my lady and N. Feild the Player'[27] (see pl. IV).

After Burbage and Field the names most prominent in theatre affairs were those of such men as Beeston and Richard Gunnell, who was a leading player with Palsgrave's in 1622—Alleyn leased the rebuilt Fortune to the company with Gunnell and Charles Massey as the chief sharers—and who built the Salisbury Court playhouse in 1629. Gunnell and Beeston were not directly involved in playing, so far as we know, in their years as impresarios. The chief fame of the last years was mainly reserved for first of all the King's Men's trio of Taylor, Lowin and Swanston, and then for the clowns of the leading companies— Shank at the Blackfriars, Timothy Reade at Salisbury Court and Andrew Cane at the Fortune. In a number of ways the notes we have on them curiously echo the praise given to the clowns of the 1580s. Shank's fame was for his knockabout and dancing,[28] as was Cane's. The latter was remembered as late as 1673, when Henry Chapman excused the presence of an appendix in his pamphlet by saying it was the fashion, 'Without which a Pamphlet now a dayes, finds as small acceptance as a Comedy did formerly, at the *Fortune* Play-house, without a Jig of *Andrew Kein's* into the bargain'.[29] Reade is linked with Cane in a pamphlet of 1641, '*The Stage-Players Complaint*, in a Pleasant Dialogue between Cane of the *Fortune* and Reed of the *Friers* [i.e. Whitefriars, or Salisbury Court]'. In the pamphlet Cane is called '*Quick*' and described as able to 'outstrip facetious Mercury in your tongue', while Reade is '*Light*', and described as nimble-footed, with heels 'as light as a *Finches* Feather'. Reade seems to have used the same trick of poking his head through the curtain as Tarlton in Nashe's anecdote. In Goffe's *The Careless Shepherdess* (1656) a character reminisces

> I never saw *Rheade* peeping through the Curtain,
> But ravishing joy enter'd into my heart

and claims to have preferred Reade's 'Craps and Quibbles' to 'the gravest speech in all the *Play*'.[30]

In noting the memories of the last decade of the Shakespearean tradition of acting, it is also worth remembering the French actors whom Beeston entertained in 1629 and 1635. Their fashion struck their contemporaries as somewhat exaggerated. In Glapthorne's *The Lady's Privilege* (1640), a character describes them as inclined to affectation:

> Very ayry people, who participate
> More fire than earth; yet generally good,
> And nobly disposition'd, something inclining
> To overweening fancy.

The same character then demonstrates their playing by mimicking a 'Comick scene', in which he '*Acts furiously*' (II.i).

The question of degrees of affectation or exaggeration in acting raises the next matter in the consideration of players and playing: the question of the boy players and the difference between their playing and that of the adults. To begin with we must distinguish between the boys of the boy companies and the boy trainees in the adult companies. The backgrounds of the two kinds of boy player were originally quite different. The boys apprenticed to the adult companies were bound for a period of several years' training in their profession before graduating, like the apprentices of the Livery Guilds, into journeymen and eventually perhaps sharers in their company. They entered their indentures between the ages of ten and thirteen, usually playing the women's parts which their small stature and unbroken voices equipped them for (though not only boys played women—there is a record of a twenty-four-year-old doing so). Burbage according to his brother's account must have been acting by the time he was thirteen,[31] and Alleyn was already outstanding by sixteen.

The boys of the children's companies on the other hand acted only with their own age group and were trained and directed not by their fellow-actors but by the managers for whose profit they worked. In 1599 and 1600 they came into existence as a venture backed by a tradition of boy playing in the choir-school companies older and far more respectable than the professional adult tumblers-turned-players had behind them. In actual fact by 1576 when Farrant started the Chapel Children at the first Blackfriars their contribution to the Court Revels had already diminished and the once predominant chorister function had been separated off altogether from the playing. They were already frankly commercial, though the bland pretence to be rehearsing for her majesty's pleasure was retained as an obvious bulwark against the hostile local authorities.

Between the boy company actors and the boy players in the adult companies there was no difference of interest, though there was some difference of organisation, since instead of being bound to individual sharers' as in the adult companies the boy players were all bound to their manager.[32] The major difference lay in their educational backgrounds. The descendants of the chorister groups played normally only once a week,[33] and some at least of the remaining time not given to rehearsing was given over to formal education. When Paul's discreetly closed down in 1606 the boys who did not join the other company returned to their nominal occupations without great difficulty. The production of plays by boy actors had always been a schoolmaster's art, and the pupils of the best schoolmasters were anxiously sought after by the managers; in some cases too anxiously, as we know from the case of the kidnapped Thomas Clifton, who was a pupil at Christ Church school. Most of Evans's boys probably came from St Paul's Grammar School, where Nathan Field was certainly a pupil. He was then thirteen, and evidently already an expertly trained player. The Master of St Paul's School was Richard Mulcaster, celebrated for several decades for the shows his boys produced at Court and elsewhere. The Citizen's Wife in *The Knight of the Burning Pestle* asks one of the boy players (of the Chapel company) if he is not one of 'Maister *Monkesters* schollars', evidently a matter for some pride. Richard Brinsley, another schoolmaster, wrote a book in 1612 called *Ludus Literarius*, praising the value of playing in the education of schoolchildren.

The background of even the post-1599 boy companies was more academic than that of the professional adult players, and their training accordingly was probably not so much in pure acting practice as in the declamatory arts of rhetoric, specifically pronunciation and gesture. Acting in plays was customary in many schools in the sixteenth century as a tail on the necessary dog of schooling in oratory. The growth of commercial interests made the acting tail wag the educational dog, but the link between the two was not entirely severed in the process.[34] Heywood in his *Apology for Actors* (1612) cited his own experience at Cambridge as a major part of his justification of his profession:

In the time of my residence in *Cambridge*, I have seen Tragedyes, Comedyes, Historyes, Pastorals and Shewes, publicly acted, in which Graduates of good place and reputation, have bene specially parted: this is held necessary for the emboldening of their Junior schollers, to arme them with audacity, against they come to bee imployed in any publicke exercise, as in the reading of Dialectike, Rhetoricke, Ethicke, Mathematicke, the Physicke, or Metaphysicke Lectures. It teacheth audacity to the bashfull Grammarian, beeing newly admitted into the private Colledge, and after matriculated and entred as a member of the University, and makes him a bold Sophister, to argue *pro et contra*, to compose his Sillogismes, Cathegoricke, or Hypotheticke (simple or compound) to reason and frame a sufficient argument to prove his questions, or to defend any *axioma*, to distinguish of any Dilemma & be able to moderate in any Argumentation whatsoever. [C3v.]

Readers of the *Parnassus* plays put on by Cambridge students at the turn of the century might feel Heywood's argument to be improbably pious; but the background of formal education in the decorums of speech and its attendant gestures must have had its effect on the theatrical foreground.[35]

We do not know how rare was the transition which brought Nathan Field, Underwood and Ostler into the leading adult companies, but Field at least was outstanding among his adult brethren for his learning. During his four years with the King's Men they put him to good use not only as an actor but as a playwright. His educational background was far different from that of such unsuccessful players as turned to pirating playbooks in the hard times of the 1590s.[36] The classical learning even of actors competent enough at writing to make up a pirated text was so deficient that they cannot be assumed to have had much schooling of any kind, let alone training in rhetoric, which usually started fairly well on in the Elizabethan school curriculum. One of Alleyn's wryer protests to his father-in-law Dr Donne claimed that his education had not been in sophistry:

Before this violence brake forth you called me a plain man. I desire always to be so for I thank God I could never disguise in my life and I am too old now to learn rhetoric of the curiousest school in Christendom.[37]

Some distinction must have existed between the unschooled professionals on the one hand, descendants of the poor players who toured and tumbled for a living only slightly better than vagabondage, and the academically tutored schoolchildren on the other, practised as they were in the long tradition of Quintillian's rhetoric with its emphasis on careful speech and studied gesture. The social and educational difference provides one reason why the playwrights who produced material for the boy companies in the years after 1600, particularly Marston and Chapman, regularly gave their little eyasses lines to belabour the common players with. Marston gave Paul's Boys in 1602 a chance to demand in *Antonio's Revenge*, I.v:

> would'st have me turn rank mad,
> Or wring my face with mimick action;
> Stampe, curse, weepe, rage, & then my bosome strike?
> Away tis apish action, player-like.

and again in 1606, in *Wonder of Women*, IV.i (acted by the Revels Children):

> I should now curse the Gods
> Call on the furies: stampe the patient earth
> cleave my streachd cheeks with sound speake from all sense
> But *loud and full* of players eloquence
> No, no, What shall we eate.

Chapman similarly gave the boys an attack on exaggerated acting in his comedy *The Widow's Tears* in about 1605 (acted by the Revels Children):

This straine of mourning with Sepulcher, like an over-doing Actor, affects grosly, and is indeede so farr forct from the life, that it bewraies it selfe to be altogether artificiall. [IV.i.]

Acting 'to the life' was of course intrinsically a more 'artificiall' business for boys acting men's parts than for the men themselves, and it would be understandable if they bolstered their performances by using the academically approved conceptions of what was natural, and criticised by their means the acting of the adults which exceeded their capacities. Equally, of course, there may be the taste of sour grapes in their distaste for the adult fustian kings and for the excesses of the 'stalking-stamping Player, that will raise a tempest with his toung, and thunder with his heeles' (*The Puritan*, 1607, III.iv: acted by Paul's). They seem to have given a very emphatic preference themselves to satirical prose comedy over the fustian plays with which they tried in the early days to match the adults.

Cynthia's Revels, the first play the Chapel Children commissioned from Jonson in 1600, contains a large number of instructions to the boys how they should act, and offers as good a guide as any to what a judicious bystander felt they could do. They are advised to 'studie to be like cracks [i.e. crackropes, boy players]; practise...language, and behaviours, and not with a dead imitation: act freely, carelessly, and capriciously, as if our veines ranne with quick-silver.'[38] Amorphus, who was probably played by Field, at one point (II.iii) demonstrates to his fellows 'the particular, and distinct face of every your most noted *species* of persons, as your marchant, your scholer, your souldier, your lawyer, courtier, &c. and each of these so truly, as you would sweare, but that your eye shal see the variation of the lineament, it were my most proper, and genuine aspect'. III.v in the same play is a full-scale rehearsal scene, a coaching session in acting run by Amorphus. Jonson's opinion of the capacities of the player of Amorphus was evidently high, and of a kind to suggest that the boy company strictures on 'player' acting as 'stalking-stamping' were simply justifiable condemnations of exaggeration.

The condemnations of exaggerated acting were not confined to the boys of 1600–8, however. Shakespeare gave Burbage as Hamlet the most famous condemnation of all in 1600 when the eyasses were carrying it away. He followed it up with Ulysses' speech in *Troilus and Cressida* about the 'strutting player whose conceit / Lies in his hamstring, and doth think it rich / To hear the wooden dialogue and sound, / 'Twixt his stretched footing and the scaffoldage' (I.iii.153–6), which might be construed as stalking–stamping. Shakespeare had produced a detailed account of over-acting much earlier than this in *Richard III*, where Buckingham says contemptuously (III.v.5–11):

> Tut, I can counterfeit the deep tragedian,
> Speak and look back, and pry on every side,
> Tremble and start at wagging of a straw:
> Intending deep suspicion, ghastly looks
> Are at my service, like enforcéd smiles;
> And both are ready in their offices,
> At any time, to grace my stratagems.

We might well suspect that academic teaching of pronunciation and gesture was less useful to either the boys or the adults than a direct eye on nature.[39] If anything the orators learnt these aspects of their occupation from the players rather than the reverse. The relationship was certainly described on that assumption by an anonymous writer in 1616 (T. G., *The Rich Cabinet*), who claimed that

as an Orator was most forcible in his ellocution; so was an actor in his gesture and personated action. [Q4r.]

The really important thing for us in the relationship between oratory and acting is its effect on the terminology used to describe acting, and the implications of the changes in terminology.

In the sixteenth century the term 'acting' was originally used to describe the 'action' of the orator, his art of gesture. What the common stages offered was 'playing'.[40] From this distinction came Jonson's bitter jibe when he inscribed the title-page of *The New Inn* as having been 'never acted, but most negligently play'd, by some, the Kings Servants'. That the academic term 'acting' should so completely become the prerogative of the common players as it did by early in the seventeenth century is the most striking testimony possible to their predominance over the orators. More significantly perhaps, what the players were presenting on stage by the beginning of the century was distinctive enough to require a whole new term to describe it. This term, 'personation', is suggestive of a relatively new art of individual characterisation, an art distinct from the orator's display of passions or the academic actor's portrayal of the character-types described by Jonson in *Cynthia's Revels* and by earlier academic playwrights such as Richard Edwardes, in the prologue to his *Damon and Pithias*, 1565. The author of the comparison between oratory and acting quoted above spoke of the player's 'personated' action; Heywood's *Apology for Actors* specified that the good actor should 'qualifie everything according to the nature of the person personated' (C4r); even the author of a puritanical reply to Heywood (I. G., *A Refutation of the Apology for Actors*, 1615) told a story in which a 'jesting-Plaier...so truely counterfeited every thing, that it seemed to bee the very persons whom he acted' (E3v). The essential virtue of the character of 'An Excellent

Actor' was held to be that 'what we see him personate, we thinke truely done before us'. The first use of the term 'personation' is recorded in the Induction to Marston's *Antonio and Mellida*, written probably in 1599–1600, at the end of the great decade in which Alleyn and Burbage made their reputations. It is probably not stretching plausibility too far to suggest that the term was called into being by the same developments—in the kinds of part given the actors to play and their own skill in their parts—that made two great tragedians succeed the extemporising clowns on the pinnacle of theatrical fame. By 1600 characterisation was the chief requisite of the successful actor.

To know that natural acting, 'counterfeiting' nature and playing a part 'to the life' or with 'lively action' was the Elizabethan norm[41] is not necessarily to know how an Elizabethan player would have rendered his part on stage, of course. Such descriptions as we have of Elizabethan displays of feeling do not entirely correspond with the postures evoked by the same feelings today. The language of gesture is more or less conventional, and therefore as liable to change as any other language. In Field's *Amends for Ladies* (1616) I.i, a gentleman complains that his mistress does not take his love seriously because he uses the wrong language:

> 'cause I doe not weepe,
> Lay mine arms ore my heart, and weare no garters,
> Walke with mine eyes in my hat, sigh, and make faces.

And the 'country man' who composed *The Cyprian Conqueror* in about 1633 wrote a preface instructing the potential actors of his play how to perform:

The other parts of action, is in ye gesture, wch must be various, as required; as in a sorrowfull parte, ye head must hang downe; in a proud, ye head must bee lofty; in an amorous, closed eies, hanging downe lookes, & crossed armes, in a hastie, fuming, & scratching ye head &c. . . [42]

Still, the difference was probably not too great. In 1644 a teacher of the deaf, John Bulwer, produced a manual of what he called with unconscious irony the 'Naturall language of the hand', describing the gesture appropriate to each emotion (*Chirologia* and *Chironomia*, 1644).[43] The thoughtful man is shown scratching his head, threats are made with a shaking of the clenched fist, a finger on the lips asks for silence, and oaths are sworn with raised palm, much as one might expect today if one were to seek out gestures with which to mime such processes. Of Bulwer's illustrations, a hundred and twenty in all, perhaps twenty would not still be readily recognisable to a modern audience. But such gestures would also be recognised today of course as more appropriate to mime than to acting. Bulwer was not writing for the stage, but for the orator, from the standpoint of the inventor of a sign-language for the deaf, and his illustrations belong more properly with dumb-show than acting with words. When the Player Queen in *Hamlet* '*makes passionate Action*' of grief during the dumb-show (III.ii.134) she in all probability raised her joined hands to heaven just in the way Bulwer's sorrowful orator does. That Queen Gertrude was expected to do the same is unlikely.

By the time *Hamlet* was written, in fact, 'Pantomimick action' was openly condemned as old-fashioned. Thomas Campion in his *Book of Airs* (1601) spoke contemptuously of the old academic acting, the

> old exploided action in Comedies, when if they did pronounce *Memeni*, they would point to the hinder parts of their heads, if *Video*, put their finger in their eye. But such childish observing of words is altogether ridiculous. [B2v.]

And in 1602 Thomas Tomkis showed that it was out of date even in Cambridge, where plays in Latin were still performed, when in his student play *Lingua* he produced an affected young man called Phantastes, showing his peers how to 'pronounce':

> PHA[NTASTES]. Pish, pish this is a speech with no action, lets here Terence: *quid igitur faciam*, &c
>
> COM[EDUS]. *Quid igitur faciam? non eam ne nunc quidam cum accusor ultro?*
>
> PHA. Phy, phy, phy, no more action, lend me your baies, doe it thus. *Quid igitur*, &c.
> > *He acts it after the old kinde of Pantomimick action*
>
> COM[MUNIS] SEN[SUS]. I shold judge this action *Phantastes* most absurd: unles we should come to a Commedy, as gentlewomen to the commencement, only to see men speake. [IV. ii.]

Tomkis at least, one presumes, would have listened to his Shakespeare as well as watching him. Bulwer's concern was primarily with the academic schooling of orators so that their audiences could, literally, 'see men speake'.

Certain conventions of gesture on the Elizabethan stage did clearly differ from what would be familiar today. The conventions were the shorthand of stage presentation, and in a packed repertory, with plays performed at high speed, there can have been little chance for deeply studied portrayals of emotions at work. There were many ways of utilising this shorthand.[44] Such conventions as love at first sight needed an established means of portrayal on stage, for use when the dramatist needed it. Marston did, in *The Insatiate Countess* (1611), where we find at one point the bald stage direction '*Isabella fals in love*'. Some method of presentation involving mimed gestures was necessary in such cases, especially with love at first sight, since it usually struck the lover dumb.[45] Another convention which seems less than natural today is the tradition of direct address to the audience. Falstaff's catechism on honour is a relic of the clown's role of 'interloqutions with the

Audients'.[46] Like explanatory prologues, the explanatory soliloquy or aside to the audience was a relic of the less sophisticated days which developed into a useful and more naturalistic convention of thinking aloud, but which never entirely ceased to be a convention.[47]

Theatrical shorthand in the conventions of action which mimed the internal passion must have been essential to the Elizabethan actor. The repertory was hardly ever the same two days running, and the opportunities for rehearsal can have been few in comparison with modern standards. With a part in every play, the leading players can have had little time for doing more while studying their parts than the essential learning of the lines. As Bernard Beckerman puts it of the Globe actor:

There was no opportunity for him to fix a role in his memory by repetition. Rarely would he play the same role two days in succession. Even in the most popular role he would not appear more than twice in one week, and then only in the first month or two of the play's stage life. The consequences of such a strenuous repertory were twofold. First, the actor had to cultivate a fabulous memory and devote much of his time to memorization; various plays testify to the scorn of the playwright for the actor who is out of his part. Secondly, the actor had to systematize his methods of portrayal and of working with his colleagues.[48]

The Chamberlain's Men had barely more than a day to revive the defunct *Richard II* for performance when the Essex conspirators paid them to do so in 1600. The temptation in such circumstances to introduce stock poses must have been strong, and would have been reinforced by the practice of allocating parts according to acting 'lines'. Such a procedure would have reduced the strain on the actor's ability to 'personate' and left him to concentrate properly on his memory.

There is a certain amount of evidence which shows how well the companies worked in this repertory system. This is to be found in the few cases where a play-text has survived in two versions, one the author's or the company's original text and the other a version based on a text copied down from a piratical actor's memory. A text like the first quarto of *Faustus* appears to have been produced by a provincial company capitalising on its assets by writing down the version it was used to performing. One such revealing text is the 1594 quarto of Greene's *Orlando Furioso*. W. W. Greg, in his edition,[49] maintains that the play was written after August 1591 and played possibly at Christmas 1591, and certainly in February 1592 by Alleyn and Strange's Men for Henslowe. The Christmas performance may have been by the Queen's Men, who would have relinquished the play to Alleyn when they left for the provinces at the beginning of 1592—unless, as the *Defence of Conny-Catching* maintained, Greene resold the play after the owners had gone. Alleyn took the play as his personal property, since it stayed with him in the Admiral's Company repertoire when he and Strange's Men parted company.

The authoritative piece of text is the 'Part' of Orlando, a fragment comprising two-thirds of a scribal transcript of the leading part. It has corrections made in Alleyn's hand, so was presumably made at the beginning of 1592, since it is unlikely that Alleyn would ever have wanted the part copied for him a second time. The only text of the full play is the quarto printed in 1594. Greg writes

The text of *Orlando* printed in 1594 proves on examination to be a version severely abridged by the excision of scenes, speeches, and passages of dialogue, as well as by compression and the omission of characters, for performance by a reduced cast in a strictly limited time. Further than this the version has been adapted, by the insertion of episodes of rough clownage and horseplay, to the tastes of a lower class of audience... Thus the quarto contains what would appear to be essentially a stage version: the text is dependent on, not antecedent to, actual performance...based almost throughout on reconstruction from memory, while there seems likewise to be an oral link in the transmission. Modifying this, however, to some extent is the fact that a couple of short passages appear to reproduce written copies that happened to be preserved in the stock of the company, while a few incidental points reveal a knowledge of the original version, though this knowledge was clearly not obtained directly from any written source. Certain features, lastly, prove that the copy used for the printed quarto was in the first instance prepared for playhouse use.[50]

Greg suggests that the cause of this compilation was the reduced circumstances of the Queen's Men, who made it while on tour, possessing the original properties (for instance the roundelay scrolls which Orlando reads from; these were certainly written out to be read on stage, since Alleyn's Part does not transcribe them), and with a company reduced to seven men and two boys. They lacked the prompt-book, since this had been sold to Alleyn before they left London. Their limited resources made them cut progressively more and more, for fewer players, made them build up the action sequences in place of words, and elaborate the comic scenes. The verse, where it was preserved, was kept, in Greg's opinion, with remarkable accuracy, at least in its metre.

The Q text as a whole stands firmly on the 'drumming decasillabon', with a few alexandrines or half-lines to interrupt the flow. Altogether it is not greatly different from Greene's original, though less adroit. It is more revealing to see the way Q irons over the patches it puts on badly mangled verses to make them as smooth as their neighbours. It even makes up rhymes. One such case is Q1019–20:

> *Part* 171–2:
> and yet forsooth Medor durst enterprise
> to reave Orlando of Angelica

Q1019–20:
    And yet forsooth, Medor, base Medor durst
    Attempt to reve Orlando of his love.

Greg conjectures that this corruption started with the change of verb, necessitating the repetition in the first line and the shortening of the second. But the repetition is a characteristic acting exclamation, and the alteration of the second line creates a rhyme with the one following, line 1021, which is identical in both texts. Greg may be right, but the creation of a new rhyme suggests something more positive operating than simply improvising to cover lost metre. It implies a strong concept of the need for high poetry. The result in Q is metrically no less correct than Greene's original as given in the transcript.

A second instance of patching is equally positive. In Q604 the actor substituted for Greene's abstruse 'Clora' the more familiar 'Flora' from two lines earlier, then added a phrase to make the reference seem more apt, and still kept his metre:

P10–11:
    kinde Clora make her couch, fair cristall springes
    washe you her Roses, yf she long to drinck
Q604–6:
    Fair Flora make her couch amidst thy flowres,
    Sweet Christall springs, wash ye with roses,
    When she longs to drinke.

The addition leaves Q with a three-foot line at 606, the first half of a rhymed couplet, but the extra phrase itself is fitted into the metrical pattern and leaves it little more nonsensical than the original.

The provincial players consistently cut long-drawn similes and passages of classical name-dropping such as P410–13:

    Extinguish proud tesyphone those brandes
    fetch dark Alecto, from black phlegeton
    or Lethe waters, to appease those flames
    that wrathfull Nemesis hath sett on fire.

And another seven lines equally crowded are cut after Q1550. It is possible of course that the provincial players simply felt they could not match Alleyn's delivery of such lines.

The exclamations which occur regularly in the quarto as obvious actor's additions are sometimes absorbed into their line, sometimes not.

    P18: venus hath graven hir triumphes here beside
    Q614: What? Venus writes her triumphs here beside

    P22: this gordyon knott together counites
    Q620: But soft this Gordion knot together co-unites

This last exclamation does not fit its context as aptly as it should, because there is no reason for the speaker to be surprised over who is co-united by the Gordian knot. A still more inapt exclamation is one which Q adds to line 1385—Orlando's 'Sacrepant', a surprised recognition of the villain of the piece, when Orlando already knows perfectly well who it is. Greg calls this 'just the sort of touch that a blustering actor would introduce'. By this criterion there was a good deal of bluster in the performances which helped to make the Q text.

Harold Jenkins has noted a similar tendency of the actors to inflate their lines in the Folio version of *Hamlet*, the classic instance being Hamlet's 'O vengeance!' in his second soliloquy, a cry which does not appear in the second quarto, the text which, unlike the Folio version, does not seem to have been touched by the players.[51]

The pirated quarto of Shakespeare's *Henry V* when compared with the accepted text, the Folio, shows that minor players wrote out the text, and probably played the parts of Exeter and Gower in the early performances.[52] On the whole they got their own speeches right but had hopeless memories for numbers and for proper names, and sometimes failed to grasp the meaning of what they had been given to speak. Their version as a whole suggests that the play was performed with an urgency that prevented any dalliance. The slow awakening of King Henry from the depths of penitence in his prayer scene, for instance, when summoned by Gloucester, which is delicately presented in the Folio version, was made in the pirates' memories into a vigorous arousing, a springing back to action:

> Folio IV. i.323–6:
> GLOUC. My Liege.
> KING. My Brother *Gloucesters* voyce? I:
>   I know thy errand, I will goe with thee:
>   The day, my friend, and all things stay for me.

> Quarto:
> GLOST. My Lord.
> KING. My brother *Glosters* voyce
> GLOST. My Lord, the Army stayes upon your presence.
> KING. Stay *Gloster* stay, and I will goe with thee,
>   The day my friends, and all things stayes for me.

The clowns too would seem to have fastened on what was set down for them, particularly their comic catchphrases. Nym's 'and theres the humor of it' turns up on three extra occasions in Q, and Fluellen's catchphrases got even harder wearing: his favourite oath, 'Godes plud' crops up three extra times, and once Q elaborates it to 'Gode plut, and his', when he has just been struck a blow which he has every intention of repaying. 'Looke you' is sprinkled at random throughout all his speeches, and four times he incongruously uses a phrase not found anywhere in F—'and it shall please your Majesty'. One late entry in the game appears twice in Q to once in F—'in the worell', an oddity of pronunciation which crops up again in *The Merry Wives of Windsor*. And there is the peculiar regularity with which Ancient Pistol is faced with his own name in the quarto, perhaps because it was pronounced 'Pizzle'.

When one attempts finally to draw up a composite picture of the characteristics of the Shakespearean actor and the main features of his trade, one is confronted with an impressionist landscape flecked with many colours, in which the design is nowhere distinct. The broad lines would suggest that from the 1570s onwards acting was always a trade, one less than wholly respectable but one in which success and money could buy a good name nearly as readily as in other trades. It was more hazardous than the guild occupations but it could also be more profitable. The trade itself always held to a standard of life-like presentation as its total artistic aim.

What remains is to attempt an assessment of the quality of the acting in so far as it can be differentiated at different points in time and among different companies or individuals. We have already seen the evidence which suggests that the discerning critic by about 1600 had rejected the scholastic 'Pantomimick action', recognised a concept of 'personation' and begun to deplore exaggerated or affected acting. After 1600 there appears to have been little substantial change. Richard Brome in 1638 looked right back to the 'dayes of *Tarlton* and *Kempe*' to find the 'barbarisme' which had been successfully purged from his own stage (*The Antipodes*, II.ii). Through the seventeenth century exaggeration was the only charge commonly flung at the players.

The actors of the northern playhouses, the Fortune and the Red Bull, were targets for attacks on 'over-doing' more commonly than any other theatre. Tomkis jibed at them in *Albumazar* (1615), Wither in *Abuses Stript and Whipt* in the same year, and Thomas Carew in verses prefixed to Davenant's *The Just Italian* in 1630.[53] Edmund Gayton ironically claimed in 1654 to have heard that 'the Poets of the Fortune and red Bull, had alwayes a mouth-measure for their Actors (who were terrible teare-throats) and made their lines proportionable to their compasse, which were *sesquipedales*, a foot and a halfe' (*Pleasant Notes upon Don Quixote*, p. 24). Soon after Gayton, Richard Flecknoe showed what a standard comparison for affectation Red Bull acting used to be, writing (in his 'Character' *Of a Proud [Wo]man*) 'She looks high and speaks in a majestique Tone, like one playing the *Queens* part at the *Bull*' (*Aenigmaticall Characters* (1658), B1v).

Gesture seems to have trodden hard on the heels of the *sesquipedales*, to judge by such incidents as one in 1622 when Richard Baxter while acting on the Red Bull stage accidentally wounded a feltmaker's apprentice, who was sitting on the stage to watch the play.[54] We might trace the acting tradition to which Baxter's swashbuckling belonged back as far as Alleyn himself. Alleyn after all was owner of the Fortune and creator of the 'majestick' roles which the Red Bull and Fortune players inherited from him (most of his repertory, including *Tamburlaine* and *Faustus*, went to his Fortune company, but some plays, including *The Jew of Malta*, went to the Red Bull). He was most remarked on for his characteristic 'stalking and roaring' in his roles as Tamburlaine, Cutlack and Orlando.[55] His peer Burbage, on the other hand, who spoke Hamlet's words to the Players about unnatural actors strutting and bellowing, was himself never spoken of except as a master of 'lively' or life-like acting. His elegist wrote of his most famous 'personation',

> oft have I seene him, leap into the Grave
> suiting the person, w[ch] he seem'd to have
> of A sadd Lover, with soe true an Eye
> that theer I would have sworne, he meant to dye,
> oft have I seene him, play this part in jeast,
> soe livly, that Spectators, and the rest
> of his sad Crew, whilst he but seem'd to bleed,
> amazed, thought even then hee dyed in deed.[56]

And Thomas May in *The Heir* (1620), also written shortly after Burbage's real death, speaks of him 'painting' another famous role:

> ROSCIO. ...has not your Lordship seene
>   A Player personate *Hieronimo*?
> POL[YMETES]. By th'masse tis true, I have seen the knave paint grief
>   In such a lively colour, that for false
>   And acted passion he has drawne true teares
>   From the spectators. Ladies in the boxes
>   Kept time with sighs, and teares to his sad accents
>   As had he truely been the man he seem'd.   [I.i.]

His technique of personation is suggested by such things as his elaboration in *Hamlet* of the hero's habit of repeating words, as a trait peculiar to a very singular character,[57] and by references like Samuel Rowland's to gentlemen copying his appearance as Richard III (*The Letting of Humours Blood in the Head-Vaine* (1600), A2r):

> *Gallants*, like *Richard* the usurper, swagger,
> That had his hand continuall on his dagger.

As in so many other ways, Shakespeare's company, more restrained than their fellows on the public stages, and more life-size if not more life-like than the boy companies, appear to have been the outstanding company of the age in the naturalism of their acting.

4. The Playhouses

The most well-trodden subject of all the background aspects of the drama is the structure of the playhouses. Partly because of this, it is easy to misunderstand their role as influences on the plays and the playing companies. Both plays and players existed before there were any structures actually reserved solely for the performance of plays. Throughout the Shakespearean period companies retained the ability at the end of an afternoon's playing to take their repertory off to a private house or to Court and play again there with no more aids to performance than the playing area itself and what they could carry. The Revels Office did supply costumes and constructions for performances at Court, but even there most of the work went into erecting stages in halls which were normally used for other things. What was in James Burbage's mind when he set about building the first playhouse proper was probably above all the control it gave him over his audience. It enabled him to collect money at the door instead of going through the audience with a hat as the travelling players did. Any improvement in the kind of playing area he could provide the players with would have been a secondary consideration.[1] Commerce certainly took precedence over art in his other dealings.

The adaptability of the Elizabethan and Jacobean player with regard to his playing area is reflected in the diverse origins of the two types of playhouse which flourished in the early years of the seventeenth century. Each type first appeared on the commercial scene in 1576, but from opposite ends of the social scale. Burbage's building, at the lower end of the scale, was a wooden, unroofed amphitheatre, close kin to the bear-baiting houses and the innyards, which were the usual places where the professional players performed when in London. It was 'public', in the sense that it catered for all comers, primarily for the crowd who stood in the open around the stage, and only secondarily for the wealthier patrons who sat at a distance in the seclusion of the surrounding galleries or lords' rooms. The so-called 'private' playhouses, on the other hand, were located to begin with in the halls of existing buildings. They had benches next to the stage, where the wealthy sat, as well as galleries, a much smaller audience capacity, and much higher admission prices.

Adult players were accustomed to playing both in public amphitheatres, as rivals to the bulls and bears, and in lordly halls, or at Court, as opportunity arose.[2] By 1610 they had commercial playhouses in London based on both kinds of venue. This testifies above all to the simplicity of their needs for staging their plays. The chief variable throughout the period was not so much the design of the stage area as the layout of the auditorium. The professional adult players began by performing in the courtyards of inns or in the arena of the circular baiting-houses, where the auditorium was arranged for maximum capacity. There the bulk of the audience paid a penny to crowd standing in the yard around the stage platform, open to the sky. Their wealthier or more comfortable fellows paid another penny or two for a seat in the surrounding tiers of roofed galleries. The only contemporary estimates of the capacity of such amphitheatres, those by Johannes de Witt on the Swan in 1596, and the Spanish Ambassador on the Globe in 1624,[3] both set the limit for such playhouses at three thousand.

Quite contrary to this were the 'private' houses, where the boy companies acted, and which the adults did not acquire until 1609. Being set in the halls of existing buildings their capacities were far smaller than those of the wooden amphitheatres, perhaps no more than five or six hundred. Their performances were candle-lit, their prices for admission were at least six times as high, and above all they reversed the priorities in the auditorium. There was no standing, and the cheapest seats were those in the galleries, the 'gods'. In comfort, cost, and in seating layout they were fitted out for the wealthy. The Restoration theatres copied their auditorium arrangement, in preference to that of the public amphitheatres, and started a tradition of theatre design which has lasted down to today.

The terms 'public' and 'private' did not appear until the boy companies started up in 1599 and 1600 in serious commercial competition with the public playhouses. There is no obvious reason why they should have been called 'private' houses (the petition protesting against the Blackfriars called it a 'common playhouse'), unless in order to differentiate them from the 'public' amphitheatres by reference to the tradition they grew out of, performing in halls of private houses for the private entertainment of the owner and his guests. The claim for social superiority this implies is borne out by the admission prices and the auditorium layout. After 1609 there was not even the distinction between boy-company and adult venues to justify the use of the terms, but they none the less survived into Caroline times.[4]

The private playhouses were better fitted for the wealthy in location as well as structure. All the early public playhouses were built outside the city's jurisdiction, in the suburbs, under the more lenient eyes of the justices of the counties of Middlesex and Surrey. The first of them, the Theatre, was built in Shoreditch, near Finsbury Fields, about a mile north of the eastern end of the city. Its first successor, the Curtain, followed it a few hundred yards nearer the city. The Fortune was

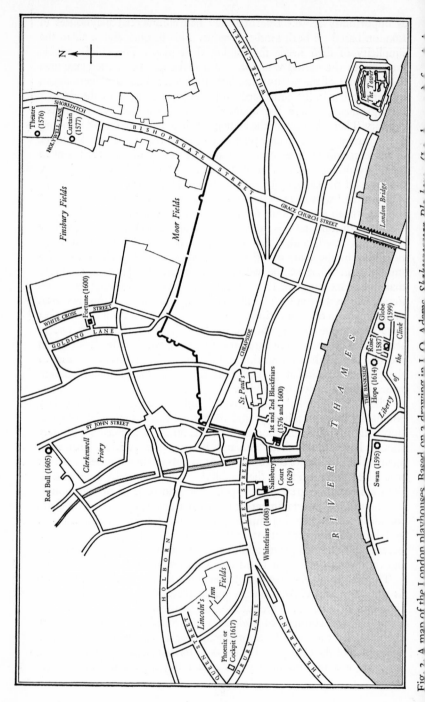

Fig. 2. A map of the London playhouses. Based on a drawing in J. Q. Adams, *Shakespearean Playhouses* (Had... and Co.)...

built closer to the city and farther west, about a mile north of St Paul's, which was on the western side of the city. The Red Bull was even farther west, and farther out, in Clerkenwell. The other public amphitheatres were all south of the river, on the Bankside (i.e. Southwark), and were reached by boat. The Swan was the farthest west, across the river from St Paul's, with the Beargarden, the Rose, and the Globe in a fairly close group to the east, about halfway to London Bridge, opposite the busiest city wharves.

The location of the private playhouses was urban rather than suburban. The first Blackfriars playhouse was situated in the old precinct or liberty of the Blackfriars, which was located inside the city walls at the western extremity, just west of St Paul's. The two Blackfriars playhouses, and the abortive Porter's Hall, were the only playhouses actually to be placed inside the walls. The Whitefriars was in a similar precinct to the Blackfriars, but on the other side of the walls, and the last of the playhouses to be built, Salisbury Court, was close to it on the city side. The Phoenix or Cockpit was half a mile or so farther west, with the Inns of Court in between and the fashionable residential area of Westminster and Whitehall Palace just to the south. The private playhouses form a central line stretching from St Paul's westwards, with the public playhouses to the north and the south, and rather more to the east.

From early Tudor times, and even before, the chorister boys had performed indoors, in venues located close to those later established as private playhouses. The first commercial private playhouse was set up in a rented hall by Richard Farrant in 1576, at Blackfriars, for his Chapel Children. It closed down in about 1584. Burbage built his Theatre in Finsbury Fields also in 1576, and its peer the Curtain opened shortly afterwards. Once the first Blackfriars theatre had closed, the Theatre and Curtain were for a few years the only venues open which had been specifically designed as playhouses. They were joined by Henslowe's Rose in 1587, and Langley's Swan in 1596, all public amphitheatres. These might broadly be said to have been the first generation of public playhouses. They were rivalled by as many as half-a-dozen innyards commonly used for playing, including the Bell and Bel Savage, both used by the Queen's Men in the 1580s, one located in Gracious (Gracechurch) Street in the city, the other on Ludgate Hill near St Paul's. The Cross Keys, also in Gracious Street, was used by Shakespeare's company in 1594. There seems to have been a tendency to use the inns as 'winter houses', presumably because of their urban location, to save their audiences too long a walk in bad weather. The Chamberlain's Men used the Cross Keys for winter in 1594. The Boar's Head in Whitechapel was substantially enlarged in 1599 for use as a winter house. This inn must have been very considerably altered for playing, in fact, by its player-lessee, Robert Browne. In 1604 Queen

Anne's Men preferred to use it for playing even though the Curtain, Swan and Rose were available to them. The Red Bull, the playhouse they occupied a year or two later as their regular home, was itself adapted from former inn buildings. Most of the innyard playing-places were suppressed in Elizabeth's time, however, and the playhouse regulations drawn up in James's time gave no licences to innyards.[5] When Shakespeare's company took over the Blackfriars in 1608 to supplement the Globe, they were following the old custom of getting a city location for the winter.

The second generation of public playhouses appeared at the turn of the century. The Theatre was pulled down in 1597 and reconstructed across the river 'in an other forme'[6] as the Globe, in 1599. The Fortune replaced the Rose as the Globe's chief rival in the following year, and the third royally-sponsored company in James's time took the Red Bull, built in about 1605. The Curtain survived for occasional plays and other spectacles through another two decades, and was still standing in 1627. Langley's unhappy Swan was used only intermittently through all its lifetime, and was largely supplanted for playing by its neighbour, the last of the public playhouses to be built, the Hope or Beargarden, in 1614. The only records of the Swan's use after 1615, apart from a hint that plays were performed there in 1621, are for fencing displays and prize fights.

The Hope was something less than the last of its kind, for it was designed from the start as a dual-purpose playhouse and bull- and bear-baiting house. Playing at first was more frequent there than baiting, three afternoons out of four, so far as we can tell. The two forms of entertainment did not work well in partnership, however, and there were quarrels over priority which led to the players more or less giving it up altogether by about 1620.

We might note, while considering the ancestry of the public play-houses, that the connection between playhouses and baiting-houses was not the only one to survive into the era of custom-built playhouses. Browne's Boar's Head kept not only its taproom when it was adapted for use as a playhouse, but also four parlours (for meals and private parties), and eleven bedrooms. Taprooms were also a feature of both the Globe and Fortune properties, and it is not unlikely that the Red Bull, having once been an inn, should have retained some part of its original function. Certainly beer was sold at performances, along with bread and fruit.[7]

Three other playhouses were opened along with the second generation of public playhouses, and another three up to 1629. These were all private. Paul's started up in the playing business again in 1599, in a hall at the school, and the Chapel Children in 1600, at the second Blackfriars theatre. In 1608 a private playhouse opened in the White-friars, in 1615 another (Porter's Hall) in the Blackfriars precinct, in

1617 the Cockpit or Phoenix in Drury Lane, and in 1629 the Salisbury
Court, near to the old Whitefriars, which had closed after only a
few years when its lease fell in. Porter's Hall opened up to replace the
Whitefriars, but was suppressed at the urging of the city and the
Blackfriars residents almost before it was completed. None the less,
the life of the three private playhouses which existed in 1629 was every
bit as healthy as the three public playhouses then still flourishing. It is
probably an accurate sign of the times that after 1609, the first year
an adult company was able to get possession of an indoor playhouse,
the only new ones built or projected were private. The whole history
of playhouse-building can be summarised in the words of the reviser
of Stow's *Annales*:

In the yeere one thousand six hundred twenty nine, there was builded a
new faire Play-house, neere the white Fryers. And this is the seaventeenth
Stage, or common Play-house, which hath beene new made within the space
of three-score yeeres within London and the Suburbs, viz.

   Five Innes, or common Osteryes turned to Play-houses, one *Cockpit*,
S. *Paules* singing Schoole, one in the *Black-fryers*, and one in the *White-
fryers*, which was built last of all, in the yeare one thousand six hundred
twenty nine, all the rest not named, were erected only for common Playhouses, besides the new built Beare garden, which was built as well for
playes, and Fencers prizes, as Bull Bayting; besides, one in former time at
Newington Buts; Before the space of threescore yeares above-sayd, I neither
knew, heard, nor read, of any such Theaters, set Stages, or Play-houses, as
have beene purposely built within mans memory.[8]

   For the first generation of playhouses the information is sparse,
and not entirely consistent. Samuel Kiechel, a German merchant visiting London in 1584, noted of its entertainments that

there are some peculiar houses, which are so made as to have about three
galleries over one another, inasmuch as a great number of people always
enters to see such an entertainment. It may well be that they take as much as
from 50 to 60 dollars [£10 to £12] at once, especially when they act anything
new, which has not been given before, and double prices are charged. This
goes on nearly every day in the week; even though performances are forbidden on Friday and Saturday, it is not observed.[9]

Another traveller, William Lambarde, within a decade or so of Kiechel
recorded that

such as goe to Parisgardein, the Bell Savage, or Theatre, to beholde Beare
baiting, Enterludes, or Fence play, can account of any pleasant spectacle,
[if] they first pay one pennie at the gate, another at the entrie of the
Scaffolde, and the thirde for a quiet standing.[10]

The public playhouses were usually round or polygonal buildings,[11]
at least on the inside of the amphitheatre, built on a timber frame with
plaster infilling, on brick and pile foundations, with thatch or tile

4-2

roofing for the galleries.[12] The yard and three ranges of galleries were reached, to judge by Lambarde's account, by one or more gates into the yard, then by steps from the yard into the galleries. To enter the yard cost a penny, to enter the galleries cost another, and to sit in comfort in the higher galleries cost another ('to get a standing' meant finding a viewing-place, whether standing or sitting). There were also lords' rooms costing sixpence, partitioned off from the galleries closest to the stage, at the Theatre, Rose and Globe, and presumably at the others too. [13] The stage was a platform measuring as much as forty feet across and extending out from one side to the middle of the yard. Some had low rails round them. At the rear of the stage was a 'tiring-house' or players' changing-room, the front face of which had two or more openings on to the stage. At the first gallery level in the tiring-house façade was a balcony or gallery (sometimes called the 'tarras' in the seventeenth century), which was not infrequently used as a supplementary playing area in conjunction with the stage itself. Near the front of the stage was a large trap-door. Over the stage, extending out from the tiring-house above the balcony or tarras was a cover or 'heavens' supported by two pillars rising from the stage. This was to shelter the stage from the weather and to provide a place from which things could be let down on to the stage. The Hope's stage was built in 1614 with a 'heavens' but no pillars, so that the stage could be removed for the baiting. Set on top of the heavens or cover was a 'hut' or huts, within which stage-hands operated the machinery for 'flights' or descents on to the stage, and where they produced thunder and lightning effects. Alongside the hut was a small platform, level with the gallery roof, from which a trumpeter announced the beginning of a performance. A flagstaff beside the platform or on the hut flew a flag during the performance. These last details appear to be true of the Swan, and were probably not dissimilar in the other playhouses.

The decor of these playhouses was 'sumptuous' and 'gorgeous' according to the Puritan preachers of the 1570s and 1580s, though unless they put themselves at risk by visiting plays we must assume their testimony to have been second-hand. We do know, from contemporary documents such as the building contract for the Fortune, that the woodwork of the interior was painted, in at least one case to imitate the appearance of marble, like the Italian theatres.[14] Some of the woodwork was carved. The underside of the 'heavens' was painted with sun, moon, and stars, and probably the signs of the zodiac. Curtains or 'hangings' covered part of the tiring-house façade, and green rushes were strewn on the stage itself.[15]

So much for what might be regarded as valid generalisations about the public playhouses in general, and more particularly the first generation. There were evidently many variations between individual houses, but they were differences mostly of detail, for which we have very little evidence. The unprecedented stoppage in theatre-building which lasted from the closure of 1642 to the Restoration made a complete break with the tradition of public playhouse-building inevitable. It has left us at the mercy of contemporary witnesses who were on the whole too familiar with the public playhouses to bother with the kind of information we need, and of the plays themselves, which were not infrequently performed on both public and private stages, and so can offer information about typical features only. The little evidence we do have needs watching carefully, particularly in order to distinguish between features unique to one playhouse and features one may have had in common with the others.

Of all the pieces of evidence which can help us to fill in the details of the picture of public playhouses, incontestably the most important is Arend van Buchell's copy of de Witt's sketch of the interior of the Swan (see pl. V). This sketch was made in 1596 shortly after the playhouse was built, and discovered in Amsterdam only in 1880.[16] De Witt was visiting London, and like most foreign tourists took particular note of the playhouses then in use, the Theatre, Curtain, Rose and Swan. As he noted in his diary,

There are four amphitheatres in London of notable beauty, which from their diverse signs bear diverse names. In each of them a different play is daily exhibited to the populace. The two more magnificent of these are situated to the southward beyond the Thames, and from the signs suspended before them are called the Rose and the Swan... Of all the theatres, however, the largest and the most magnificent is that one of which the sign is a swan, called in the vernacular the Swan Theatre; for it accommodates in its seats three thousand persons, and is built of a mass of flint stones (of which there is a prodigious supply in Britain), and supported by wooden columns painted in such excellent imitation of marble that it is able to deceive even the most cunning. Since its form resembles that of a Roman work, I have made a sketch of it.

The sketch shows the three galleries noted by other tourists, with two entries to the galleries from the yard. There is a stage, with three players performing on it. The tiring-house façade has two pairs of closed doors, and a partitioned gallery or tarras containing several spectators (or players, or musicians). There are two carved stage-posts supporting the cover or heavens, which is tiled. The hut, trumpeter and flag appear above the cover. The various sections are labelled by de Witt with the equivalent names from the Roman theatres, which the Swan reminded him of.

To say that a number of the features illustrated by de Witt are debatable is to put it mildly. Many other items of evidence about the public playhouses seem to conflict with what is shown in the sketch, and have accordingly created doubts about de Witt's accuracy, or that of van Buchell as copyist, or both. For one thing, what is supposed to be happening in the picture is not clear—the trumpeter would seem to be announcing the commencement of the performance, but the players are in full swing. The audience is there (if it is audience) in the tiring-house gallery, but nobody is portrayed in the circular galleries or the yard (it has even been conjectured that de Witt is bearing witness to a rehearsal). If the gallery figures are audience, where is the playing area above the stage? The two double doors are at odds with evidence that there were three or more stage entrances in many Elizabethan and Jacobean plays. There is certainly no 'inner stage' or 'discovery-space', as many plays require, and no hangings. There are curious 'bulks' or 'trestles' underneath the stage, which seem to be upholding it in a very awkward position. And there is the question of the stairs which appear to allow entry to the galleries. Their positioning accords with the contemporary statements that the audience first entered the play-house, presumably the yard, before going up into the galleries, but they are at odds with the two external staircases which are noted in the contracts for the Fortune and the Hope. Where would external staircases be going to if not into the galleries? The internal stairs which de Witt illustrated would hardly have been used as exits only. The 'ingressus' label which de Witt gave them might mean either that they were entries from the yard to the galleries, or to the yard, presumably from outside the playhouse. They do look most like stairs up into the galleries from the yard. Some resolution of these questions is necessary before we can accept either that de Witt's sketch is an accurate depiction of the Swan or that it is inaccurate and the evidence which seems to contradict it preferable.

Most commentators today are inclined to accept its accuracy, and therefore its primacy as evidence, and I would not disagree. To my mind what is happening in the sketch is unimportant. Each of the figures, the players on stage, the people in the stage gallery, the trumpeter, and the flag, were most likely put in the sketch to clarify the function of the features where they are shown. The two stage-doors are quite sufficient for the staging of the only plays we know to have been performed at the Swan. *A Chaste Maid in Cheapside* actually specifies in a stage direction entries 'at one Dore . . . At the other Doore'.[17] It has been pointed out that one pair of double doors opened out would have been sufficient for any normal 'discovery' or display scene, or for the pushing out of a bed on to the stage, or the carrying out of large properties. The hangings might either have been omitted by de Witt because they would have obscured the location of the stage doors, or more likely they could have hung in the doorways behind the doors, so that when the doors were open the hangings would be visible to conceal a 'discovery', and when they were closed the hangings would be hidden and so would not impede the normal use of the doors.

The figures watching the players from above the stage have caused as much controversy as the discovery-space. Something like half the extant plays written in the period when the Swan was in use require a playing space 'above' or 'aloft', but there is little space apparent in de Witt's sketch. The partitions of the gallery suggest that they are the Swan's equivalent to the 'gentlemens roomes' of the Fortune contract, or the 'lords roome' which Jonson describes as 'over the stage' at the Globe in *Every Man Out of his Humour*. It has been suggested that the players simply moved into one of the gentlemen's rooms when they required an area aloft, and shared it temporarily with the gentlemen.[18] There would then be no loss of revenue from the rooms, and perhaps a gratifying proximity to the action for the gentlemen. Or one of the rooms might be the musicians' room, in which case there would be no problem in asking them to move over.

The 'bulks' or 'trestles', as they have been called, underneath the stage, are curious chiefly because they seem to be drawn so crudely and so out of proportion in comparison with the rest of the sketch. I have a suspicion that they are in fact quite accurately if incompletely drawn, and that they represent not under-stage supports but gaps in the hangings which were draped round the stage to conceal the under-stage area. Some form of concealment there must have been—at the Fortune it was wooden palings—or the operation of the stage trap could hardly be secret. There must have been apertures, because it was from under the stage that devils were expected to run amongst the audience in *England's Joy*, a non-existent play for which an ingenious trickster attracted large crowds to the Swan in 1602.[19] The crowd, when it realised it had been caught by fraud, are said to have revenged themselves upon the playhouse, including the 'hangings', of which the most accessible would have been those surrounding the stage. Such a theory would explain the curiously soft outlines of the shapes and the splay of their feet, as being a depiction of soft material hanging to the ground, in contrast with the sharp outlines of the wooden features in the sketch. All that is missing are the vertical lines at the outer edges of the stage marking the corners of the hangings. De Witt could have sketched the apertures to show where the devils emerged from.

The question of the interior stairs, if that is what they are, and the clash of their evidence with the Fortune's external staircases, is harder to determine. It may be that external staircases were a development which belonged only to the second generation of playhouses. Possibly they provided access not from the outside direct to the galleries as one would expect, but only from the first galleries to the two above. But if so the two entries from outside which the later playhouses are known to have had require explanation. No outside doors are apparent in the Swan sketch, and there would hardly have been any need for more than one in the half-circle of the amphitheatre which lies behind the artist's standpoint in the sketch. The second might have been the tiring-house door, of course, which seems to have been the means of access to the lords' rooms. The evidence is inconclusive. For what it is worth, I would conjecture a change between the two generations of playhouses (we do know the Globe was built from the Theatre's timbers 'in an other forme'). The change introduced a smoother entry system, with two doors instead of one, at the foot of the two external staircases. These entries sent the penny-payers on into the yard and the gallery-goers straight up the stairs into the galleries without having to pass through the yard first. De Witt's drawing shows the old system, with the audience progressing penny by penny from the outside to the yard and from the yard to the galleries. Wenceslas Hollar's 'Long View' of the second Globe has been thought to show two entrances at the foot of roofed external staircases to the north-east and south-east of the building.[20] This was probably the configuration of the 'second generation' Globe, Fortune and Hope.

The best information we have of this second generation of public playhouses is the builder's contract for the Fortune. The Fortune was built in about six months, from 17 January 1600, in competition with the Globe. The builder, Peter Streete, was the man who had supervised the demolition of the old Theatre and its reconstruction on the Bankside. Unfortunately much of his contract simply instructs him to copy what he had done in the previous year with the Globe, or to follow a plan which has not survived. It is none the less worth quoting in detail:

Phillipp Henslowe & Edward Allen, the daie of the date hereof, have bargayned, compounded & agreed with the saide Peter Streete ffor the erectinge, buildinge & settinge upp of a new howse and Stadge for a Plaiehouse in and uppon a certeine plott or parcell of grounde appoynted oute for that purpose, scytuate and beinge nere Goldinge lane in the parishe of Ste Giles withoute Cripplegate of London, to be by him the saide Peeter Streete or somme other sufficyent woorkmen of his provideinge and appoyntemente and att his propper costes & chardges, for the consideracion hereafter in theis presentes expressed, made, erected, builded and sett upp in manner & forme followinge (that is to saie); The frame of the saide howse to be sett square and to conteine ffowerscore foote of lawfull assize everye waie square withoutt and fiftie five foote of like assize square everye waie within, with a good suer and stronge foundacion of pyles, brick, lyme and sand bothe without & within, to be wroughte one foote of assize att the leiste above the grounde; And the saide fframe to conteine three Stories in heighth, the first or lower Storie to conteine Twelve foote of lawfull assize in heighth, the second Storie Eleaven foote of lawfull assize in heigth, and the third or upper Storie to conteine Nyne foote of lawfull assize in height; All which Stories shall conteine Twelve foote and a halfe of lawfull assize in breadth througheoute, besides a juttey forwardes in either of the saide twoe upper Stories of Tenne ynches of lawfull assize, with ffower convenient divisions for gentlemens roomes, and other sufficient and convenient divisions for Twoe pennie roomes, with necessarie seates to be placed and sett, aswell in those roomes as througheoute all the rest of the galleries of the saide howse, and with suchelike steares, conveyances & divisions withoute & within, as are made & contryved in and to the late erected Plaiehowse on the Banck in the saide parishe of Ste Saviours called the Globe; With a Stadge and Tyreinge howse to be made, erected & settupp within the saide fframe, with a shadowe or cover over the saide Stadge, which Stadge shalbe placed & sett, as alsoe the stearecases of the saide fframe, in suche sorte as is prefigured in a plott thereof drawen, and which Stadge shall conteine in length Fortie and Three foote of lawfull assize and in breadth to extende to the middle of the yarde of the saide howse; The same Stadge to be paled in belowe with good, stronge and sufficyent newe oken bourdes, and likewise the lower Storie of the saide fframe withinside, and the same lower storie to be alsoe laide over and fenced with stronge yron pykes; And the saide Stadge to be in all other proporcions contryved and fashioned like unto the Stadge of the saide Plaie howse called the Globe; With convenient windowes and lightes glazed to the saide Tyreinge howse; And the saide fframe, Stadge and Stearecases to be covered with Tyle, and to have a sufficient gutter of lead to carrie & convey the water frome the coveringe of the saide Stadge to fall backwardes; And also all the saide fframe and the Stairecases thereof to be sufficyently enclosed withoute with lathe, lyme & haire, and the gentlemens roomes and Twoe pennie roomes to be seeled with lathe, lyme & haire, and all the fflowers of the saide Galleries, Stories and Stadge to be bourded with good & sufficyent newe deale bourdes of the whole thicknes, wheare need shalbe; And the saide howse and other thinges beforemencioned to be made & doen to be in all other contrivitions, conveyances, fashions, thinge and thinges effected, finished and doen accordinge to the manner and fashion of the saide howse called the Globe, saveinge only that all the princypall and maine postes of the saide fframe and Stadge forwarde shalbe square and wroughte palasterwise, with carved proporcions called Satiers to be placed & sett on the topp of every of the same postes, and saveinge also that the said Peeter Streete shall not be chardged with anie manner of Pay[ntin]ge in or aboute the saide fframe howse or Stadge or anie parte thereof, nor rendringe the walls within, nor seeling anie more or other roomes then the gentlemens roomes, Twoe pennie roomes and Stadge before remembred. Nowe theiruppon the saide Peeter Streete dothe covenant, promise and graunte ffor himself, his executours and administratours, to and with the saide Phillipp Henslowe and Edward Allen and either of them, and thexecutours and administratours of them and either of them, by theis presentes in manner & forme followeinge (that is to saie); That he the saide Peeter Streete, his executours or assignes, shall & will att his or their owne propper costes & chardges well, woorkmanlike & substancyallie make, erect, sett upp and fully finishe in and by all thinges, accordinge to the true meaninge of theis presentes, with good, stronge and substancyall newe tymber and other necessarie stuff, all the saide fframe and other woorkes whatsoever in and uppon the saide plott or parcell of grounde (beinge not by anie aucthoretie restrayned, and havinge ingres, egres & regres to doe the same) before the ffyve & twentith daie of Julie next commeinge after the date hereof; And shall alsoe at his or theire like costes and chardges

93

provide and finde all manner of woorkmen, tymber, joystes, rafters, boordes, dores, boltes, hinges, brick, tyle, lathe, lyme, haire, sande, nailes, lade, iron, glasse, woorkmanshipp and other thinges whatsoever, which shalbe neede-full, convenyent & necessarie for the saide fframe & woorkes & everie parte thereof; And shall alsoe make all the saide fframe in every poynte for Scantlinges lardger and bigger in assize then the Scantlinges of the timber of the saide newe erected howse called the Globe; And alsoe that he the saide Peeter Streete shall furthwith, aswell by himself as by suche other and soe-manie woorkmen as shalbe convenient & necessarie, enter into and uppon the saide buildinges and woorkes, and shall in reasonable manner proceede therein withoute anie wilfull detraccion untill the same shalbe fully effected and finished.[21]

In summary, the significant points are that the shape was to be square inside and out, unlike the Globe, probably imitating the innyards instead of the baiting-houses. The square measured eighty feet on the outside and fifty-five inside. It was to be built in timber clad with plaster ('lathe lyme & haire') on a brick and pile foundation, and roofed with tiles over the 'fframe Stadge and Stearecases'. The first gallery was to be twelve feet high, the second eleven and the third nine, a total height of thirty-two feet, each of the upper galleries having a ten-inch overhang into the yard. The stage, tiring-house and cover were set up inside the main framework, the stage measuring forty-three feet across and extending half-way, i.e. twenty-seven feet six inches, into the yard. The stage and lowest gallery were 'paled in' with oak boards, and the gallery paling was reinforced with iron 'pykes'. The tiring-house was to have glass windows, presumably at the rear, on the outer face of the framework.

The cost of building the playhouse was £520, the total cost to Henslowe and Alleyn £1,320.[22] It cost £120 a year in upkeep between 1602 and 1608. Its sign was a picture or statue of Dame Fortune,[23] who smiled on the building until 9 December 1621, when it was burnt to the ground. Alleyn promptly rebuilt it in brick at a cost of £1,000, possibly with a circular design. James Wright described it as 'a large, round Brick building'.[24] It was finally dismantled in 1649.

Our knowledge of the other Elizabethan and Jacobean playhouses is more fragmentary, deriving mainly from casual mentions in contem-porary writing, including the inevitable lawsuits, and from the analysis of stage-directions in the plays, filled in with deductions based on the Swan sketch and Fortune contract. Of the original Theatre in Shore-ditch we know from lawsuits that it was built in timber with some ironwork, and had a tiring-house and galleries, one of which had rooms for gentlemen to sit in.[25] The leading companies used it regularly in the 1580s, but by 1597 it was empty because of trouble with the lease of the land on which it stood. After Christmas 1598 the players, under the supervision of Peter Streete, began to pull it down, and on 20

January 1599 they transported its timbers across the river to a new site near the Rose and Swan. Exit Theatre.

The techniques of building in timber were on the decline in Tudor times, partly under the influence of Renaissance brick and plaster construction, partly because timber became more costly as the oak forests were cut back. We can see the changes at work in theatre-building, in the Swan's marbling, and in the switch from timber framing to brick at the second Fortune and the later private playhouses. Early playhouses like the Theatre, however, belong in the old tradition, understandably enough since James Burbage was by training a carpenter. Building in timber involved highly standardised construction techniques, and a very precise module or dimensional code for interlocking beams. The beams were morticed and tenoned, and held at the joints only by dowel pegs (iron nails were expensive). The component timbers were prefabricated, since construction by means of interlocking pieces required a whole section or bay of a framework to be fitted together before they could stand in their places—the beams could not easily be interlocked once they were in place. The main component beams were numbered if they were prefabricated in large numbers or if they were to be transported from one site to another. This is what Streete would have done in dismantling the Theatre's framework.[26]

We have very little direct evidence of the playhouse which was built out of the transportation over the Thames, the venue for which Shakespeare wrote all but a few of his plays. It was built in six months, was round or polygonal on the outside and more or less round inside.[27] It had two narrow entry doors, to judge by a reference made in 1613, when it was burnt down.[28] Its galleries were roofed with thatch, which gave the fire of 1613 its chance when some smouldering wadding from a cannon lodged there during a performance of *Henry VIII*. The fittings, especially the stage area, could have gone into the Fortune as Streete's contract describes it. Its sign is thought to have been a figure of Hercules carrying the globe, and its motto, adapted from John of Salisbury, was *Totus mundus agit histrionem*.[29] The rebuilding after the fire of 1613 was on the old foundation piles again in timber but with tiles for the roofing this time, at a cost of £1,400. The rest of our knowledge of either the first or the second Globe is conjecture based on what can be deduced from the plays performed there.

There is a large measure of agreement amongst the many scholars who have studied the Globe plays in detail, that like the Swan the Globe's stage area had a tiring-house façade; a stage extending to the middle of the yard; a large stage-trap, big enough for two men to descend at once; two pillars supporting the heavens; and two stage doors.[30] The last item is less certain, or less agreeable, but it seems to be confirmed by a stage direction in *Pericles* which speaks of '*one door*' and '*the other*'. References to two characters entering at '*several*' doors, as Viola and Malvolio do in *Twelfth Night*, II.ii, of course meant merely separate doors. The question is complicated by uncertainty over the curtained 'discovery-space' or 'inner-stage' (neither of them Shakespearean terms), which seems to be required for the staging of nearly half the extant Globe plays. It may have served as a third means of entrance in addition to the two doors. Such a feature would represent a major departure from the Swan's stage, of course, and we have no pictorial evidence for what it might have looked like, or even where it might have been located. Was it a recess in the tiring-house façade between the two doors, a booth or curtained scaffold built out on the stage in front of the façade, or simply one of the entry doors, double like those of the Swan, opened out and curtained across? On this, and on the parallel question of the playing area 'above', which might have been a gallery, 'tarras', chamber or window, an enormous body of argument has built up, with few positive answers coming out of it. The design of the whole tiring-house façade remains a matter for conjecture.

Taking the lesser question first, the playing-space 'above', we find that rather more than half of the plays associated with the Globe between 1599 and 1609 require some use of an area above or aloft to supplement the action on the stage proper.[31] For some of the scenes, a '*window*' above the stage is mentioned in the stage directions or the text, in others the players appear '*on the walls*' or above the gates of a besieged town. Other scenes require a non-specific locality above as a place of observation. In Shakespeare, fourteen references indicate the place simply as '*aloft*' or '*above*'. Ten references, not all of them plays written for the Globe, call it '*on the walls*', four '*the window*', one '*the Tarras*', and others are simply implied in the dialogue.[32] Two references to a place '*on the top*' occur in plays not written specifically for the Globe, though most likely staged there. They seem to refer to places above the upper playing area. These may have been the topmost spectators' galleries, or a place adjacent to the heavens or the huts—possibly even the trumpeter's place, if the Globe had one like de Witt's sketch. Thirteen scenes in Shakespeare need descents from the upper area to the stage, and five require ascents, three by way of the tiring-house interior.

The action above was usually brief, twenty-eight of Shakespeare's instances averaging only thirty-seven lines there, and a maximum of three players.[33] They use speech rather than movement. From these observations it is easy to deduce that the area available above the stage was limited. Scholars have accordingly been quick to point out that an above-stage gallery area given over to spectators, like the partitioned gallery of the Swan sketch, could easily have accommodated the above-stage requirements of the Globe plays. Therefore it is not unlikely that the upper levels of the Globe tiring-house façade were constructed in a manner not essentially different from those of the Swan. Jonson's reference to 'the lords roome over the stage' at the Globe would seem to confirm this. The players may have simply reserved one of the rooms for playing in when a play demanding such an area was to be put on.

One other matter relates to the gallery over the stage. This is the possibility that one of the rooms in the gallery was normally reserved as a 'music-room', and—a further conjecture—that it was this room which doubled as the above-stage playing area. It has even been suggested that the figures in the third and fourth sections of the gallery (the middle two) in de Witt's sketch represent musicians.[34] There certainly was a music-room at the Swan in 1611, when *A Chaste Maid in Cheapside* was performed, because it calls at one point for '*a sad Song in the Musicke-roome*'.[35]

The question is complicated by what appears to have been a change in the function of music in the public playhouses during the first decade of the seventeenth century. The Induction to the version of *The Malcontent* played at the Globe speaks of the 'not received custome of musicke in our Theater'. This presumably means that they lacked concert musicians performing with strings and woodwinds. Drums, trumpets, fiddles and flutes were standard accessories to performances from early in the history of playing. The fashion for string and wood-wind chamber-music began in the private theatres, where it was played as a kind of overture, and between the acts. The Blackfriars musicians had a considerable reputation even in 1602, when the visiting Duke of Stettin-Pomerania heard an hour-long concert before the play by a consort of lutes, mandolins, bandores, violins and flutes.[36] The Black-friars music-room was probably a curtained room above the stage,[37] rather like the musicians' gallery in a Tudor hall screen. In the public playhouses, on the other hand, at least up to the end of the sixteenth century, music seems always to have sounded from '*within*', i.e. from the tiring-house, not in a chamber above the stage.[38] This not only makes it unlikely that de Witt's gallery portrays a music-room, but also makes it doubtful whether the Globe tiring-house gallery originally had one either. Not until some time after 1604, when the players ack-nowledged that they were still not accustomed to providing music as part of the afternoon's entertainment, would a music-room have been established. Somewhere between 1607 and 1609, at about the time the boys at Blackfriars relinquished their playhouse to the King's Men, is a likely time for the change. We do know that the public-theatre playwrights after 1607 began to follow the private-theatre practice of dividing their plays into acts.[39] This may signal the adoption of the related practice of inter-act music. The *Chaste Maid* was per-formed at the Swan in 1611, by which time Langley could well have taken over one of the lords' rooms for music. The Red Bull had a music-room 'above' by about 1608, and the second Globe's music-room certainly had fiddlers, in a curtained alcove 'above',[40] as we learn from a passage in *Late Lancashire Witches*, performed at the Globe in 1634:

ARTH[UR]. Play fidlers any thing.
DOUGH[TY]. I, and lets see your faces, that you play fairely with us.
Musitians shew themselves above.

There is a strong possibility that it was the musicians' alcove in the private playhouses which the players used for action above.[41] The players at the Globe could have done the same, but there is only one slight piece of evidence that they did so before 1609. Jasper Mayne praised Jonson in 1638 for his care in staging, his realism, in that 'Thou laid'st no sieges to the music room'.[42] Sieges of the tiring-house were less fashionable in the seventeenth than the sixteenth century at the Globe, but in any case Mayne's memory could not have stretched back to much before 1609.

The second and more vexed question, of what was below the tiring-house gallery, is less easy to resolve, if only because the evidence provided by the plays is difficult to reconcile with any single kind of structure. Twenty-one of the thirty plays known to have been performed at the Globe between 1599 and 1609 need no inner-stage or discovery-space at all.[43] Of the remaining nine seven use the feature only once. So it was not pressed into use with great enthusiasm. It can hardly have been a really prominent feature, or if it was, then it must have been erected only for those plays needing it—a prominent feature of the stage's structure which rests unused throughout a performance would be a sore distraction to players and audience alike.

There must in fact have been two kinds of feature. One was permanent, a curtained alcove or discovery-space in the tiring-house wall, which served as a shop, tomb, cell, study or closet. The other was a special property, a raised platform, or even a curtained 'booth' set up on stage, of the kind used in the early years by the travelling players as their tiring-house. It seems to have had various shapes. It might be a tent, a canopied 'state' (a regal throne on a dais), or in *Antony and Cleopatra* a 'monument' big enough to hold Antony's body and several women on top, but low enough for the women to lift the body up on to it. Several plays need a raised area like the dais of the 'state', for such actions as the mountebank speeches in *Volpone*. A platform with steps up to it, which could be used as an executioner's scaffold, is needed in *The Fair Maid of Bristow*. These structures could not have been the same thing as the 'discovery-space', unless they were curtained and the discovery-space was the area inside, a kind of discovery-booth. If it were such a structure, it would have had to be attached to the tiring-house in some way, at a door, so that the objects and players to be discovered could be changed without the audience seeing. *The Devil's Charter* uses the discovery-space six times for different tableaux, as well as two '*tents*', all requiring changes to be made inside the discovery-space. And as there seem to have been two doors at the Globe, which could be used even when the discovery-space was in service, a discovery-booth can hardly have been set in front of one of the doors. In *The Devil's Charter* apparitions enter by one door and leave by the other while the discovery-space is in use. Moreover, one of the same play's stage directions speaks of a discovered player coming '*upon the Stage out of his study*'. This is not the kind of terminology likely to be used if the discovery-space study were really a booth already set up on the stage.[44] If the platform or booth construction were put up only for plays needing it, and the discovery-space was simply a curtained alcove in the tiring-house wall, neither feature would have been obtrusive when plays not using them were performed.

There was certainly some sort of enclosed space at the back of the stage which could be pressed into use for the Globe plays. Its use seems to have been essentially for static tableaux, in accordance with a long-established theatrical tradition. The '*brazen Head*' which was revealed '*in the middle of the place behind the Stage*' in *Alphonsus of Aragon* (c. 1587) is echoed in Volpone's unveiling of his gold. The players who are 'discovered' in the Globe plays are almost all single figures who do not usually move, unless to step out on to the stage. They are almost all studying, sleeping, or dead. In Shakespeare's plays seven are studiers, six sleepers, and five corpses.[45] This kind of static display is the clearest distinguishing feature of the discovery scenes. Recognition that they are designed as tableaux can save us from thinking of all scenes which are said in the dialogue to be in bedchambers or other interiors as being tucked away at the back of the stage.

The discovery-space seems to have had a number of lesser uses, some of which can explain other details about the staging. Most importantly it probably made a third entry-point. In *The Devil's Charter*, IV.v, the leading character enters '*out of his studie*', and later exits '*into his studie*', which we might suppose to be through one of the normal entry doors if it were not that in two other scenes he is discovered in his study and speaks six or eight lines there before moving out on to the stage. Secondly, the curtain or hangings of the discovery-space could also be used for concealment, for Polonius's arras in *Hamlet*, or Galatea in *Philaster*, who eavesdrops from '*behind the Hangings*'. Volpone peers over a curtain to watch his gulls ('Ile get up / Behind the Curtain, on a stool, and hearken; / Some time peep over'). And of course noises off or music '*within*' could most easily be heard from behind a curtain.

The raised platform, canopied 'state' or curtained booth was a more variable feature. It was usually employed for animated action, as would befit a construction set up on the stage proper. It or they might have been portable enough to be brought in for a particular scene—certainly substantial properties such as canopied beds as well as tables were carried on and off the stage, and Volpone's rostrum is explicitly said to be carried out on stage. They were less common than discoveries, but they certainly were used. They took the form of tents (*The Devil's Charter*, *Richard III*, and *Troilus and Cressida*), a dais, 'state' or scaffold (*The Fair Maid of Bristow*, and the rostrums in *Volpone* and *Julius Caesar*), or a raised monument as in *Antony and Cleopatra*. All in all, the various possible faces which the tiring-house may have presented to the stage could be said to be like a good nose in a face, flexible and not obtrusive.

Only one other public playhouse, the Red Bull, has been granted the kind of detailed analysis of the staging of its repertory which Shakespeare's playhouse has received. As with the Globe, the conclusion to be drawn from the analysis is that the Red Bull plays 'could be given on a stage structurally like that of the Swan, with the single important addition of a third stage door'.[46] The Red Bull was evidently square in shape, like its near neighbour the Fortune. As we learn from a petition by Martin Slater, a player involved in the enterprise, the builder

altered some stables and other rooms, being before a square court in an inn, to turn them into galleries, with the consent of the parish.[47]

Like the Fortune it was probably similar to the round Globe and Swan in its stage fittings. It had stage-posts, a heaven and a large trap. It offered only a small upper playing-area, normally reached by stairs in the tiring-house. It had a fair number of discovery-scenes, and possibly a removable curtained booth, as well as a dais for the 'state', or throne, which was also removable. The Red Bull was more inclined to favour spectacle than Shakespeare was, so the Red Bull plays contain a greater use of properties of all kinds amongst their stage effects. But there is nothing which indicates any significant structural differences in the design of the stage area from the Globe, nor of the other public playhouses.

One other fairly substantial piece of evidence about the public playhouses remains to be considered: a contract for building the Hope, similar to Streete's contract for the Fortune. The Hope was erected in 1613–14 by Henslowe and Alleyn, primarily out of their interest in bull- and bear-baiting. It replaced the old Bear-garden (also known as Paris Garden), though that place of entertainment had provided only baitings with occasional jigs as interludes.[48] Alleyn and Henslowe planned a regular alternation of baiting and playing. The contract stipulates the usual timber construction on a brick foundation, with three galleries of the same height as the Fortune's, tile roofing, and two external staircases. Its other fittings were to be like those of the Swan, except that it was to have boxes in the lowest gallery level, and the stage had to be removable and therefore without pillars to support the heavens. The contractor was to

not onlie take downe or pull downe all that same place or house wherin Beares and Bulls have been heretofore usuallie bayted, and also one other house or staple wherin Bulls and horsses did usuallie stande, sett, lyinge, and beinge uppon or neere the Banksyde in the saide parish of St Saviour in Sowthworke, comonlie called or knowne by the name of the Beare garden, but shall also at his or theire owne proper costes and charges uppon or before the saide laste daie of November newly erect, builde, and sett upp one other same place or Plaiehouse fitt & convenient in all thinges, bothe for players to play in, and for the game of Beares and Bulls to be bayted in the same, and also a fitt and convenient Tyre house and a stage to be carryed or taken awaie, and to stande uppon tressells good, substanciall, and sufficient for the carryinge and bearinge of suche a stage; And shall new builde, erect, and sett up againe the saide plaie house or game place neere or uppon the saide place, where the saide game place did heretofore stande; And to builde the same of suche large compasse, fforme, widenes, and height as the Plaie house called the Swan in the libertie of Parris garden in the saide parishe of St Saviour now is; And shall also builde two stearecasses without and adjoyninge to the saide Playe house in suche convenient places, as shalbe moste fitt and convenient for the same to stande uppon, and of such largnes and height as the stearecasses of the saide playehouse called the Swan nowe are or bee; And shall also builde the Heavens all over the saide stage, to be borne or carryed without any postes or supporters to be fixed or sett uppon the saide stage, and all gutters of leade needfull for the carryage of all suche raine water as shall fall uppon the same; And shall also make two Boxes in the lowermost storie fitt and decent for gentlemen to sitt in; And shall make the particions betwne the Rommes as they are at the saide Plaie House called the Swan; And to make turned cullumes uppon and over the stage; And shall make the principalls and fore fronte of the saide Plaie house of good and sufficient oken tymber, and no furr tymber to be putt or used in the lower most, or midell stories, except the upright postes on the backparte of the saide stories (all the byndinge joystes to be of oken tymber); The inner principall postes of the first storie to be twelve footes in height and tenn ynches square, the inner principall postes in the midell storie to be eight ynches square, the inner most postes in the upper storie to be seaven ynches square; The prick postes in the first storie to be eight ynches square, in the seconde storie seaven ynches square, and in the upper most storie six ynches square; Also the brest sommers in the lower moste storie to be nyne ynches depe, and seaven ynches in thicknes, and in the midell storie to be eight ynches depe and six ynches in thicknes; The byndinge jostes of the firste storie to be nyne and eight ynches in depthe and thicknes, and in the midell storie to be viii and vii ynches in depthe and thicknes. Item to make a good, sure, and sufficient foundacion of brickes for the saide Play house or game place, and to make it xiii^{teene} ynches at the leaste above the grounde.[49]

It was a round or polygonal building, like its predecessor.[50]

Jonson's *Bartholomew Fair* was one of the first plays written for the new Hope, and played there by the reconstituted Lady Elizabeth's Men, in 1614. Not surprisingly, Jonson put in a number of pointed references to the dual-purpose nature of the playhouse. The play begins with a stage-keeper coming out to beg the audience's patience for a delay while one of the players' costumes is sewn up, and is later accused of collecting the apples thrown by the impatient audience to feed 'the bears within'. Jonson claims to have kept a 'special decorum' in the depiction of his Fairground, since the playhouse is 'as durty as *Smithfield* [the real venue of the fair], and as stinking every whit'. He also speaks of a spectator paying sixpence at the door—a further hint that the old system of paying out penny by penny may have been dropped for the second generation of playhouses.

It may be an indication of the reduced status of the public playhouses, that the last of them should have been built as a dual-purpose place of entertainment. It should be noted, though, that the building it replaced was solely a baiting-house, and to add playing to its bill of fare actually gave the players an extra venue which they had not had before. Since baiting could not be provided every day (for the animals' sake), it was a sound commercial device for Alleyn and Henslowe to combine their two interests at the one house in this way. None the less, it was not a happy notion. The players and the playhouse-owners quarrelled frequently over the priorities the owners gave to baiting over playing,[51] and after 1620 the Hope was hardly used by players at all. By the 1630s it had reverted to the old name of Bear-garden. There were enough public playhouses then—the Globe and Fortune were both rebuilt more lavishly after their fires, and substantial improvements seem also to have been made to the Red Bull in the 1620s, if we can trust William Prynne's claim that it was 'reedified' and 'enlarged' somewhere near the time the Fortune was rebuilt.[52]

These then were the kinds of venue which the adult companies and their audiences became used to after 1576. The other main venues, the private playhouses, are less well documented. Two fairly general initial presumptions are all that we can make with any confidence: first, that the auditorium area probably differed markedly from those of the public playhouses, in view of the different origins of each kind of structure; secondly, that the actual playing areas of the two kinds of playhouse are less likely to have differed, if only because the builder of the most important of them was James Burbage, and because the King's Men had so little apparent trouble after 1608 in switching themselves and their repertory between the Globe and Blackfriars. Queen Anne's Men also passed from the Red Bull to the Cockpit and back again in 1617.

Of the first commercial indoor playhouse, Richard Farrant's first Blackfriars, we know very little. It had an advantage enjoyed only by its later namesake, of being located inside the city walls, and yet free of the city's jurisdiction. As a former monastic precinct the five acres of Blackfriars were technically a 'liberty', with a vague form of local self-government like that of a rural parish. Its independence was a continued irritation to the Lord Mayor of the city, and the City Charter of 1608 finally abolished all the liberties and brought them under city government. By that time, of course, the playhouses were not only long-established but under the royal protection.[53] Farrant leased property there late in 1576, in order to obtain a room for his Chapel Children to perform in. The room he used was the frater of the original monastery. When Farrant rented it, it was divided into smaller rooms by partitions which Farrant promptly pulled down. William More, the owner of the building, liked neither Farrant's pulling down of the partitions nor his use of the room as a playhouse. After Farrant's death in 1580 his successors as company manager kept the lease from More by various dodges, but More none the less repossessed the building and turned the players out in 1584.

A similar attitude to playing in the precinct showed up amongst the residents when James Burbage tried to set up a new playhouse there in 1596. He bought a considerable property from the same William More who had closed the first playhouse, for the sum of £600.[54] It did in the end prove to be a splendid investment, but Burbage himself did not live to see it. He bought the property, so it could not be taken from him as Farrant's property had been. None the less, he could be stopped from using it as a playhouse, and a petition of Blackfriars residents promptly made sure he was stopped, though not until after he had made all the alterations to turn the building into a playhouse. The petition told the Privy Council that

one Burbage hath lately bought certaine roomes in the...precinct neere adjoyning unto the dwelling houses of the right honorable the Lord Chamberlaine and the Lord of Hunsdon, which romes the said Burbage is now altering and meaneth very shortly to convert and turne the same into a comon playhouse, which will grow to be a very great annoyance and trouble, not only to all the noblemen and gentlemen thereabout inhabiting but allso a generall inconvenience to all the inhabitants of the same precinct, both by reason of the great resort and gathering togeather of all manner of vagrant and lewde persons that, under cullor of resorting to the playes, will come thither and worke all manner of mischeefe, and allso to the great pestring and filling up of the same precinct, yf it should please God to send any visitation of sicknesse as heretofore hath been, for that the same precinct is allready growne very populous; and besides, that the same playhouse is so neere the Church that the noyse of the drummes and trumpetts will greatly disturbe and hinder both the ministers and parishioners in tyme of devine service and sermons;—In tender consideracion wherof, as allso for that there hath not at any tyme heretofore been used any comon playhouse within the same precinct, but that now all players being banished by the Lord Mayor from playing within the Cittie by reason of the great inconveniences and ill rule that followeth them, they now thincke to plant them selves in liberties.[55]

Burbage died soon after, and his sons Cuthbert and Richard could do nothing with their inheritance till Evans offered to make use of it in 1600 for his boy company. The rest of its story has already been told.

The property included the paved hall of the old Priory, and a great chamber, sometimes called the Upper Frater. Like Farrant's property it was subdivided, and consisted of:

All those Seaven greate upper Romes as they are nowe devided being all upon one flower and sometyme beinge one greate and entire rome wth the roufe over the same covered wth Leade...And also all that greate paire of wyndinge staires wth the staire case thereunto belonginge wch leadeth upp unto the same seaven greate upper Romes oute of the greate yarde.[56]

It was probably this hall of seven rooms rather than the one in the Old Priory which Burbage made into his theatre. The 'greate paire of wyndinge staires' is implied in various references to the entry being 'below', and to the theatre being up a set of stairs.[57] The total dimensions of the upper frater were 110 feet by 46 feet, though the actual dimensions of the theatre are stated to have been 66 feet north to south and 46 feet east to west.[58] The stairway, and, as we know from other evidence,[59] the theatre entrance, were to the north. It was all beautifully convenient for an indoor playhouse.

The dimensions of 66 feet by 46 feet given in lawsuits for the Blackfriars compare with the outside dimensions of 80 feet for the public Fortune. The stage was at one end, presumably the south, since the entrance up the great staircase was at the north end. It occupied the full width of the hall, less any space required for boxes or lords' rooms, which were probably located at stage level on each side of the stage itself. This would have reduced the width of the stage to less than forty feet (the Fortune was 43 feet), which might justify Shirley's claim, made in 1641, in the Prologue to *The Doubtful Heir*, that the Globe stage was 'vast' in comparison with the Blackfriars'. Lawsuits tell us that the auditorium was paved, and equipped with benches and galleries.[60] Whether it was rectangular like the original shape of the hall, or polygonal or round like other playhouses, we do not know. Nor is there any clear information as to how many galleries there were. The reference in the lawsuit is in the plural, which would imply at least two levels if they ran right round the hall, but might mean only one level if there was one gallery along each of the long sides of the hall, with a break at the entrance end to the north. Two references to 'the middle region' at Blackfriars[61] possibly apply to the middle gallery of a range of three, but may equally well apply to the pit, the benches on the floor of the hall in between the galleries.

Admission prices at Blackfriars began at a basic sixpence, which gained entry to the galleries. A further shilling provided a bench in the pit. As many as ten gallants, who wished to display themselves at the same time as they got a close view of the play, could pass through the tiring-house and hire a stool to sit on the stage itself, for a total of two shillings.[62] A box cost half-a-crown.

The location of the boxes has been in doubt until recently, and it still is open to some question. A reference to a tiff between two

Fig. 3. Fludd's *Theatrum Orbis*. Etching from Robert Fludd,
Ars Memoriae (1623), p. 55.

spectators at the playhouse in 1632 proves that boxes were close enough to the stage for a spectator standing on the stage to obscure a box-holder's view, and for the standing spectator to lunge with his sword at the box-holder when told to move out of the way. That they were at the side rather than the back of the stage is a matter of conjecture, but it seems more likely. It accords with the location of the 'two Boxes in the lowermost storie' of the galleries in the Hope contract. It allows the 'discovery-space' more room at the back of the stage. And it perhaps explains the increasing popularity of boxes and stools on the stage at the expense of the tiring-house gallery, where of course the spectators would have had difficulty in seeing any discoveries. It would also accord with an illustration which is thought to be of the Blackfriars stage area, the 'memory theatre' in Robert Fludd's *Ars*

Memoriae of 1623.[63] Fludd's illustration shows a nearly square stage, flanked on each side at stage level by four partitioned boxes, with a tiring-house wall containing in the centre a large pair of doors, flanked by two arched doorways. Above the double doors is a huge corbelled structure containing two small windows facing forward, and on either side of it a battlemented gallery, each with an arched doorway behind. The whole structure is faced with what is probably wood painted to resemble stone. The drawing may be fanciful, it may be an accurate picture of the Blackfriars, or it may be a mixture of both. Its balcony area does not accord very readily with what can be deduced from the plays.

The plays suggest that the stage fittings were basically similar to those of public playhouses. There are no references to stage posts, though there must have been a 'heaven', because flights were not unusual. There was a mid-stage trap, according to *Poetaster*, which begins with '*Envie. Arising in the midst of the stage*'. There was a playing-area above which Chapman in *May-Day* several times calls a '*tarras*', and which is used as a window or balcony. Jonson in *Poetaster*, iv.ix, shaped his stage directions ambiguously, as in '*Shee appeareth above, as at her chamber window*'; but in *The Devil is an Ass*, ii.vi, he noted in the margin of the text '*This Scene is acted at two windo's, as out of two contiguous buildings*'. Elizabethan windows were not necessarily glazed, of course, nor necessarily even papered, and it need not be assumed that more than two adjacent apertures, possibly curtained like the musicians' alcoves, were called for.

What may have been below the tarras or windows is as much a matter of conjecture as it is in the public playhouses. There is much less evidence for large constructions than in public-theatre plays, and not much more for a curtained discovery-space. The opening stage direction of *Eastward Ho!* is as explicit as one could hope for:

Enter Maister Touchstone, and Quicksilver at several dores; . . . At the middle dore, Enter Golding discovering a Goldsmiths shoppe, and walking short turnes before it.

This implies three doors, the central one large enough to conceal a shop. It matches the arrangement suggested by Fludd's illustration, of central double-doors flanked by single doorways. Some authors evidently expected one of the doors, presumably the middle one if it was used for discoveries, to be curtained. Davenant's prologue to *The Unfortunate Lovers* speaks of a half-dressed player peeping through the hangings before the play starts, to see how the theatre is filling up. The 'silke cortaine, come to hang the stage here', mentioned in the Induction to *Cynthia's Revels*, would have hung in the doorway or a similar place. It was not hung in front of the stage to conceal the understage area, because the Citizen and Wife who sit on the stage in

The Knight of the Burning Pestle comment on stage hangings within their view. Understage hangings would have been out of sight for them. Either the double doors or the hangings could have opened for discoveries like the one in *A Staple of News*, when ' *The study is open'd where she sit in state*'.

Evidence about the other private playhouses is more fragmentary, but presents a picture largely consistent with that of the Blackfriars. The playhouse used by Paul's Boys, and particularly the stage area, seems to have been smaller, since the stage was not large enough to allow gallants to sit on stools on it. The space 'above' had a window/balcony which included a place for musicians. There was a large trap, and two entry doors probably flanking a discovery-space. A structure called a 'canopy' in two of the plays[64] was big enough to seat five boys holding books.

The Whitefriars theatre, which came into being in 1608 after Paul's had closed down, and its abortive successor, Porter's Hall, are almost totally obscure. It is not even clear that they were private rather than public houses, though the fact that both were intended for use by children and that all the urban playhouses were indoors makes it more than likely. A little more is known of the Cockpit, or Phoenix, which Beeston built in 1617, and of Salisbury Court, built by Richard Gunnell and William Blagrave in 1629. James Wright said that they and the Blackfriars were almost exactly the same size.[65] The Cockpit was probably a circular building,[66] but the Salisbury Court, built out of a barn with walls largely of brick at a cost of £1,200, was most probably rectangular, at least on the outside. A specification to build a dancing-school room forty feet square over the stage at Salisbury Court suggests that the width of the hall was forty feet, a little less than that of the Blackfriars.

An analysis of stage directions in plays put on at the Cockpit suggests that its stage area had two doors, a tiring-house gallery or '*Balcone*', capable of holding a maximum of three players, and that a curtained booth was erected for some plays, either more or less or exactly as in the public playhouses.[67]

We should not pass from considering the playhouses without a look at the third major venue for the plays, the halls at Court. Some companies performed at Court in the festivities almost every Christmas throughout the period. Used in the murk of winter, indoors, on stages and 'degrees' or tiers of seating set up for the occasion, the Court venues resembled the private playhouses rather than the public. Under Elizabeth most performances were held in the Banqueting House in Whitehall, a substantial building in the shape of a 'long square', measuring 332 feet in circumference, forty feet high, and fitted with 292 glass windows. In 1607 under James it was pulled down and rebuilt on a rather larger scale, 120 feet by 53 feet. Pillars supported galleries along the east, north and west sides, under which scaffolding for the 'degrees' or tiers of seats was installed by the Revels Office when a play was to be put on. The seating was partitioned into boxes, and the stage was set at one end, as in the private playhouses. It was at first used only for masques, matters of spectacle rather than story, which were no doubt felt to be more suitable for a lavishly equipped new building. It opened with Jonson's *Masque of Beauty* in 1608. Plays were put on there from 1610, though usually they were assigned to the Hall or Great Chamber, or the Cockpit, an enclosed wooden amphitheatre built under Henry VIII for cockfighting. The Revels men were paid in January 1618 for six days' work preparing 'the Banquettinghouse the Cockpitt and the Hall...for three severall plaies'.[68] There is little evidence for the design of any of these buildings.[69]

Just after the 1618–19 Christmas season, on 12 January 1619, the Banqueting House burned to the ground. It was replaced by a building which has rightly been called the most substantial architectural project of the whole early Stuart period. This was Inigo Jones's Banqueting House in Whitehall, a building which was so valued by Wren that when the rest of Whitehall went up in flames in 1698 he directed the fire-fighters to save Jones's building at all costs, even at the cost of his own designs. Its survival into this century is rather like that of George Washington's axe, but it is none the less still an impressive monument to its time, and the only theatrical venue of its time to survive. It was finished in 1622 at a cost of £9,850; it measures 110 feet by 55 feet, and 55 feet in height. Being magnificently decorated, it attracted masques more than plays, beginning with Jonson's *Masque of Augurs* on twelfth night, 1622. The stage was set at the north or lower end, in front of the entrance screen, across the whole width of the hall, a matter of forty feet once allowance is made for the flanking galleries. The depth of the stage varied for different occasions between twenty-seven and forty feet, and it was usually about four feet high.[70]

Some of the Court stages of the last years were complex affairs. One, designed by Jones for the Queen's masque *Florimène* in 1635, for which the ground plan has survived, had a rear stage closed off by shutters, with in front of it a stage proper, flanked on each side by wings in perspective, and finally a shallow forestage framed by a proscenium arch, with steps at each side for the final descent of the masquers on to the floor for dancing.[71] It must be remembered that this was a royal spectacle, put on by the Queen herself and her French ladies-in-waiting, not a professional theatrical performance.

For the presentation of masques an empty space was left in front of the stage for the dancing which concluded each masque. This space ended at the King's 'State', his dais and throne, to which all the sight-lines of the perspective scenery were drawn. Behind the King was the great screen and window which marked the upper end of the hall.

The first-floor windows were either covered with gorgeous tapestry hangings or were 'bastard' false windows, to allow the 'State' to be haloed by the light from the high south window.[72]

Florimène was one of the last shows to be put on at the Banqueting House, because in 1635 the Rubens ceiling-paintings arrived, and the King put a ban on performing there, for fear of damage to the paintings by candle-smoke. A new masquing-house was built in its place, of wood. As Davenant, whose *Britannia Triumphans* was the first masque to open the new house in January 1638, recorded,

There being now past three yeers of Intermission, that the King and Queenes Majesties have not made Masques with shewes and Intermedii, by reason the roome where formerly they were presented, having the seeling since richly adorn'd with peeces of painting of great value, figuring the acts of King *James* of happy memory, and other inrichments: lest this might suffer by the smoake of many lights, his Majestie commanded the Surveyor of his workes, that a new temporary roome of Timber, both for strength and capacitie of spectators, should bee suddenly built for that use; which being performed in two moneths, the Scenes for this Masque were prepared.[73]

It cost £2,500, the walls being of fir weather-board cladding, and it was set on the Whitehall 'tarras' next to the Banqueting House, which it resembled in size.[74]

Plays had already been found a venue of their own in the Cockpit-at-Court. This was another of Inigo Jones's buildings, replacing Henry VIII's old structure, and set on the same foundation, octagonal internally like the old building but square externally. It was built during 1629–30. For this building not only have detailed accounts of the interior decoration survived, but even drawings of the ground-plan by Jones himself.[75] They show a building about fifty-eight feet square, with an octagonal auditorium each side about twenty-eight feet across the gallery front. One side of the octagon is the entrance, and four sides, two to the left and two to the right of the entrance, make up the galleries. The stage occupies the space of the sixth, seventh and eighth sides, extending almost to the middle of the building. It is shaped like a shallow apron, about thirty-five feet by five feet, with the tiring-house front as a concave bay behind it, giving a maximum stage depth at the centre of the tiring-house front of about sixteen feet. The tiring-house is lavishly pilastered, and pierced by a large central doorway and four smaller doorways arranged symmetrically. Above the central opening is an equally wide 'window' or balcony. The small, shallow stage would prohibit anything at all elaborate in the way of spectacle. It is clearly designed purely for playing.

Not that the theatre was bare. It was lit by at least fifteen iron candelabra, had matting on the floors, and was royally finished. As the Office of the Works accounts show,

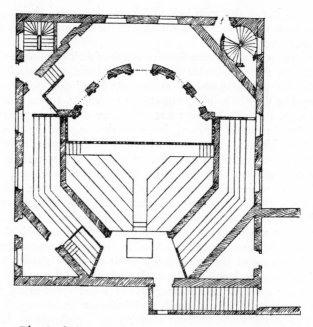

Fig. 4. The Cockpit-at-Court. From a drawing by Inigo Jones,
Worcester College, Oxford.

for pryminge stoppinge and payntinge stone Cullor in oyle divers Cornishes pendaunt[es] and mouldings in the viii^t Cant[es] of the Cockepitt wth the postes both belowe and in the gallery above in the insyde all Cont: in measure ccclvi ya^{ds} did at xvi^d the yarde £xxiii xv^s iiii^d, for new Couleringe over wth fayre blewe the viii^t upper squares on the wall three of them beinge wholy shaddowed and the rest mended xl^s, for pryminge and payntinge like glasse xx^{ty} panes wch had bin Lightes xxx^s and for Clenzinge and washinge the gold of the pendaunt[es] and Cornishes and mendinge the same in divers places wth gold Cullor in oyle and mendinge the blew of the same in sondry places I^s . . .

Carvers for moulding and clensinge of twoe great Statuaes of Plaster of Parris for the Cockpitt mouldinge and castinge three Ballastleavo^{rs} and cuttinge and flutinge the Bodies of twoe Corinthian Columnes ciiii^s . . .

Candlestickes of Iron beautified wth branches Leaves and garnished wth other ornament[es] to beare Lights in the Cockpitt x^{en} at xxx^s the peece £xv . . .

John Walker Property maker viz:^{t} for hanging the Throne and Chaire in the Cockpit wth cloth bound about wth whalebone packthred and wyer for the better foulding of the same to come downe from the Cloud[es] to the Stage cutting fitting and soweing of Callicoe to cover all the roome over head wth in the Cockpitt cutting a great number of Starres of Assidue and setting them one the Blew Callicoe to garnish the cloath there setting one a great number of Coppring[es] to drawe the cloth to and fro . . . for divers times Cullouring in Gould cullo^r the Braunches of xv^e Candlesticks in the Cockpitt wherof tenn smaller and twoe greater then thother about and before the Stage and for Hatching and Guilding them wth fine gould cullouring the great Braunches in the front of the stage and Hatching and Guilding all the ptes to be seene forwards allowed by agrem^t £x in all.[76]

At least some of the playhouses went out in a blaze of glory.

5. The Staging

We have already looked at the quality of the players and the structure of the stages. The next matter for consideration is the product of the two put together, the staging. If there were a suitable plural to use for the singular word 'staging', I would use it, because syncretism is tempting in this section more than any other. The classification into public and private, which serves as at least a basic division for the playhouse structures, is not very accurate for categorising the staging, and in some respects it may be actively misleading. At first sight there is some justification for following the division. It is easy to see the staging as chiefly done on a bare stage with portable properties in the public playhouses on the one hand, and according to more modern practices with pictorial scenery and set-pieces in the indoor venues on the other, as in the Restoration theatres, which resemble them much more than they do the public amphitheatres. The boy companies which first occupied the private playhouses had stability of tenure as well as a roof over their heads, some of them had access to the resources of the Revels Office, and their early repertory, especially under John Lyly, shows the kind of sophistication which could well have found the Italian influence of Vitruvian perspective scene-presentation agreeable. Perspective staging was certainly entirely predominant on the Restoration stages. The adult companies by contrast might be seen reflecting their different origins and their susceptibility to the travelling sickness in their preference for representing bedchambers simply by the presence of a bed, and battlefields by the flourishing of swords. Such a division would be quite misleading. The evidence for the staging of plays at the private playhouses shows if anything that even the plays staged with the most elaborate of Inigo Jones's Vitruvian scenery at Court in Caroline times were put on without it when they returned to the private playhouses.[1] A recent examination of the Phoenix repertory draws the conclusion that 'in usual practice the playwrights for the Phoenix were following the conventions of the earlier Elizabethan "open stage" rather than anticipating the modes of presentation usually associated with the Restoration period'.[2]

The differences in staging went more by individual playhouses than by the basic types of playhouse. They varied according to repertory and to historical changes in fashion. Some playhouses, like the Red Bull and the Fortune, kept through the seventeenth century a lot of the plays which they inherited from the sixteenth, and so their fashions probably changed relatively little. Others, notably the Globe, linked as it was to the Blackfriars, kept up with the changes. The use of jigs, for instance, varied quite markedly between the different repertories. They provide a clear, if perhaps over-simplified demarcation of the different tendencies.

The dance which we now think of as the jig is related to the stage jig of Elizabethan times, but the stage versions usually involved song as much as dance, and relate most closely of all to the popular ballads. In their fullest form they were offered as end-pieces after the plays were finished, an item of entertainment quite separate from the play. Short songs or dances might be used as interludes in the course of a play, as in Peele's *James IV*, but the full-scale jigs led an independent existence. The most popular were bawdy knockabout song-and-dance farces, though extempore rhyming on given themes and various forms of dance were equally common, so far as we can judge. John Harington in *Metamorphosis of Ajax* (1596) mentions '*Machachinas*', or sword dances.

Jigs not infrequently resembled the popular ballads in their function as commentaries on topical matters, political, religious or personal. Will Kempe has a hostile word at the end of his *Nine Days' Wonder* for the 'Jig-monger' who manufactured ballads about his morris-dance to Norwich in 1599, and Tarlton involved himself in the Mar-prelate controversy ten years before that, most probably in his jigs and extemporising. The author of the tract *Mar-Martine* claimed that the violence of abuse which was a feature of the controversy began with the clown:

> These tinkers termes, and barbers jestes first
> > *Tarleton* on the stage,
> Then *Martin* in his bookes of lies, hath put in every page.[3]

Tarlton was the first of the famous jigging clowns. He had parts to perform in the plays his company presented, but he was renowned above all for his comedy as a country clown in jigs, and as an extemporising ballad-maker. One of the *Jests* describes how, when travelling with a company of players, 'Tarlton's use was, the play being done, every one so pleased to throw up his theame'.[4] He seems to have worn a standard country garb for his end-piece, 'his sute of russet, his buttond cap', and to have entered beating a taber or drum which was slung around his neck (see pl. VI).

After Tarlton's death in 1588 the famous clowns were Will Kempe and the Admiral's George Attewell. One jig performed by each of them found its way into print, and the two, the rhyming ballad known as 'Attewell's Jig', and the ballad of 'Singing Simkin', are the best examples we have of the kind.[5] The second is not specifically named as

Kempe's, though if it is not, it must have borne a very close resemblance to 'Kemps newe jygge betwixt, a souldiour and a Miser and Sym the clown'. 'Singing Simkin' is a rhyming farce for four players, a housewife, the clown, who appears as the housewife's first lover, a soldier, her second lover, whose arrival causes the clown to hide in a chest, and the old husband, who is told when he enters that the soldier is hunting for a thief. The wife and husband persuade the soldier to leave, and let Simkin out of the chest. The husband leaves, Simkin makes up to the wife, the husband catches him at it, and wife and husband together beat the clown off the stage.

The jig reached the height of its fame with Tarlton and Kempe. In the seventeenth century the word became conspicuous chiefly as a term of contempt used by one type of playgoer against another. In the eyes of the satirists it epitomised all that was disgusting in popular entertainment. Jonson in the Epistle to *The Alchemist* and the Induction to *Bartholomew Fair* disowned 'the concupiscence of jigs and dances'. Hamlet speaks dismissingly of Polonius's taste in light entertainment as happy with 'a jig or a tale of bawdry'. Massinger's dedication to *The Roman Actor* (1626) specifically rejects the censure of those who prefer 'jigs and ribaldry'. Mostly it was the obscenity which drew the attacks of the satirists. In 1612 the jigs at the Fortune even drew the official displeasure of the Middlesex magistrates, for the disturbances they caused and the kind of audience they attracted:

Complaynte have beene made at this last Generall Sessions that by reason of certayne lewde Jigges songes and daunces used and accustomed at the play-house called the Fortune in Goulding-lane divers cutt-purses and other lewde and ill disposed persons in greate multitudes doe resorte thither at th' end of everye playe many tymes causinge tumultes and outrages where-bye His Majesties peace is often broke and much mischiefe like to ensue thereby.

Some such picture is painted by Dekker in his *Strange Horse-Race* (1613), where he testifies,

I have often seene, after the finishing of some worthy Tragedy, or Catastrophe in the open Theaters, that the Sceane after the Epilogue hath beene more blacke (about a nasty bawdy Jigge) then the most horrid Sceane in the Play was.

The audience at such a time are in commotion, he says, 'the stinkards speaking all things, yet no man understanding any thing' (C4v).

It is probably significant of the divergence in taste and fashion that after 1600 (or to be precise, after Kempe left the Chamberlain's Men in 1599) the only playhouses which are named as presenting jigs were the three to the north of the city, the Fortune, Curtain and Red Bull.[6] These were the playhouses covered by the Middlesex County Order of 1612 suppressing jigs. William Turner's *Dish of Lenten*

Stuffe (1613) seems to contrast the northern playhouses against the two Bankside playhouses so far as the performing of jigs went:

> That's the fat foole of the Curtin,
> and the leane foole of the Bull:
> Since *Shanke* did leave to sing his rimes,
> he is counted but a gull.
> The players of the Banke side,
> the round Globe and the Swan,
> Will teach you idle trickes of love,
> but the Bull will play the man.[7]

If we discount the contrived word-play of the last line, we can read this as meaning that Shank has left the Fortune and jig-making to join the Globe company (which he in fact did in 1613), a change for the worse so far as Turner is concerned. The contrast is between the romantic love offered by the Bankside playhouses and the bawdy jigs of the northern playhouses.

Jigs certainly did persist, in spite of the voice of official displeasure, through to the closure, though their history is obscure. Some jigs, including 'Singing Simkin', were printed with the prose farces and drolls which the playhouses continued furtively and fugitively to offer during the Commonwealth. Their persistence is a sign of how the fashion in plays which they accompanied survived in the north after it had been supplanted to the south of the city.

The differences in fashion which went with the different repertories are complicated by a number of further differences which did grow out of the differences between the public and private playhouses. The fact that the private playhouses were roofed, for instance, inevitably created variations in staging. The firing of cannon and the use of fireworks were neither of them pleasant devices indoors. The cannon which fired at the Globe for the death of Hamlet and which burnt it for *Henry VIII* obviously had to be reproduced for similar performances at the Blackfriars. They were, however, reduced in scale. In *Love's Pilgrimage*, played at the Blackfriars in 1635, an order is given to shoot off a cannon (iv.i); the folio text of the play accordingly has a book-holder's direction '*Joh. Bacon ready to shoot off a Pistol*'.[8] Besides the volume of noise, there was the smell, an objection that also applied to fireworks. Marston's *The Fawn* (1605) has the following passage (i.ii):

> PAGE. There be squibs sir, which squibs running upon lines like some of our gawdie Gallants sir, keepe a smother sir, with flishing and flashing, and in the end sir, they do sir,—
> NYMPHADORO. What sir?
> PAGE. Stink sir.

One important change in staging which does seem to have been universal may also have been brought about by the influence of the indoor playhouses. This was the practice of breaking off the performance between each act, which spread from the private to the public repertories after about 1607. In the private playhouses pauses were necessary, if only to keep the candles which lit the stage trimmed. All the early public-theatre plays seem to have run continuously, the incidental entertainment being confined to before and after the performance. Beer and bread were sold during the performance, so unless the play itself actually called for a pause, there was little need. Some plays do contain a few hints of pauses, but they are slight. The lovers in *A Midsummer Night's Dream* '*sleep all the Act*', that is, between the end of Act III and the beginning of IV; but that direction is to be found in the Folio text printed in 1623, and might have found its way there at any time up to 1622. *James IV* (1590) has songs or dances, including a hornpipe and a jig, after Acts I, II, and IV, to mark pauses in the story, and the plot of the Admirals' *Dead Man's Fortune*, which dates from about 1590,[9] has a line of crosses drawn at each act break, with a note '*musique*' alongside. The manuscript also has lines drawn at each scene-end, however, which were certainly not marked by pauses in the staging even in the private playhouses. They may be simply scribal markings, or relics of the authorial manuscript. I would be inclined to believe that some authors in the 1590s acknowledged act breaks by inserting song-interludes or by placing their mid-play choruses at them, but not that they necessarily expected the players to mark them with the kind of pause which appears in later staging.

The significance of act breaks, which were usually occupied with music and dancing,[10] is that they altered the practice of continuous staging traditional on the public stages. Scene divisions in the earlier plays are identifiable only by the departure of one group of players as another group enters. Act divisions were probably treated similarly, except when the chorus, or in the early academic plays like *Gorboduc* a plot-foreshadowing dumb-show, came to herald the next act. Speech was almost non-stop. The only silences were for heavy breathing in hand-to-hand fights (in *Orlando Furioso*, '*they fight a good while and then breathe*'), or in the voiceless uproar of battles. Real silences are truly noteworthy, as in Tamburlaine's exit after he has caught Agydas denigrating him to Zenocrate (I *Tamburlaine*, III.ii):

Tamburlaine goes to her, & takes her away lovingly by the hand, looking wrathfully on Agidas, and sayes nothing.

There are only three such eloquent silences in Shakespeare.[11]

The words were rattled off at speeds markedly higher than we are used to now, if the contemporary references to the duration of performances are any guide. Plays of 2,500 or so lines which now take three or more hours to speak, even on recordings when no scene-changing is needed, then took two hours. Even *Bartholomew Fair*, an exceptionally long play in its own time at over 4,000 lines, was said by its author to take 'the space of two houres and an halfe, and somewhat more'.[12] The Lord Chamberlain wrote to the Lord Mayor in October 1594 that his new company had given an undertaking

that where heretofore they began not their Plaies til towardes Fower a clock, they will now begin at two and have done betwene fower and five.

Considering that time was taken for the jigging veins of rhyming clowns before and after each performance, this undertaking allowed precious little time for the 3,700 lines of *Richard III*, still less the 4,000-odd of *Hamlet*.

Continuous and fast-paced staging went hand-in-hand with unlocalised settings. The 'scene' was changed simply by one person departing and another entering. *Catiline* offers as similes for rapid movement 'a veil put off, a visor changed, / Or the scene shifted'.[13] The word 'scene' provides some problems, because it could mean the tiring-house (Florio's dictionary defines it as 'a skaffold, a pavillion, or fore part of a theater where players make them readie, being trimmed with hangings, out of which they enter upon the stage'), or it could mean the fictional localities where the action of a play was supposed to happen. Later it also came to mean the canvas flats of scenery which provided backgrounds for such localities. The use of the word in these three senses has misled some scholars into thinking that scenery was used in the private theatres. Thomas Nabbes has been cited as using the word to mean scenery in the following passage in the prologue to *Covent Garden* (1633):

> The places sometimes chang'd too for the Scene
> Which is translated as the musicke playes
> Betwixt the acts...

but the rest of the passage shows he meant fictional localities:

> ...wherein [the author] likewise prayes
> You will conceive his battailes done.

The same play specifies all the entries for its characters as '*by the right* Scoene', '*by the middle* Scoene', and '*by the left* Scoene' (using the 'tiring-house' sense of the term), and '*in the* Balcone'.

Almost all the action took place on the stage or platform, the only area known at the time as the 'stage' (which is why I have been trying to avoid using the terms 'upper stage' and 'inner stage'). Analyses of staging in the repertories of the Globe on the one hand and the Cockpit on the other give little indication that the stage was ever empty of characters.[14] There was no separation of players from audience by a proscenium arch, of course,[15] and the crowd of 'understanders' jostling alongside the public-theatre platforms would have had little patience with players who left them to their own devices for any period.

References to audiences hurling apples at the hangings in order to get the players to start their play are widespread.

With unlocalised staging or variable 'scenes' all that the playwright had to do was slip in a reference early on in his scene to the locality to be imagined, if he wanted a specific one. Jonson in *Every Man Out of his Humour* went to the length of providing two Presenters who inform the audience of each change of locality. At the beginning of Act III, for instance, one says 'we must desire you to presuppose the stage, the middle isle in *Paules*; and that, [pointing to the tiring-house?] the west end of it'. Occasionally the stage doors might be called on to serve as specifically separate locations, as in the Globe's *Merry Devil of Edmonton* (1607), where a group of characters are tricked about the names of two inns by a switch of sign-boards—presumably one over each stage-door. Title-boards were occasionally hung by the boys in the private playhouses. *Wily Beguiled* at Paul's and *The Knight of the Burning Pestle* at Blackfriars in 1607 both begin with some by-play about changing their play's title-boards, and *Cynthia's Revels* at Blackfriars in 1601 mentions them. Some sixteenth-century Court plays appear to have used both title and locality boards. Locality boards were on the whole an early phenomenon, a cumbersome way of locating scenes.

The business of public and private theatre staging can conveniently be divided into a number of categories: stage realism, stage business and effects, properties, costumes (known as apparel), and perspective scenery. The most awkward of these by far to assess is realism. Without the proscenium-arch to separate players from audience, as it has generally done since the Restoration, the presentation of illusion as reality was inevitably more complicated. The players were closer for one thing, in the midst of the audience, and lacked the facilities for presenting the pictorial aspects of illusion because they were appearing in three dimensions, not the two which the proscenium-arch picture-frame establishes. Awareness of the illusion as illusion was therefore much closer to the surface all the time. It is presumably because of this that so many of the plays begin with prologues and inductions openly acknowledging that the play which follows is a fiction. The illusion is acknowledged to be illusion. From there it was a slight further twist to develop inductions in which the players come on stage to talk about their play and in so doing actually play themselves, performing what the playwright has written for them to speak in their own personality. *Cynthia's Revels*, the 1604 *Malcontent*, *Bartholomew Fair*, and other Jonson plays, all use such realistic fictions. Playwrights such as Beaumont in *The Knight of the Burning Pestle* bring players disguised as audience on stage to comment on the play they are seeing, confusing the illusion/reality borderline with a sophistication rarely matched in any drama at any time. *Twelfth Night* is crammed with jokes about the stage illusion. At III.iv.131–2, for instance, Fabian watches Malvolio making a gull of himself and says, 'If this were played upon a stage now, I could condemn it as an improbable fiction'. In *The Malcontent*'s Induction Will Sly comes on stage pretending to be a gallant looking for a stool, and accuses his attendant 'Ile hold my life thou took'st me for one of the plaiers'. Later he asks to see 'Harry Cundele, D: Burbidge and W: Sly', and begins to flourish his hat like Osric in *Hamlet*, presumably in imitation of his own playing of the part. The fictional reality was a pleasant paradox, a matter of 'Tragedy / Played in jest, by counterfeiting actors', as Shakespeare put it in 3 *Henry VI*.

Interplay between illusion and reality went easily with the conventions of continuous staging and unlocalised settings. Sidney's mockery of the playwrights and players who failed to remember that their reality was illusion stayed in the minds of at least some of the dramatists. In his *Defence of Poesy* (*c.* 1583) Sidney wrote

you shal have *Asia* of the one side, and *Affrick* of the other, and so many other under-kingdoms, that the Player, when he commeth in, must ever begin with telling where he is, or els the tale wil not be conceived. Now ye shal have three ladies walke to gather flowers, and then we must beleeve the stage to be a Garden. By and by, we heare newes of shipwracke in the same place, and then wee are to blame if we accept it not for a Rock. Upon the backe of that, comes out a hidious Monster, with fire and smoke, and then the miserable beholders are bounde to take it for a Cave. While in the meantime two Armies flye in, represented with foure swords and bucklers, and then what harde heart will not receive it for a pitched fielde?[16]

Shakespeare used a presenter as chorus in the last of his history plays in 1599, and acknowledged the inadequacy of his illusion by asking the audience to 'piece out our imperfections with your thoughts'. Jonson echoed Sidney in a prologue to *Every Man in his Humour*, published with the Folio text in 1616, when he claimed that:

> he himselfe must justly hate,
> To make a child, now swadled, to proceede
> Man, and then shoote up, in one beard, and weede,
> Past threescore yeeres: or, with three rustie swords,
> And helpe of some few foot-and-halfe-foote words,
> Fight over *Yorke*, and *Lancasters* long jarres:
> And in the tyring-house bring wounds, to scarres.
> He rather prayes, you will be pleas'd to see
> One such, to day, as other playes should be.
> Where neither *Chorus* wafts you ore the seas;
> Nor creaking throne comes downe, the boyes to please;
> Nor nimble squibbe is seene, to make afear'd
> The Gentlewomen; nor roul'd bullet heard
> To say, it thunders; nor tempestuous drumme
> Rumbles, to tell you when the storme doth come.

Stage realism did have its simpler levels, of course. Bladders or sponges of vinegar concealed in the armpit and squeezed to produce the semblance of blood were not unknown, and many other realistic details testify to the esteem the players had for realism on this level. In the plot of the Admiral's *Battle of Alcaʒar* three characters are executed and disembowelled on stage. The appropriate book-holder's instruction is '3 violls of blood & a sheeps gather', that is, a bladder holding liver, heart and lungs. The annotator calls blandly for 'raw flesh' a little earlier in the same plot. It may even have been real blood; calves' or sheep's blood does not usually congeal. In *The Spanish Tragedy*, though, a letter said to be written in blood is accompanied by a marginal note '*red ink*'. Some plays had execution scenes involving decapitation. A late anonymous play printed in 1649, *The Rebellion of Naples*, has a stage direction for such an execution, '*He thrusts out his head, and they cut off a false head made of a bladder fill'd with bloud. Exeunt with his body*'. The odds are that this was fanciful, since the play was written during the closure of the theatres, but it might explain how the decapitations in plays like *Faustus*, *The Insatiate Countess*, and *Sir John Van Olden Barnavelt* were done.[17] In the 1616 text of *Faustus* the decapitation is preceded by a direction '*Enter Faustus with the false head*'. A list of other realistic devices in staging might include the appearance of the mariners '*wet*' after the shipwreck in *The Tempest*, a device used also in the horse-courser scene of *Faustus*. Smoke was provided to make mists and fog, as in the masque in Act I of *The Maid's Tragedy*, which starts with Night coming up through the trap '*in mists*'.

Realism could easily be supplied by means of noises off, and was. Marston in *The Insatiate Countess*, II.vi, ordered '*a trampling of Horses heard*', and Fletcher in *The Chances*, III.iv, similarly asked for '*A noise within like horses*'. Massinger's *The Guardian* has '*a noyse within, as the fall of a Horse*' (IV.i), after which a character enters and shouts 'Hell take the stumbling Jade'. The firing of cannon and peals of bells were other means of producing noises off, especially in the public playhouses, and the private playhouses seem to have been able to produce bird-song when required. Middleton's *Blurt Master Constable*, a Paul's play of 1601, has the stage direction '*Musicke sodainly plaies and Birds sing*', and Marston's *Dutch Courtesan* at the Blackfriars in 1603 has '*the Nittingalls sing*'. *The Pilgrim*, performed by the King's Men in 1621, has two stage directions, one simply '*Musicke and birds*', the other '*Musick afar off. Pot birds*'. The last reference is probably not to capons but to the Elizabethan device of producing a warbling note by blowing through a pipe into a pot of water.[18]

Realism of this kind was by no means uniform, of course. It appears usually as a special effect designed to intensify the inherent comedy or tragedy of its occasion. 'When the bad bleedes,' as Vindice says in

The Revenger's Tragedy, 'then is the Tragedie good.' We must measure such effects against totally non-realistic conventions of the kind suggested by Henslowe's note of a 'robe for to goo invisibell' (*Diary*, p. 325). In the anonymous *Two Noble Ladies*, a Red Bull play of 1619–23, two soldiers are drowned on stage, in the following passage:

> 1ST [SOLDIER]. what strange noise is this?
> 2ND [SOLDIER]. dispatch, the tide swells high. what feind is this?
> 1ST. what furie ceazes me?
> 2ND. Alas, I'm hurried headlong to the streame.
> 1ST. And so am I, wee both must drowne and die.

The accompanying stage directions show how the players managed to drown themselves. Opposite 'what strange noise is this?' is written '*Thunder. Enter 2 Tritons with silver trumpets*', and after 'what feind is this?' '*The tritons ceaȝ the souldiers*'. They drown as '*The Tritons dragge them in sounding their trumpets*'.[19]

Realism is closely linked with spectacle, and with stage business and effects, which themselves were likely to vary according to the nature of each playing company's repertory. Here the distinction drawn earlier, between the plays dating before about 1600 and the plays at the northern playhouses after that on the one hand, and the private-theatre plays and Globe plays on the other, once again crops up. Some general impression of the former can be found in the English Wagner Book of 1594, a fantasy on the life and death of Faustus strongly coloured by memories of the play in performance:

there might you see the ground-worke at the one end of the Stage whereout the personated divels should enter in their fiery ornaments, made like the broad wide mouth of an huge Dragon...the teeth of this Hels-mouth far out stretching.[20]

The hell-mouth which is 'discovered' in the 1616 text of *Faustus* has usually been identified with the 'i Hell mought' in Henslowe's inventory of the Rose's properties. The Fortune players offered *Faustus* up in the same way in 1620, when, as a contemporary witnessed,

a man may behold shagg-hayr'd Devills runne roaring over the Stage with Squibs in their mouthes, while Drummers make Thunder in the Tyring-house, and the twelve-penny Hirelings make artificiall Lightning in their Heavens.[21]

The public theatre players had considerable resources, and resourcefulness, for this kind of staging. A foreign visitor wrote this account of what he saw at the first Beargarden in 1584:

There is a round building three stories high, in which are kept about a hundred large English dogs, with separate wooden kennels for each of them. These dogs were made to fight singly with three bears, the second bear being larger than the first and the third larger than the second. After this a horse was brought in and chased by the dogs, and at last a bull, who defended himself bravely. The next was that a number of men and women came forward from a separate compartment, dancing, conversing and fighting with each other: also a man who threw some white bread among the crowd, that scrambled for it. Right over the middle of the place a rose was fixed, this rose being set on fire by a rocket: suddenly lots of apples and pears fell out of it down upon the people standing below. Whilst the people were scrambling for the apples, some rockets were made to fall down upon them out of the rose, which caused a great fright but amused the spectators. After this, rockets and other fireworks came flying out of all corners, and that was the end of the play.[22]

There is a suggestion of the traveller's tale about this, though the baiting and the jig which followed it are easily enough authenticated, and fireworks were freely used. The pyrotechnics in Heywood's *Ages* plays at the Red Bull in 1610–12 involved some extraordinary feats. In *The Silver Age*, for instance, '*Enter* Pluto *with a club of fire, a burning crowne...and a guard of Divels, all with burning weapons*'; '*Jupiter appeares in his glory under a Raine-bow*'; '*Thunder, lightnings,* Jupiter *descends in his majesty, his Thunderbolt burning...As he toucheth the bed it fires, and all flyes up*'. One stage direction in *The Silver Age* concludes '*fire-workes all over the house*'. The private play-houses, and on the whole the Globe, made less use of such resources.

The fact that the public playhouses used daylight and the private houses relied on candles seems to have made surprisingly little difference to the means of presenting night scenes. In plays written for both kinds of playhouse night scenes are signified in words and by the players or stage-hands bringing on flaming torches. Other atmospheric effects, thunder, lightning, and mists, noises off, and mood music of various kinds, all occur in plays put on at all the playhouses. Thunder came from the 'roul'd bullet' on a sheet of metal, or a 'tempestuous drum', as Jonson said, lightning from squibs, and mists from smoke. There are even some hints that the heavens were not beyond dropping a gentle rain upon the earth beneath, in *The Brazen Age*, and in Dekker's *If it Be Not Good, the Devil is in It*, both at the Red Bull. Atmospherics in a metaphorical sense appeared in the stage hangings, which might be black for a tragedy,[23] and in off-stage music. The Blackfriars, with its famous consort of musicians, made this readily available in plays like *The Duchess of Malfi*, where the Madmen sing '*to a dismall kind of Musique*'. In Marston's *Sophonisba* there is a stage direction '*Infernall Musicke plaies softly whilst Erictho enters and when she speakes ceaseth*'. Martin Peerson, who had a financial interest in the second Blackfriars boys, was a professional musician. He left the Blackfriars to become singing master at Paul's School. Phillip Rosseter, who started the abortive Porter's Hall playhouse in 1615, was another professional musician. Music in the public playhouses was commonly introduced as song, with or without accompaniment, and the usual musical atmospherics were supplied in the form of a sennet or flourish of trumpets of the kind which heralded the commencement of a play. Drums provided martial music as well as thunder, and accompanied battle scenes in consort with the trumpets.[24] The equipment of the Admiral's Men in 1598 included three trumpets, one drum, a treble and bass viol, a bandore, a sackbut, 'iii tymbrells' and 'i chyme of bells'.

Displays and discoveries were matters of stage business as spectacle, besides their function in the dramatic action. The early playhouses offered displays of properties, like the brazen head in *Friar Bacon and Friar Bungay* and in *Alphonsus of Aragon,* or the hell-mouth of *Faustus.* The Globe displayed Volpone's gold, while the revelations of the Red Bull included a Trojan Horse. On the whole the private playhouses went in for more functional displays. Shops, studies and cells in all the playhouses appeared furnished to show what they were, as in the Red Bull's *If It Be Not Good,* where a cell has '*A table...set out with a candle burning, a deaths head* [i.e. a skull] *a cloke and a crosse'. The Devil's Law-case* at the same playhouse discovered a table with '*two Tapers, a Deaths head, a Booke'.* The study in the Globe's *Devil's Charter* is equipped for one discovery with '*bookes, coffers,* [a] *triple Crowne upon a cushion...'* and in another a player is '*beholding a Magicall glasse with other observations'.*

Properties were tangible assets to a play-acting company, and the list of properties which Henslowe compiled in March 1598 is a businessman's inventory of his stock. It is also the most precise indication we have of a company's normal resources in time of prosperity. The full list is as follows:

Item, i rocke, i cage, i tombe, i Hell mought.
Item, i tome of Guido, i tome of Dido, i bedsteade.
Item, viii lances, i payer of stayers for Fayeton.
Item, ii stepells, & i chyme of belles, & i beacon.
Item, i hecfor for the playe of Faeton, the limes dead [a heifer for the sacrifice?]
Item, i globe, & i golden scepter, iii clobes.
Item, ii marchepanes, & the sittie of Rome.
Item, i gowlden flece; ii rackets; i baye tree.
Item, i wooden hatchett; i lether hatchete.
Item, i wooden canepie; owld Mahemetes head.
Item, i lyone skin; i beares skyne; & Faetones lymes, & Faeton charete; & Argosse heade.
Item, Nepun forcke & garland.
Item, i crosers stafe; Kentes woden leage.
Item, Jerosses head, & raynbowe; i littell alter.
Item, viii viserdes; Tamberlyne brydell; i wooden matook.
Item, Cupedes bowe, & quiver; the clothe of the Sone & Mone.

Item, i bores heade & Serberosse iii heads.
Item, i Cadeseus; ii mose banckes, & i snake.
Item, ii fanes of feathers; Belendon stable; i tree of gowlden apelles; Tante-
louse tre; ix eyorn targates.
Item, i copper targate, & xvii foyles.
Item, iiii wooden targates; i greve armer.
Item, i syne for Mother Readcap; i buckler.
Item, Mercures wings; Tasso picter; i helmet with a dragon; i shelde, with
iii lyones; i elme bowle.
Item, i chayne of dragons; i gylte speare.
Item, ii coffenes; i bulles head; and i vylter.
Item, iii tymbrells; i dragon in fostes.
Item, i lyone; ii lyone heades; i great horse with his leages; i sack-bute.
Item, i whell and frame in the Sege of London.
Item, i paire of rowghte gloves.
Item, i poopes miter.
Item, iii Imperial crownes; i playne crowne.
Item, i gostes crown; i crown with a sone.
Item, i frame for the heading in Black Jone.
Item, i black dogge.
Item, i cauderm for the Jewe.

The lists of Revels Office properties for Court performances of about
the same time as this inventory are broadly similar.

A few of these properties were evidently designed for display, but
the majority are portable, equipment rather than set-pieces.[25] The
portable nature of most properties means that somebody or some bodies
had to be employed to bring on those properties which were not actually
worn or carried on and off the stage by players. *King Lear's* direction
at II.ii, '*Stocks brought out*', means that a pair of anonymous hirelings
carried the required object on and set it down at a suitably conspicuous
place. There is an elaborate stage direction in the 1604 Blackfriars play
Bussy D'Ambois, v.i, '*Montsurry bare, unbrac't, pulling Tamyra in,* . . .
one bearing light, a standish, and paper, which sets a Table'. This requires
an entry by a hatless Montsurry (we have to remember that hats were
worn indoors and therefore on stage), with his doublet unlaced, drag-
ging the boy playing Tamyra in, followed by an invisible boy (a which
not a who), with a candle, an inkstand, and a sheet of paper, which he
sets out on a table already in position on stage.

So far as the evidence of stage directions enables us to judge, even
the most substantial properties were likely to be carried on to the stage
more often than they were discovered. The terminology is ambiguous,
though, and a stage direction like '*Enter X upon a bed*' may mean
either that the bed was pushed out on to the stage or that it was discovered, and the term '*set out*' seems sometimes to mean 'carried on to
the stage', and sometimes 'discovered'.[26]

One very spectacular form of display utilising only portable properties was of course the procession. Like a mannequin parade it showed off costumes and accessories to advantage, and like mannequin parades its members 'passed over the stage' in solemn march, probably out on to the stage by one door and into the tiring-house again by the other. It has been conjectured that 'passing over the stage' meant exactly that—climbing on to the stage from the yard on one side and descending to the yard again on the other.[27] I find this doubtful, if only because the stage doors leading straight from the tiring-house were already in existence, and because there is no evidence that steps ever existed from the yard up to the stage. Certainly at the Blackfriars there was no easy way up on to the stage for the Citizen's wife in *The Knight of the Burning Pestle*. An archetype for stage processions can be found in the several stately pomps of *Tamburlaine*, like the one at the death of Zenocrate:

Tamburlaine, with Usumcasane, and his three sons, foure bearing the hearse of Zenocrate; and the drums sounding a dolefull martch; the Towne burning.

All the companies liked processions, though the earlier companies and those playing at the Fortune and Red Bull made more of the martial and pompous aspects, and the private playhouses more of the sumptuous and elegant. Both kinds of venue not infrequently joined processions to dumb-shows, or at the private playhouses to masques. Nathaniel Richards, in his tragedy *Messallina*, written for the King's Revels at Salisbury Court in 1635, appended this hopeful direction:

Cornets sound a Flourish, Enter Senate who placed by Sulpilius, cornets cease, and the Antique maske consisting of eight Bachinalians, enter guirt with vine leaves, and shap'd in the middle with Tunne Vessells, each bearing a Cup in their hands, who during the first straine of Musick playd foure times over, enter two at a time, at the tune's end, make stand; draw wine and carouse, then dance all: the antimasque gone off, and solemne musicke playing; Messallina and Silius gloriously crown'd in an Arch-glittering Cloud aloft, court each other.

Descents and ascents of deities from the stage heavens were matters of spectacle, too. The earlier plays tended to allow their gods to walk on like any mortal; the first of Shakespeare's gods to fly in being Jupiter on his eagle in *Cymbeline*. Flights were more favoured by the boy companies than the adults; they had a weight advantage, of course. The ingenuities of Inigo Jones in the Court spectacles of later years, which allowed boys to fly in not only vertically but at a slant, may have encouraged imitation in the commercial theatres.

Dumb-shows were affairs of pure spectacle, and employed relatively far more properties than the plays in which they were incorporated. At their simplest they were parades of spectacle, formal processions using the most gorgeous apparel, crowns, sceptres, torches and swords, in the company's possession. State occasions like the coronation in *The Devil's Charter* or the funeral at the beginning of Act II in *Antonio's*

Revenge were characteristic of this kind. The stage direction for the latter gives a hint of what they were like:

The Cornets sound a cynet.

Enter two mourners with torches, two with streamers: Castilio & Forobosco, with torches: a Heralde bearing Andrugio's helme & sword: the coffin: Maria supported by Lucio and Alberto, Antonio by himselfe: Piero, and Strozzo talking: Galeatzo and Matzagente, Balurdo & Pandulfo: the coffin set downe: helme, sworde and streamers hung up, placed by the Herald: whil'st Antonio and Maria wet their handkerchers with their teares, kisse them, and lay them on the hearse, kneeling: all goe out but Piero. Cornets cease, and he speakes.

The earlier classical plays such as *Gorboduc* and *Jocasta* used dumbshows at the end of each act to summarise the plot of the following act. Some later plays of the boy companies also filled some of their interacts with dumb-shows, as in *Histriomastix* III, *Antonio and Mellida* III, at Paul's, and *The Malcontent* II, at Blackfriars. By the turn of the century, though, dumb-shows which mimed a plot-story were seen by some of the more acid playwrights as laughably archaic, to judge by the contempt for 'pantomimick action'. They were deliberately used as oldfashioned devices in *Hamlet* and Middleton's *Your Five Gallants*. Heywood, in a prologue to a Red Bull Play printed in 1615, *The Four Prentices of London*, still insisted on the value for abridging a story

> in dumbe shewes, which were they writ at large,
> Would aske a long and tedious circumstance.

and as late as 1634 a Cockpit play by the same author, *A Maidenhead Well Lost*, had a dumb-show as plot-thickened as this:

Musicke. A Dumbe Shew. Enter Millaine, to him Storza, and brings in Lauretta masked. the Duke takes her and puts her into Bed, and Exit. Enter both the Dukes and Julia, they make signes to her and Exit; Storza hides Julia in a corner, and stands before her. Enter againe with the Prince to bring him to bed: They cheere him on, and others snatch his points, and so Exit. The Dukes Imbrace and Exeunt.[28]

Stage business and spectacle of this kind should not be allowed to obscure the fact that the stages themselves were essentially bare, and that as a general rule the better the playwright the less spectacle there was likely to be in his plays. Eighty per cent of all Shakespeare's scenes written for the Globe, it has been estimated, could have been performed on a completely bare stage platform.[29] The one play of Shakespeare's which makes great use of stage spectacle and business is *The Tempest*, a play in which Shakespeare seems almost to have been mocking his own art by the closeness with which he observed the neo-classical unities of time and place. The contrast with *The Tempest*'s immediate predecessor, *The Winter's Tale*, which swings in time through a whole generation and in place between Sicily and the sea-coast of

Bohemia, is as complete as it well could be. *The Winter's Tale* has no stage-business or properties to display at all, apart from the bear, which took a turn as a player (if it was a real bear) in a masque as well as the play in 1611. The stage-business in *The Tempest* operates as a metaphor of Prospero's and Shakespeare's arts, of course, and is closed to our questions for that reason. But it does raise a suspicion about how deeply embedded Shakespeare's tongue was in his cheek in the last plays.

The relative frequency with which properties were discovered for display rather than brought on is hard to tell, because of the ambiguity in the stage directions. The Globe, Red Bull and Cockpit, the three playhouses whose plays have been most closely scrutinised for the evidence of their stage directions, all seem to have favoured either method without much consistency. In any case, the occupants of beds, the most substantial properties of all, usually emerged from them on to the stage. The Swan's doorways may not have provided a large enough discovery-space for such properties, since *The Chaste Maid* opens with a bed being '*thrust out*'; but this is no evidence to draw general conclusions from. Tables and chairs, more easily portable than beds, were revealed in the discovery-space when they represented a study or a cell, but were equally often carried on. Benches and stools, the 'state' or throne, a 'bar' for judgement scenes, trees and arbours, and a mossy or flowery bank could all be carried on. The 'throne' which descends from the heavens in *Faustus* and *A Looking-Glass for London and England*, the 'creaking throne' scorned by Jonson, which Henslowe notes as being stored in the heavens, was a chair for flights and nothing else, quite distinct from the 'state'.[30] The dais on which the 'state' throne usually rested was as much as four steps high, to judge by the counting of Mariana in II.i of *The Dumb Knight*. She ascends it to be executed, saying

> this first step lower,
> Mounts to this next; this, thus and thus hath brought
> My bodies frame unto its highest throne.

This dais or scaffold was also carried on by stage-hands, to judge by the stage direction in the same play, '*Enter Chyp, Shaveing and others with a Scaffold*'.[31] Hirelings always brought banquets on, sometimes already set out on a table. The 'quaint device' by which Ariel makes the banquet vanish in *The Tempest* was, I would think, a kind of reversible table-top with dishes fastened to one surface and the other bare—in which case the banquet would certainly have been brought out already fastened to the table.

Given storage space the wealthier and longer-lived companies could accumulate a good many standard properties. Some of course had to be custom-built for particular plays in the repertory. William Percy's curious plays, which seem to have been written for Paul's in the years after 1599, contain lists of the properties needed for performing them. *Cuckqueans and Cuckolds Errant* needed two inn-signs specially painted, besides a title board, a rope-ladder and a bench:

The Properties
Harwich, In Middle of the Stage Colchester with Image of Tarlton, Signe and Ghirlond under him also. The Raungers Lodge, Maldon, A Ladder of Roapes trussed up neare Harwich. Highest and Aloft the Title The Cuck-Queanes and Cuckolds Errants. A Long Fourme.

The Faery Pastorall was more demanding:

The Properties
Highest, aloft, and on the Top of the Musick Tree the Title The Faery Pastorall, Beneath him pind on Post of the Tree The Scene Elvida Forrest. Lowest of all over the Canopie ΝΑΙΙΑΙΤΒΟΔΑΙΟΝ or Faery Chappell. A kiln of Brick. A Fowen Cott. A Hollowe Oake with vice of wood to shutt to. A Lowe well with Roape and Pullye. A Fourme of Turves. A greene Bank being Pillowe to the Hed but. Lastly A Hole to creepe in and out.

Pretty well all of these properties, with the exception of the 'greene Bank' and possibly the enigmatic 'Fowen Cott' would have had to be constructed for the performance. The modesty of Shakespeare's demands for his plays may reflect his financial interests as well as his dramatic sophistication.

The impresarios and players invested much more money in apparel than in properties. When the Globe and the Fortune were burnt, and when Beeston forsook Queen Anne's Men for his own enterprises, it was the loss of playbooks and apparel which the players bewailed, not the properties. Alleyn's accounts list some startling totals for clothing by present-day priorities: £20. 10s. 6d. for a 'black velvet cloak with sleeves embroidered all with silver and gold', more than a third of Shakespeare's price for a house in Stratford.[32] No wonder Henslowe had a rule against players leaving the playhouse wearing his apparel. It was the magnificence of playing apparel which made the players common symbols of the distance between appearances and reality in Elizabethan society. Greene in *A Quip for an Upstart Courtier* (1592) wrote of a player wearing a

murrey cloth gowne...faced down before with gray conny, and laide thick on the sleeves with lace, which he quaintly bare up to shew his white Taffata hose, and black silk stockings. A huge ruffe about his necke wrapt in his great head like a wicker cage, a little Hat with brims like the wings of a doublet, wherein he wore a Jewel of Glasse, as broad as a chancery seale.

The image of the player jetting it in borrowed apparel is given point by the custom which Thomas Platter noted in 1599:

it is the English usage for eminent lords or knights at their decease to bequeath and leave almost the best of their clothes to their serving men, which it is unseemly for the latter to wear, so that they offer them then for sale for a small sum to the actors.[33]

The colours of the costumes matched the gorgeous painting of the playhouses. Henslowe's and Alleyn's papers list cloaks in scarlet with gold laces and buttons, and in purple satin adorned with silver; doublets in copper lace (for Tamburlaine), carnation velvet, flame, ginger, red and green; and women's gowns of white satin and cloth of gold. There is one complete inventory of apparel in Alleyn's hand, undated but probably of the same time as Henslowe's list of properties made in March 1598 (*Diary*, pp. 291–4). It speaks for itself.

Clokes

1 A scarlett cloke wth ii brode gould Laces: w^t gould buttens of the sam downe the sids
2 A black velvett cloke
3 A scarlett cloke Layd downe wth silver Lace and silver buttens
4 A short velvett cap clok embroydered w^t gould and gould spangles
5 A watshod sattin clok w^t v gould laces
6 A purpell sattin welted w^t velvett and silver twist
7 A black tufted cloke
8 A damask cloke garded w^t velvett
9 A longe blak tafata cloke
10 A colored bugell for a boye
11 A scarlett w^t buttens of gould fact w^t blew velvett
12 A scarlett fact w^t blak velvett
13 A stamell cloke w^t gould lace
14 blak bugell cloke

Gownes

1 hary ye viii gowne
2 the blak velvett gowne w^t wight fure
3 A crimosin Robe strypt w^t gould fact w^t ermin
4 on of wrought cloth of gould
5 on of red silk w^t gould buttens
6 a cardinalls gowne
7 wemens gowns
8, 9   i blak velvett embroyde^d w^t gould
10 i cloth of gould candish his stuf
11 i blak velvett lact and drawne out w^t wight sarsnett
12 A black silk w^t red flush
13 A cloth of silver for pan
14 A yelow silk gowne
15 a red silk gowne
16 angels silk
17 ii blew calico gowns

Antik sutes

1 a cote of crimosen velvett cutt in payns and embryderd in gould
2 i cloth of gould cote w^t grene bases

3   i cloth of gould cote w^t oraing tawny bases
4   i cloth of silver cott w^t blewe silk & tinsell bases
5   i blew damask cote the more
6   a red velvett horsmans cote
7   A yelow tafata pd
8   cloth of gould horsmans cote
9   cloth of bodkin hormans cote
10   orayng tany horsmans cot of cloth lact
11   daniels gowne
12   blew embroyderde bases
13   will somers cote
14   wight embroyd^r bases
15   gilt lether cot
16   ii hedtirs sett w^t stons

Jerkings and dublets

1   A crymosin velvett pe^s w^t gould buttens & lace
2   a crymasin sattin case lact w^t gould lace all over
3   A velvett dublett cut dimond lact w^t gould lace and spang^s
4   A dublett of blak velvett cut on sillver tinsell
5   A ginger colored dublett
6   i wight sattin cute on wight
7   blak velvett w^t goul^d lace
8   green velvett
9   blak tafata cut on blak velvett lacte w^t bugell
10   blak velvett playne
11   ould wight sattin
12   red velvett for a boye
13   A carnation velvett lact w^t silver
14   A yelow spangled case
15   red velvett w^t blew sattin sleves & case
16   cloth of silver Jerkin
17   faustus Jerkin his clok

frenchose

1   blew velvett embr^d w^t gould paynes blew sattin scalin
2   silver paynes lact w^t carnation satins lact over w^t silver
3   the guises
4   Rich payns w^t long stokins
5   gould payns w^t blak stript scalings of canish
6   gould payns w^t velvett scalings
7   gould payns w^t red strypt scaling
8   blak bugell
9   red payns for a boy w^t yelo scalins
10   pryams hoes
11   spangled hoes

venetians

1   A purpell velvett cut in dimonds lact & spangels
2   red velved lact w^t gould spanish
3   A purpell vellvett emproydored w^t silver cut on tinsell

4   green velvett lact w^t gould spanish
5   blake velvett
6   cloth of silver
7   gren strypt sattin
8   cloth of gould for a boye

The age was not only gorgeous but also intensely fashion-conscious. The range of available fabrics was enormous, and the turnover of fashionable fabrics and cuts was enormous too, which probably helped the players a little in acquiring lordly cast-offs. It was an age of glorious variety, in which, as always in the world of fashion, new names had constantly to be chosen as new shades of colour were invented. Pepper, tobacco, sea-water, and puke (a dark brown) were a few of the many Elizabethan inventions.[34]

Colour symbolism was inevitable and universal throughout the Renaissance, though the range of possible interpretations of the significances of colours was almost as wide as the range of colours. Red for blood, yellow for the sun, white for purity, black for gloom or evil and death were all traditional. Tamburlaine's famous degrees of mercy, signified by his white, red and black tents, and on stage by the changing colours of his robes, reflect a set of values for colours which can still be recognised. Other significances were more local. When Malvolio in *Twelfth Night* is gulled into appearing cross-gartered, like a lover, his yellow hose as well as his crossed garters indicate his new role. When he says he is 'not black in my mind, though yellow in my legs', he means that his yellow stockings show him to be a lover, but that he is not a melancholy (black-minded) one.

There were costumes to match vocations, of course: doctors' gowns of scarlet, lawyers' gowns in black, blue coats for serving-men, a 'friars gown of gray', a 'cardinalls gowne' in scarlet, shepherds' coats, fool's coats with cap and bauble, and of course soldiers' coats. These were worn with little concern for historical accuracy, if Henry Peacham's drawing of a scene from *Titus Andronicus*, made in 1595, is any indication. In the drawing the leading character is in a form of Roman dress reasonably like a toga, but the men flanking him are clearly dressed as Elizabethan soldiers[35] (see pl. VII). 'Turkish bonnets' get a mention in *Soliman and Perseda*, and Henslowe's lists include 'ii Danes sutes', 'i mores cote', four 'Turkes heds' and 'the suit of motley for the Scotchman' which sounds suspiciously like a plaid.

Costumes for 'Negro Moors', as Peele called them, were spectacular rather than realistic.[36] None the less, considerable efforts were made on occasions to simulate the dark skin and curly hair of the negro. Face masks and elbow gloves of velvet, and black leather leggings were topped with 'Corled hed Sculles of blacke Laune'[37] in early Court performances. Paint superseded masks in the seventeenth century, on the initiative of Queen Anne herself, who appeared with eleven of her ladies in blackface for the *Masque of Blackness* in 1605 (see pl. VIII). Sir Dudley Carleton acidly reported that

instead of Vizzards [i.e. masks], their Faces and Arms up to the Elbows, were painted black, which was Disguise sufficient, for they were hard to be known; but it became them nothing so well as their red and white, and you cannot imagine a more ugly Sight, then a Troop of lean-cheek'd Moors.[38]

Exotic costumes existed for various gods; for Juno, Phaeton, Neptune and Iris in Henslowe's lists, together with an intriguing 'Eves bodice'. He also had a 'fairys gown of buckram', a 'pair of gyants hose', and 'coats for giants', and a ghost's suit and bodice. From his function as bear-ward he could no doubt have imitated *The Winter's Tale* by introducing a real bear on stage, but his players, perhaps understandably, seem to have preferred doing it themselves, and his lists accordingly show 'i bears head', and 'i bears skin', as well as a bull's head and a head of Cerberus, 'i lions skin' and 'ii lions heads'.

In the later years, under the lavish Stuarts, the players collected the cast-offs from Court shows of plays and masques. Suckling paid out several hundred pounds to stage his play *Aglaura* at Court over Christmas 1637, and afterwards passed the costumes on with the play to the King's Men, who put the play on at Blackfriars. In the words of a contemporary:

Two of the King's Servants, Privy-Chamber Men both, have writ each of them a Play, Sir *John Sutlin* and *Will. Barclay*, which have been acted in Court, and at the *Black Friars*, with much Applause. *Sutlin's* Play cost three or four hundred Pounds setting out, eight or ten Suits of new Cloaths he gave the Players; an unheard of Prodigality.[39]

Several other plays, similarly produced, benefited the professional players who took them back to their own playhouses.

It has been argued that in Caroline times the players also took with them from Court the elaborate perspective 'scenes' which Inigo Jones gave to the plays.[40] I think it has been fairly conclusively proved that they did not. Scenic apparatus was less costly, less portable, and less readily re-usable than apparel. Furthermore the Court stages, which used perspectives regularly for masques and plays, always took several days to prepare. The commercial playhouses could not have afforded the loss of playing-time involved in setting up such non-traditional devices. Still less could they have spent time and money making their own scenery. There are occasional references to pieces of scenery being employed in the private playhouses from the earliest days, but they cannot ever have been a prominent feature of the staging, or they would have drawn more comment. *Periaktoi*, great prisms with a different scene painted on each of the three faces, set on a pivot to revolve when required, are mentioned in connection with the first

Blackfriars,[41] and Jonson speaks of a 'piece of *perspective*' in the Induction to *Cynthia's Revels*, but there are few other references except to Court staging. The bare stage backed with a curtain on which the Tudor moralities and farces were played forms the basis of the Elizabethan staging tradition, and seems to have remained firmly entrenched at all the Stuart playhouses up to the closure. The Court, largely through the person of Jones, the English Bernini, was converted to the Italian perspective staging early on, but tradition and commerce combined to keep it off the common stages.

The Court performances of masques and 'devices' which used Italianate scenery do not impinge directly on the main target-area of this book. As Bentley has said, scenery was conceived of as 'a special display exhibition'.[42] It seems to have been a feature reserved for special occasions, rather than for particular plays, as an extra adornment, a garnish to the entertainment. Jonson's opinion of scenery and his war with Jones are well known. As he put it in a scathing couplet,

> Oh, to make Boardes to speake! There is a taske
> Painting & Carpentry are ye Soule of Masque.[43]

If many people shared Jonson's hatred of the Mannerist artificiality of masque staging, the players could have had little to do with it.

Scenery was not a necessary feature of any play, to judge by the frequency with which the players seized on plays which had been staged at Court with scenery, in order to perform them without scenery on the commercial stages. They did participate in performances at Court using scenery, however, and it may be worth looking at a contemporary description of one such Court spectacle if only to see what the players were familiar with. The best description of all is of a show at Court in 1618, reported by Orazio Busino, chaplain to the Venetian Embassy, with all the frankness of a homesick expatriate writing in confidence about his outlandish hosts. I make no apology for quoting it at length.

In London, as the capital of a most flourishing kingdom, theatrical representations without end prevail throughout the year in various parts of the city, and are invariably frequented by crowds of persons devoted to pleasure who, for the most part dress grandly and in colours, so that they all seem, were it possible, more than princes, or rather comedians.

In the king's court, in like manner, after Christmas day there begins a series of sumptuous banquets, well-acted comedies, and most graceful masques of knights and ladies. Of the masques, the most famous of all is performed on the morrow of the feast of the three Wise Men according to an ancient custom of the palace here. A large hall is fitted up like a theatre, with well secured boxes all round. The stage is at one end and his Majesty's chair in front under an ample canopy. Near him are stools for the foreign ambassadors. On the 16th of the current month of January, his Excellency was invited to see a representation and masque, which had been prepared with extraordinary pains, the chief performer being the king's own son and heir, the prince of Wales, now seventeen years old, an agile youth, handsome and very graceful. At the fourth hour of the night we went privately to the Court, through the park. On reaching the royal apartments his Excellency was entertained awhile by one of the leading cavaliers until all was ready, whilst we, his attendants, all perfumed and escorted by the master of the ceremonies, entered the usual box of the Venetian embassy, where, unluckily we were so crowded and ill at ease that had it not been for our curiosity we must certainly have given in or expired. We moreover had the additional infliction of a Spaniard who came into our box by favour of the master of the ceremonies, asking but for two fingers breadth of room, although we ourselves had not space to run about in, and I swear to God that he placed himself more comfortably than any of us. I have no patience with these dons; it was observed that they were scattered about in all the principal places. The ambassador was near the king; others with gold chains round their necks sat among the Lords of the Council; others were in their own box taking care of the ambassadress and then this fellow must needs come into ours. Whilst waiting for the king we amused ourselves by admiring the decorations and beauty of the house with its two orders of columns, one above the other, their distance from the wall equalling the breadth of the passage, that of the second row being upheld by Doric pillars, while above these rise Ionic columns supporting the roof. The whole is of wood, including even the shafts, which are carved and gilt with much skill. From the roof of these hang festoons and angels in relief with two rows of lights. Then such a concourse as there was, for although they profess only to admit the favoured ones who are invited, yet every box was filled notably with most noble and richly arrayed ladies, in number some 600 and more according to the general estimate; the dresses being of such variety in cut and colour as to be indescribable; the most delicate plumes over their heads, springing from their foreheads or in their hands serving as fans; strings of jewels on their necks and bosoms and in their girdles and apparel in such quantity that they looked like so many queens, so that at the beginning, with but little light, such as that of the dawn or of the evening twilight, the splendour of their diamonds and other jewels was so brilliant that they looked like so many stars. During the two hours of waiting we had leisure to examine them again and again. Owing to my short-sightedness I could not form an accurate idea of distant objects, and referred myself in everything to my colleagues. They informed me that they espied some very sweet and handsome faces, and at every moment they kept exclaiming Oh do look at this one! Oh see her! Whose wife is that one on the row and that pretty one near, whose daughter is she? However, they came to the conclusion that amongst much grain there was also a mixture of husk and straw, that is to say shrivelled women and some very devoted to St. Charles, but that the beauties outnumbered them. The dress peculiar to these ladies is very handsome for those who like it, and profits some of them as a blind to nature's defects, for behind it hangs well-nigh from the neck down to the ground, with long, close sleeves and no waist. There are no folds so that any deformity, however monstrous, remains hidden. The farthingale also plays its part. The plump and buxom display their bosoms very liberally, and those who are lean go muffled up to the throat. All wear men's shoes or at least very low slippers. They consider the mask as indispensable for their face as bread at table, but they lay it aside willingly at these public entertainments.

At about the 6th hour of the night the king appeared with his court, having passed through the apartments where the ambassadors were in waiting, whence he graciously conducted them, that is to say, the Spaniard and the Venetian, it not being the Frenchman's turn, he and the Spaniard only attending the court ceremonies alternately by reason of their disputes about precedence.

On entering the house, the cornets and trumpets to the number of fifteen or twenty began to play very well a sort of recitative, and then after his Majesty had seated himself under the canopy alone, the queen not being present on account of a slight indisposition, he caused the ambassadors to sit below him on two stools, while the great officers of the crown and courts of law sat upon benches. The Lord Chamberlain then had the way cleared and in the middle of the theatre there appeared a fine and spacious area carpeted all over with green cloth. In an instant a large curtain dropped, painted to represent a tent of gold cloth with a broad fringe; the background was of canvas painted blue, powdered all over with golden stars. This became the front arch of the stage, forming a drop scene, and on its being removed there appeared first of all Mount Atlas, whose enormous head was alone visible up aloft under the very roof of the theatre; it rolled up its eyes and moved itself very cleverly. As a foil to the principal ballet and masque they had some mummeries performed in the first act; for instance, a very chubby Bacchus appeared on a car drawn by four gowns-men, who sang in an undertone before his Majesty. There was another stout individual on foot, dressed in red in short clothes, who made a speech, reeling about like a drunkard, tankard in hand, so that he resembled Bacchus's cupbearer. This first scene was very gay and burlesque. Next followed twelve extravagant masquers, one of whom was in a barrel, all but his extremities, his companions being similarly cased in huge wicker flasks, very well made. They danced awhile to the sound of the cornets and trumpets, performing various and most extravagant antics. These were followed by a gigantic man representing Hercules with his club, who strove with Antaeus and performed other feats. Then came twelve masked boys in the guise of frogs. They danced together, assuming sundry grotesque attitudes. After they had all fallen down, they were driven off by Hercules. Mount Atlas then opened, by means of two doors, which were made to turn, and from behind the hills of a distant landscape the day was seen to dawn, some gilt columns being placed along either side of the scene, so as to aid the perspective and make the distance seem greater. Mercury next appeared before the king and made a speech. After him came a guitar player in a gown, who sang some trills, accompanying himself with his instrument. He announced himself as some deity, and then a number of singers, dressed in long red gowns to represent high priests, came on the stage, wearing gilt mitres. In the midst of them was a goddess in a long white robe, and they sang some jigs which we did not understand. It is true that, spoiled as we are by the graceful and harmonious music of Italy, the composition did not strike us as very fine. Finally twelve cavaliers, masked, made their appearance, dressed uniformly, six having the entire hose crimson with plaited doublets of white satin trimmed with gold and silver lace. The other six wore breeches down to the knee, with the half hose also crimson, and white shoes. These matched well their corsets which were cut in the shape of the ancient Roman corslets. On their heads they wore long hair and crowns and very tall white plumes. Their faces were covered with black masks. These twelve descended together from above the scene in the figure of a pyramid, of which the prince formed the apex. When they reached the ground the violins, to the number of twenty-five or thirty began to play their airs. After they had made an obeisance to his Majesty, they began to dance in very good time, preserving for a while the same pyramidical figure, and with a variety of steps. Afterwards they changed places with each other in various ways, but ever ending the jump together. When this was over, each took his lady, the prince pairing with the principal one among those who were ranged in a row ready to dance, and the others doing the like in succession, all making obeisance to his Majesty first and then to each other. They performed every sort of ballet and dance of every country whatsoever such as passamezzi, corants, canaries see Spaniards and a hundred other very fine gestures devised to tickle the fancy (*fatte a piʒʒego*). Last of all they danced the Spanish dance, one at a time, each with his lady, and being well nigh tired they began to lag, whereupon the king, who is naturally choleric, got impatient and shouted aloud Why don't they dance? What did they make me come here for? Devil take you all, dance. Upon this, the Marquis of Buckingham, his Majesty's favourite, immediately sprang forward, cutting a score of lofty and very minute capers, with so much grace and agility that he not only appeased the ire of his angry lord, but rendered himself the admiration and delight of everybody. The other masquers, thus encouraged, continued to exhibit their prowess one after another, with various ladies, also finishing with capers and lifting their goddesses from the ground. We counted thirty-four capers as cut by one cavalier in succession, but none came up to the exquisite manner of the marquis. The prince, however, excelled them all in bowing, being very formal in making his obeisance both to the king and to the lady with whom he danced, nor was he once seen to do a step out of time when dancing, whereas one cannot perhaps say so much for the others. Owing to his youth he has not yet much breath, nevertheless he cut a few capers very gracefully.

The encounter of these twelve accomplished cavaliers being ended, and after they had valiantly overcome the sloth and debauch of Bacchus, the prince went in triumph to kiss his father's hands. The king embraced and kissed him tenderly and then honoured the marquis with marks of extraordinary affection, patting his face. The king now rose from his chair, took the ambassadors along with him, and after passing through a number of chambers and galleries he reached a hall where the usual collation was spread for the performers, a light being carried before him. After he had glanced all round the table he departed, and forthwith the parties concerned pounced upon the prey like so many harpies. The table was covered almost entirely with seasoned pasties and very few sugar confections. There were some large figures, but they were of painted pasteboard for ornament. The repast was served upon glass plates or dishes and at the first assault they upset the table and the crash of glass platters reminded me precisely of a severe hailstorm at Midsummer smashing the window glass. The story ended at half past two in the morning and half disgusted and weary we returned home.[44]

The masque Busino saw was Jonson's *Pleasure Reconciled to Virtue*, performed at the first Banqueting House. It is our loss that Busino gave no comparable account of any of the occasions when the King's Men or Cockpit company performed plays at Court on stages designed by Jones, as they did during the Christmas festivities in some years.

In Caroline times, of twelve plays we know were performed for the Court with scenery, three were put on privately by the Queen's ladies, two privately by the Earl of Pembroke's household, three at Oxford by the university, three at Court by the King's Men, and one at Court by the Cockpit company of 1634.[45] All but two or three used Jones's designs. The four plays performed by the professional players were all transferred to the private playhouses, some with the costumes used in the Court performance, none with the scenery. One of the Oxford plays went to London for a second performance before the Court, this time by the King's Men, at the instigation of the Chancellor, Archbishop Laud (who, incidentally, claimed that the professionals performed the play less well than the students). It cost £100 just to make the costumes and scenery ready again for the second performance. Laud showed an understandable anxiety about the university's property which he had committed to London, and the Queen had to assure him

you may be confident that no Part of these things y^t are come to our hands, shall be suffered to bee prostituted upon any Mercenary Stage, but shall bee carefully Reserv'd for our owne Occasions and particular Entertainments att Court.

The mercenary players on the whole probably expected little else, though they were obviously known to be waiting for any scraps which might fall from the royal stage.

The impossibly various concerns of staging through the period cannot be left without a word on the question of whether or how much anyone may have served as stage director. With such large and rapidly changing repertories no company could afford to spend much time on the niceties of production, of course. The manipulation of the business, the stage-management side, fell naturally into the hands of the only member of the company who had to be reasonably familiar with the whole text of the play, the book-holder or book-keeper. He was responsible for seeing that players were ready on their cues, and for having properties to hand for carrying on or being discovered as and when they might be needed. He had several 'stage-keepers' to help him, who also served as supernumeraries. A marginal note in Heywood's *The Captives* orders '*stage keepers as a guard*'. He lurked in the tiring-house, as we learn from such references as the one in

The Maid in the Mill, a King's Men's play of 1623, where a woman's screams are heard '*within*', and a character says 'they are out of their parts sure: it may be 'tis the Book-holder's fault; I'll go see'. Ben Jonson, probably with an excess of modesty, disclaimed any direct responsibility for the staging of *Cynthia's Revels* by getting one of the boys in the Induction to say

wee are not so officiously befriended by him, as to have his presence in the tiring-house, to prompt us aloud, stampe at the booke-holder, sweare for our properties, curse the poore tire-man, raile the musicke out of tune, and sweat for everie veniall trespasse we commit.

In view of the pains Jonson obviously took preparing this play especially for the boys to show their paces in, it is likely that this denial is another of his minglings of appearance and reality. His direct interest in the production of his plays was to become a by-word in the playhouse world, one which he himself exploited in the Induction to *Bartholomew Fair*, where the stage-keeper complains aggrievedly that the author has taken no notice of his experienced advice.

It was easier to tell youths how to perform their play than adult sharers, of course, which may be why the only other known statement about a supervising or directing hand is about a manager of a young company. William Beeston was commended for training his young players in their trade, in Brome's epilogue to *The Court Beggar*:

But this small Poet vents [no wit] but his own, and his by whose care and directions this Stage is govern'd, who has for many yeares both in his fathers dayes, and since directed Poets to write & Players to speak till he traind up these youths here to what they are now. I some of 'em before they were able to say a grace of two lines long to have more parts in their pates then would fill so many Dry-fats.

This is training in playing, of course, not directing the performance.

Apart from Jonson, the only clear hints I know of to suggest that a playwright participated in the staging of his plays come from the first cause of all the attention paid to Shakespearean drama in the last four centuries. The couplet quoted above about Burbage's mannerism in playing Richard III with 'his hand continuall on his dagger' refers to a gesture for which there is some historical justification. Holinshed's account of Richard reads in part

When he stood musing, he would bite and chaw busilie his nether lip; as who said, that his fierce nature in his cruell bodie alwaies chafed, stirred, and was ever unquiet: beside that, the dagger which he ware, he would (when he studied) with his hand plucke up & downe in the sheath to the midst, never drawing it fullie out.[46]

There was at least one fellow of Burbage who knew Holinshed and could have told him of the mannerism. The same author would most

likely have been the one to elaborate on the bare stage direction
'*Enter Clifford wounded*' in the Folio text of 3 *Henry VI*, and who told
the player or tire-man what to do. The equivalent stage direction in the
reported text reads '*Enter Clifford wounded, with an arrow in his necke*',
the correct place for the wound according to the sources of the play.
And thirdly, the second reported text, of 2 *Henry VI*, tells us that the
stage direction '*Enter Richard, and Somerset to fight*', was also amplified
in the staging by a similar reference to the play's source. Somerset was
said to have died at St Albans under an inn-sign, and the play follows
the report, as the stage direction in the reported text says: '...*enter
the Duke of* Somerset, *and* Richard *fighting and Richard kils him under
the signe of the Castle in saint* Albones.*' These three instances of
authorial intervention in the staging, incidentally, confirm that Shakespeare must have been a fellow with Burbage and the others in Pembroke's Company, some members of which made up the reported
texts of the two *Henry VI* plays, and who were familiar with *Richard III*.

6. The Audiences

A Catholic Archpriest named William Harison discovered in 1623 that some of his priests were in the habit of seeing plays at the public theatres. With pained understanding he pointed out to them that

such playes are made to sport, and delight the auditorie, which consisting most of young gallants, and Protestants (for no true Puritanes will endure to bee present at playes) how unlikely is it, but that there are, and must bee, at least some passages in the playes, which may relish, and tickle the humor of such persons, or else good night to the players.[1]

Similar presumptions and similar deductions about the relationship between Elizabethan plays and their audiences have been made for the last three hundred years. Working in the reverse direction to Harison and noting that events shown in the plays were bloody and bawdy, scholars have found it easy to assume that the audiences to whom such plays were fed were correspondingly riotous and self-willed. The trouble is that this kind of presumption has no particular validity. One might look at twentieth-century television and by the same presumption conclude that audiences now are quite as lecherous and disorderly in their living rooms as those of Shakespeare's day are thought to have been in their theatres.

It may for all we know be true that the basic mentality of the Elizabethan and early Stuart audiences is not essentially different from that of the majority audiences of today. It is the knowing which is difficult. Also of course the returns on the labour of summarising and generalising about such intangibles are likely to be small. There was on average over that seventy years or so of London commercial theatre as many as a million visits to the playhouse a year. Any generalisation which covered that number would have to be stretched thinly. Three of the four estates of the theatre, the playhouses, staging, and even the playing, can evoke generalisations with far more strength. None the less, the audiences were there, and our picture of the Shakespearean theatre is incomplete without some impression of them as one of the factors conditioning performances. Unless one makes Harison's kind of presumption one cannot draw conclusions about their mentality or their causative influence on playwriting, but there is evidence about their constituent members, those sections of society which did help the players to stay prosperous, their behaviour, their favourite habits and tastes, and one can draw from these things a recognisable if impressionistic picture of the theatre's fourth estate. Like other fourth estates, we can know something of its disposition, though we can only guess at its influence.

To take the grand perspective first: from 1574 to 1642 the London playhouses found their audiences amongst a population of between 150,000 and 200,000 people. In 1595 the estimates suggest that the two acting companies were visited by about 15,000 people weekly. In 1620 when six playhouses were open, three of them the smaller private houses, the weekly total was probably nearer 25,000.[2] Probably about 15 or 20 per cent of all the people living within reach of Shoreditch and Southwark were regular playgoers. Modern estimates of the capacities of public theatres converge on about 2,500 as a maximum figure (De Witt estimated 3,000 for the Swan).[3] According to Henslowe, the only theatre impresario whose accounts we have in any detail, the largest audiences attended for new plays and on public holidays, the average attendance being more like half of the capacity. Seasonal variation was less than might be expected, Henslowe's daily receipts dropping from £44. 19s. 0d. in May only to £37. 11s. 0d. in January.[4] The auditorium area in private playhouses such as Blackfriars seems to have been less than half that of the public playhouses, to judge by Beaumont's description in 1609 of the Blackfriars as a place where 'a thousand men in judgement sit'. But of course their admission charges were much higher.

Figures such as these, rough estimates as they are, do not say much about the more revealing but less tangible matters, like the place playgoing occupied in Shakespearean society, how largely it figured in the flood of contemporary social life, or what image it offered the public. Shakespearean London more than most conurbations had a many-headed public divided against itself, and the images its members painted of playhouses and playgoing were highly variable and of very doubtful reliability, particularly from the non-playgoing 80 per cent. The spokesmen for Puritan London described the audiences as riotous and immoral; the playwrights described them as ignorant and wilful; the City Fathers regarded them as riotous and seditious. If any of these images had been in any large degree true the playhouses would have been closed much earlier than 1642. As it was, on the one distressing occasion when officialdom did investigate the playhouses—in 1602 on the instructions of the Privy Council to clear places of resort of idle and disorderly persons and press them for the army—it found the image had misled them. According to contemporary gossip the City Fathers chose to clear the playhouses first, even before the taverns and brothels, and found 'not only...Gentlemen, and servingmen, but Lawyers, Clarkes, country men that had lawe cawses, aye the Quens men, knightes, and as it was credibly reported one Earle'.[5]

Any general picture one may be able to construct from contemporary evidence will have to be built up piecemeal. It will rather be a series of pictures, changing in space and time as the audiences changed, varying from theatre to theatre, from the audiences for Marlowe to the audiences for Davenant. Even contemporary generalisations of acknowledged impartiality need qualifying when the 'contemporary' label covers seventy years of rapid social and cultural change.

One of the more reliable types of witness here as elsewhere was the traveller from abroad. The Elizabethan players were famous across Europe and many of the foreigners who passed through London took care to see them. As tourists they also not infrequently recorded what they saw for the benefit of their fellow-countrymen in the kind of detail which the Londoner, to whom such things were automatic knowledge, usually omitted. Thomas Platter, a German who travelled widely in England in 1599, told of seeing a play at the Curtain:

in conclusion they danced very charmingly in English and Irish fashion. Thus daily at two in the afternoon, London has two, sometimes three plays running in different places, competing with each other, and those which play best obtain most spectators. The playhouses are so constructed that they play on a raised platform, so that everyone has a good view. There are different galleries and places, however, where the seating is better and more comfortable and therefore more expensive. For whoever cares to stand below only pays one English penny, but if he wishes to sit he enters by another door, and pays another penny, while if he desires to sit in the most comfortable seats which are cushioned, where he not only sees everything well, but can also be seen, then he pays yet another English penny at another door. And during the performance food and drink are carried round the audience, so that for what one cares to pay one may also have refreshment.[6]

This is a typical (if minimal) portrait of a public theatre scene on the eve of the rebirth of the private theatres. Platter's admission prices are confirmed in William Lambarde's *Perambulation of Kent* (1596). There were, in addition to the standing room in the yard and the penny and twopenny galleries, in all the public houses one or more lords' rooms, where the charge was sixpence. There is no positive evidence that these prices altered at any time in the period. In the private playhouses, as we have noted, the basic admission was sixpence, which gained the spectator access to the top gallery only. Access to the benches in the pit was a shilling at first, and later 1s. 6d., and a stool on the stage itself cost a further sixpence. The boxes at the side of the stage cost half-a-crown.[7]

Prices understandably tended to determine the distribution of social classes in the playhouses. The basic penny at the Globe in 1600 was cheap by the standards of most forms of entertainment at any time, though the private theatres' basic sixpence, one twelfth of the London artisan's weekly wage,[8] was by public theatre standards indeed a lord's

price for the two hours of stage traffic. The other major pastimes available, however, gambling, whoring and drinking, were all by that
standard lordly sports. Tobacco was threepence for a small pipeful,
and even the nuts which spectators commonly chewed during performances cost up to sixpence. Only bearbaiting was as cheap as the yard
of the public playhouses. The working classes seem to have paid up
to twopence for their plays according to the author of *Father Hubburd's
Tales* (1603), who writes of 'a dull Audience of Stinkards sitting in
the Penny Galleries of a Theater, and yawning upon the Players'. Sir
Humphrey Mildmay, a landed gentleman about town in the 1630s,
used to pay for a twelvepenny room (in the middle gallery?) at the
private playhouse, and paid a similar price, presumably for a lord's
room, when he went to the Globe in the summer months.[9] The public
playhouse's shilling may have been made up to that total in his accounts
by a boatman's fee. With such exceptions, the different pricing did
apparently make a difference in the audiences. The praeludium to
Goffe's *Careless Shepherdess*, played at a private playhouse in 1629, has
a Citizen say

> I will hasten to the money Box,
> And take my shilling out again, for now
> I have considered that it is too much;
> I'le go to th'Bull, or Fortune, and there see
> A Play for two pense, with a Jig to boot.

If a merchant or craftsman found the shilling too much, it is not likely
that apprentices would have been tempted.

One of the fundamental differences between all the various audiences
must have existed between the social classes, in simple financial terms
of those who could not afford the private playhouse charges and those
who could. It is easy to exaggerate the difference, and certainly the
Globe at least after 1610 as the King's Men's summer resort attracted
the playgoers used to seeing them at the Blackfriars. Mildmay's diary
records several plays seen at Court, eighteen visits to Blackfriars and
four to the Cockpit, but also four to the Globe. The Globe company
even in the decade before 1610, the first years of the private theatres,
was summoned to play at Court twice as often as any other company,
in fact as often as all the other companies put together. It is unlikely
that those who favoured them so much at Court would have ignored
them at the Globe. The rich and the poor audiences were not mutually
exclusive; rather the rich went to public and private theatre alike, the
poor more exclusively to the public.

Looking back from 1699 the antiquary James Wright summed up the
general impressions of the different Caroline theatres as they evolved
after 1608 as follows:

Before the Wars, there were in being all these Playhouses at the same time.
The *Black-friers*, and *Globe* on the *Bankside*, a Winter and Summer House,

belonging to the same Company called the King's Servants; the *Cockpit* or *Phoenix*, in *Drury-Lane*, called the Queen's Servants; the private House in *Salisbury-court*, called the Prince's Servants; the Fortune near *White-cross-street*, and the Red Bull at the upper end of St. *John's-street*: The two last were mostly frequented by Citizens, and the meaner sort of People. All these Companies got Money, and Liv'd in Reputation, especially those of the *Black-friers*, who were Men of grave and sober Behaviour.[10]

Most of the evidence for the composition of audiences at these various playhouses supports Wright's description, though by no means so simply. The boy companies at the new private theatres in 1600 seem not so much to have drawn wealthy audiences away from the public theatres as for a time and in ways which changed to have excluded the poorer patrons. Marston, writing about St Paul's Boys in 1600, in *Jack Drums Entertainment*, v.i, told his listeners

> I like the Audience that frequenteth there
> With much applause: A man shall not be choakte
> With the stench of Garlicke, nor be pasted
> To the barmy Jacket of a Beer-brewer.

And called them 'a good gentle Audience'. It was a hopeful pronouncement, and probably meant more that the stinkard was banished from the yard to the top gallery than that he was totally excluded. By 1609 Jonson was writing of 'six-penny mechanicks' and the 'shop's foreman ...that may judge for his sixpence' at Blackfriars. It is also worth bearing in mind that the first performance of Beaumont's *Knight of the Burning Pestle* at the Blackfriars in 1607 was a total flop because, as the publisher of the first quarto (1613) said, the audience missed 'the privie mark of irony about it'. That a burlesque of citizen plays should be construed by the audience as a straight citizen play rather implies that the citizen element in the audience was stronger than Beaumont bargained for.

   The wealthy had of course patronised the public playhouses readily enough before 1600. Nashe in 1592 listed the classes with leisure to spend on the players as 'Gentlemen of the Court, the Innes of the Courte, and the number of Captaines and Souldiers about London'. Foreign dignitaries patronised public as much as private at least into the 1620s. The French ambassador took his wife to the Globe to see *Pericles* in 1607–8. Still more outlandishly the Spanish ambassador and his train chose the Fortune in 1621 and afterwards banqueted with the players. The scandal over the performance of *A Game at Chesse* in August 1624 produced the following note from a contemporary observer:

I doubt not but you have heard of our famous play of Gondomar, which hath been followed with extraordinary concourse, and frequented by all sorts of people old and younge, rich and poore, masters and servants, papists and puritans, wise men *et. ct.*, churchmen and statesmen, as Sir Henry Wotton, Sir Albert Morton, Sir Benjamin Ruddier, Sir Thomas Lake, and a world besides; the Lady Smith wold have gon yf she could have persuaded me to go with her. I am not so sowre nor severe but I could not sit so long, for we must have ben there before one a clocke at farthest to find any roome.

The concourse at such a *succès de scandale* was not of course extraordinary for its social altitude but for its wide range. We have a more customary account from Busino, the wide-eyed Venetian, who visited the Fortune in 1617, and was impressed

to see such a crowd of nobility, so very well arrayed that they looked like so many princes, listening as silently and soberly as possible. These theatres are frequented by a number of respectable and handsome ladies, who come freely and seat themselves among the men without the slightest hesitation.

He goes on to describe being solicited by one such masked gentlewoman, in two languages; she was probably set on him as a joke by his ambassador.

John Earle writing of a leading actor in 1628 coupled gentlewomen and law students as the most frequent playgoers, claiming with characteristic malice that

The waiting-women Spectators are over-eares in love with him, and Ladies send for him to act in their Chambers. Your Innes of Court men were undone but for him, hee is their chiefe guest and imployment, and the sole businesse that makes them Afternoones men.

A more detailed, though not necessarily more typical catalogue of a Blackfriars audience under the Stuarts was given in 1617 by the Inns of Court student Henry Fitzgeoffrey, in a book of verses called *Satyres and Satyricall Epigrams: with Certaine Observations at Black-Fryers*. In a looser version of the Theophrastan 'Characters' manner he describes a '*Captaine Martio*, he ith' *Renounce Me* Band, / That in the middle Region doth stand', 'Sir *Iland Hunt*, a Travailer that will tell / Of stranger Things then *Tatterd Tom* ere li't of ', 'A *Cheapside* Dame' (i.e. a Citizen's wife), a high-heeled 'world of fashions' (male), 'A *Woman* of the *masculine Gender*', a 'plumed *Dandebrat*, / Yon Ladyes *Shittle-cocke*', and a 'misshappen *Prodigall*' who passes on to the stage from the tiring-house as if he had not a debt in the world. Later, and perhaps a little inconsistently, the audience is described as 'this *Microcosme*, Man's societie'.

Both Earle's and Fitzgeoffrey's descriptions are of the Blackfriars, unquestionably the most reputable playhouse of the whole later period. In 1630 it was the focus of a literary quarrel which in a small way illustrates the differences between the theatres at that time. Davenant's second commercial theatre play, *The Just Italian*, failed when put on by the King's Men. His friends promptly supplied him with sympathetic prefatory verses for the publication of the play early in 1630. One of them was Thomas Carew, who wrote of the audience:

> they'l still slight
> All that exceeds Red Bull, and Cockpit flight.
> These are the men in crowded heapes that throng
> To that adulterate stage, where not a tong
> Of th'untun'd Kennell, can a line repeat
> Of serious sence: but like lips, meet like meat;
> Whilst the true brood of Actors, that alone
> Keepe naturall unstrayn'd Action in her throne
> Behold their benches bare, though they rehearse
> The tearser *Beaumonts*, or great *Johnsons* verse.

This slur, linking Beeston's company at the Cockpit with the tear-throat citizen fare of the Red Bull, found a prompt reply in verses attached to Shirley's *Grateful Servant*, one of the only two plays by Shirley to be printed with prefatory verses. One defender of Shirley and the Cockpit repertory, for which Shirley was the leading playwright, replied that

> I must
> Be to my conscience and thy Poem just,
> Which grac'd with comely action, did appeare
> The full delight of every eye and eare,
> And had that stage no other play, it might
> Have made the critticke blushe at cock-pit flight,
> Who not discovering what pitch it flies
> His wit came down in pitty to his eyes
> And lent him a discourse of cock and bull
> To make his other commendations full:
> But let such Momi passe, and give applause
> Among the brood of actors, in whose cause,
> As Champion he hath sweat, let their stale pride
> Finde some excuse in being magnified,
> Thy Muse will live, and no adulterate pen
> Shall wound her, through the sides of common men
> Let 'em unkennell malice, yet thy praise
> Shall mount secure, hell cannot blast thy bayes.[11]

Others of Shirley's sympathisers upheld his 'So smooth, so sweet' verse against the 'mighty rimes, / Audacious metaphors' of Davenant. Shirley himself defended his actors—'the most of them deserving a name in the file of those that are eminent for gracefull and unaffected action'. It has been suggested that what gave Shirley's supporters so much exercise was not only the 'untun'd Kennell' charge but more particularly the 'cock and bull' association of the 'Cocke-pit flight' with that of the Red Bull.[12] The suggestion is plausible, though one should perhaps note that the Red Bull's quondam playwright took offence as well as the Cockpit's. In Book IV of his religious poem *The Hierarchy of the Blessed Angels* (1635) Heywood broke out against Carew and Davenant in righteous if postponed indignation:

> Whence growes this Innovation? How comes it
> Some dare to measure mouthes for every bit
> The Muse shall tast? And those Approv'd Tongues call
> Which have pleased Court and City, indeed All;
> An untuned Kennel: when the populous Throng
> Of Auditors have thought the Muses sung,
> When they but spake? How comes it (ere he know it)
> A puny shall assume the name of poet,
> And in a Tympa'nous and Thrasonicke stile
> (Words at which th'Ignorant laugh but the learn'd smile
> Because Adulterate and Undenizen'd) he
> Should taske such Artists, as have took Degre
> Before he was a Fresh-man?

It was more a personal quarrel than a war about dramatic standards, since Heywood for one took it personally. But the question of differing standards did exist. Carew's view of the superiority of the Blackfriars repertory was reasserted by Leonard Digges in commendatory verses attached to Shakespeare's *Poems* of 1640. Digges exhorted contemporary scribblers not to pollute Shakespeare's stage:

> But if you needs must write, if poverty
> So pinch, that otherwise you starve and die,
> On Gods name may the Bull or Cockpit have
> Your lame blancke Verse, to keepe you from the grave:
> Or let new Fortunes younger brethren see,
> What they can picke from your leane industry.
> I do not wonder when you offer at
> Blacke-friers, that you suffer.[13]

This is a celebration of the superior standards offered at the Blackfriars, rather than any essential difference in the repertory. The whole quarrel shows an awareness in the rival playwrights of the homogeneity of each playhouse's audiences, and their tendency to differ.

The chief problem in differentiating the theatre audiences is not in fact so much between the public and citizen Red Bull and Fortune on the one hand, and the private and courtier Blackfriars on the other, as in locating the place held by the Globe after 1608–9, when the King's Men became private theatre players as well as public, and used the Globe for the summer season from May to September and Blackfriars through the rest of the year. By 1630 the Blackfriars was taking twice as much money as the Globe on the average, and was used for twice as long in the year. The title-pages of play-quartos published between 1616 and 1642 mention performances at the Blackfriars alone forty-nine times; ten name both Blackfriars and Globe, and only five give the Globe alone as the venue. It is unlikely that many or even any of these plays had really only been acted at one of the playhouses, because the repertory of the King's Men seems to have been almost completely interchangeable, at least down to the last decade. The Globe of course was open mainly while the Inns of Court were in vacation and the aristocracy out of town, and it is likely to be this circumstance as much as its more 'popular' public theatre image which made it less distinguished than the Blackfriars. Henry Glapthorne's *Poems* (1639) contains a prologue '*To a Reviv'd Vacation Play*' which puts forward the hope that its wit will find some response from an audience of citizens, but on the other hand Davenant's *News from Plymouth*, acted at the Globe in vacation, has a prologue expressing joy at the appearance there of a Blackfriars audience:

> A Noble Company! for we can spy
> Beside rich gawdy Sirs, some that rely
> More on their Judgments, then their Cloathes, and may
> With wit as well as Pride, rescue our Play:
> And 'tis but just, though each Spectator knows
> This House, and season, does more promise shewes,
> Dancing, and Buckler Fights, then Art, or Witt.

Davenant's last lines suggest that the Globe provided jigs and spectacles despite the success of the King's Men's musicians at the Blackfriars. The prologue to Shirley's *Doubtful Heir* (1640) supplies a detailed catalogue of the differences between the offerings of the two playhouses in a heavily grudging apology for presenting a play written for the Blackfriars at the Globe:

> Our Author did not calculate this Play
> For this Meridian; the Bankside, he knows,
> Are far more skilfull at the Ebbes and flows
> Of water, than of wit, he did not mean
> For the elevation of your poles, this scene.
> No shews, no dance, and what you most delight in,
> Grave understanders, here's no target fighting.

The catalogue goes on at some length. What the Globe audience thought of the apology is not recorded. It has an undertone to it which implies resentment that the players have chosen to demean the play in this fashion, and one might deduce from this that players and audiences were less concerned about the difference between the two playhouses than were the playwrights.

The trappings of public and private performance remained at each theatre, and the repertories of plays were possibly in the later years also divided, though not as much as some playwrights wished. On Davenant's testimony and evidence such as Mildmay's diary it also appears that in summer the Blackfriars audiences did not forsake the

King's Men just because they moved to the Globe and were producing their plays with public theatre appurtenances. In these late years both audiences were socially mixed, to judge by Lovelace's epilogue to his lost play *The Scholars*, published in 1649. The difference at Blackfriars between the gallery and the pit required two plays in one:

> His *Schollars* school'd, sayd if he had been wise
> He should have wove in one two comedies.
> The first for th'gallery, in which the throne
> To their amazement should descend alone,
> The rosin-lightning flash and monster spire
> Squibs, and words hotter than his fire.
> Th'other for the gentlemen o'th' pit
> Like to themselves all spirit, fancy, wit.

The price differential no doubt reduced the proportion of commoners in the gallery of the Blackfriars in the winter, compared with the numbers standing around the Globe stage. The disappearance of the landed gentry to their estates and of the afternoon men from the Inns of Court no doubt similarly reduced the proportions of gallants at the Globe in summer. But at neither playhouse could the King's Men expect a complete change of audience.

Evidence for the behaviour of Shakespearean audiences is much more plentiful than for their constitution; rather too plentiful in fact. As Alfred Harbage puts it, most of the testimony for audience behaviour 'expresses a social attitude or comes from disappointed poets, disgruntled preachers, wary politicians, or spokesmen for threatened commercial interests'.[14] Harbage makes the point that the bulk of the unfavourable testimony can be discounted by analogy with the similar body of testimony against the depraved and corrupted nature of plays. Since the one set of testimonies can be proved false by reference to the plays accused of corruption, the equivalent testimonies for riotous behaviour among the audiences can similarly be distrusted. One's inclination to do so is strengthened on finding that Stephen Gosson, once an actor and playwright and one of the most eloquent testifiers against the playhouses, took his descriptions of Elizabethan audiences from Ovid's accounts of Roman audiences in the *Amores*.[15] Harison's cautious and not implausible deduction about the nature of plays, quoted at the beginning of this chapter, was a safer argument for a non-playgoer to use than the accusations levelled by the non-playgoing Puritans and City Fathers. One might expect the playwrights to carry more weight with their condemnations, and they were certainly more eloquent: Nashe attacked audiences in 1592, Heywood in 1595, Marston in 1597, 1603 and 1604, Chapman in 1599, Beaumont in 1607 and 1609, Fletcher in 1609 and 1613, Dekker in 1609 and 1610, Webster in 1611, Middleton in 1613, Carew in 1630, and Jonson at frequent

6 149

intervals throughout his career.[16] But all their attacks were on bad judgement rather than behaviour, and cannot therefore be looked on as reasonably disinterested. A few playwrights sometimes went to the other extreme of flattery, but with no more sign of disinterest than when they condemned.

There is some evidence of violence and lawlessness in the playhouses between 1574 and 1642, but there is nothing to show that it was more than the occasional consequence of large crowds gathering together for a length of time. Chambers[17] lists instances of lawlessness in playhouses including a case of stealing at the Red Bull in 1613, a stabbing (the Fortune in the same year), fighting (the Red Bull in 1610), and receiving a stolen diamond (the Curtain in 1594). There were also such minor consequences of ill manners as the lawsuit brought in Star Chamber by a Captain Essex against the Irish Lord Thurles (a few weeks later to be the Duke of Ormond) in 1632, resulting from a brawl with swords when Thurles took up a position on the stage at the Blackfriars and obstructed the view of Captain Essex and the Earl of Essex's new wife, whom the Captain was escorting, in their box.[18]

As in any crowd of course pickpockets and prostitutes were to be found at work, but even for them the taverns were better employment. A pickpocket caught in 1600 at one of the Middlesex public theatres was the only one amongst 118 proven cases in that year to be taken at a playhouse.[19] In the case of the Fortune, there was even a rather self-conscious pride in the association of cut-purses and similar rogues with the house. Dekker and Middleton wrote a play, *The Roaring Girl*, celebrating one Marion Frith, a well-known female transvestite who herself favoured the Fortune. In 1605 the *Consistory of London Correction Book* recorded Roaring Moll's bad reputation, and especially that

being at a play about three quarters of a yeare since at ye Fortune in man's apparel and in her boots and wth a sword at her syde she told the company then present y[t] she thought many of them were of opinion that she was a man, but if any of them would come to her lodging they should finde she is a woman, and some other immodest and lascivious speaches she also used at y[t] time and also sat upon the stage in the public viewe of all the people there present in man's apparel and played upon her lute and sange a song.[20]

The play itself, written a year or two later, utilised Moll to identify her associates in the playhouse audience, in v.i. In i.ii a leading gentleman character presents a detailed description of the Fortune audience and also identifies a cutpurse amongst them:

The furniture that doth adorne this roome,
Cost many a faire gray groat ere it came here,
But good things are most cheape, when th'are most deere,
Nay when you looke into my galleries,
How bravely they are trim'd up, you all shall sweare
Y'are highly pleasd to see whats set downe there:

Stories of men and women (mixt together
Faire ones with foule, like sun-shine in wet wether)
Within one square a thousand heads are laid
So close, that all of heads, the roome seemes made,
As many faces there (fill'd with blith lookes)
Shew like the promising titles of new bookes,
(Writ merily) the Readers being their owne eyes,
Which seeme to move and to give plaudities,
       And here and there (whilst with obsequious eares,
Throng'd heapes do listen) a cut purse thrusts and leeres
With haukes eyes for his prey: I need not shew him,
By a hanging villanous looke, your selves may know him,
The face is drawne so rarely. Then sir below,
The very flowre (as twere) waves to and fro,
And like a floating Iland, seemes to move,
Upon a sea bound in with shores above.

It was the Fortune which was singled out in the Middlesex order of 1612 for the suppression of jigs because of the cutpurses they attracted.

The presence of criminals was a much more common phenomenon than civil brawls in the playhouse crowds. The only major breaches of the peace were likely to happen during the apprentices' traditional Shrovetide saturnalia, when they sometimes turned on the playhouses instead of their more usual target the bawdy houses. As we have seen, they seriously damaged the Cockpit in 1617. It is this annual and on the whole exceptional occasion that Edmund Gayton enthusiastically described in 1654:

the players have been appointed, notwithstanding their bills to the contrary, to act what the major part of the company had a mind to. Sometimes *Tamerlane*, sometimes *Jugurtha*, sometimes *The Jew of Malta*, and sometimes parts of all these; and at last, none of the three taking, they were forced to undress and put off their tragick habits, and conclude the day with *The Merry Milkmaides*. And unless this were done, and the popular humour satisfied (as sometimes it so fortun'd that the players were refractory), the benches, the tiles, the laths, the stones, oranges, apples, nuts, flew about most liberally; and as there were mechanicks of all professions, who fell every one to his trade, and dissolved a house in an instant, and made a ruin of a stately fabric.

The plays Gayton mentions were in the Red Bull and Fortune repertories, and it is understandable that the more riotous happenings, like the lawbreaking, occurred there more than elsewhere. Captain Essex's altercation is the only kind of incident recorded at the Blackfriars.

Riots, brawls and lawbreaking were hardly everyday happenings, and it is impossible to gauge the behaviour of a typical audience by them. Habitual practices tell us more than such exceptions. The most obtrusive habits were to be seen in the private playhouses in the gallants who sat on stools on the stage, and, in all the playhouses, in the nut-cracking which was a favourite exercise for everybody. A gallant talking and smoking on a stool on the periphery of the stage was, and meant himself to be, an extremely obtrusive feature of the performance. It was a popular habit from the time the private playhouses first opened, and however objectionable to the mass of the audience and the players it survived. The preface to the first Shakespeare Folio in 1623 complained of wits sitting 'on the Stage at Black-friers, or the Cock-pit, to arraigne Playes dailie'. The players were similarly unhappy about the noise of nuts being cracked during their performances; nut-cracking in fact was the only regular complaint apart from the Prologue's customary plea for silence.[21] Jasper Mayne's prologue to *The City Match* bravely declares that the author has no fear of 'them who sixpence pay and sixpence crack', but according to Thomas Palmer in the 1647 Beaumont and Fletcher Folio it took Falstaff to keep the audience from their cracking. Bottle ale, which was sold during the performance, was also occasionally remarked on for the potentially misunderstood hiss it gave when opened.

Hisses or 'mewes', like applause, were given freely, and not only at the end of the play. Drayton speaks of

> Showts and Claps at ev'ry little pawse,
> When the proud Round on ev'ry side hath rung.[22]

And they were highly responsive in sentiment too. An academic spectator seeing a performance of *Othello* by the King's Men at Oxford in 1610 wrote that

not only by their speech but also by their deeds they drew tears.—But indeed Desdemona, killed by her husband, although she always acted the matter very well, in her death moved us still more greatly; when lying in bed she implored the pity of those watching with her countenance alone.[23]

The famous anecdote of the audience at *Faustus* being startled when the theatre fabric gave a loud crack speaks of the tension which audiences could generate. Not of course that they were often easily satisfied. Middleton echoed several fellow-playwrights in complaining of the variousness of audience tastes, in the prologue to *No Wit, No Help like a Woman's*:

> How is't possible to suffice
> So many Ears, so many Eyes?
> Some in wit, some in shows
> Take delight, and some in Clothes;
> Some for mirth they cheifly come,
> Some for passion, for both some;
> Some for lascivious meetings, that's their arrant;
> Some to detract, and ignorance their warrant.
> How is't possible to please
> Opinion tos'd in such wilde Seas?

The playwrights' complaints about the intelligence of their audiences sometimes took the form of accusations that they came for the spectacle, not the words, 'only to see men speak'.[24] As Jonson put it, plays should be

> *offered, as a* Rite,
> *To* Schollers, *that can judge, and faire report*
> *The sense they heare, above the vulgar sort*
> *Of Nut-crackers, that onely come for sight.*[25]

One can count as many as thirty-four complaints from almost all the dramatists of the time (except Shakespeare) of the kind of reception their plays were given. And yet very few of the plays which failed then, with the sole exceptions of *The Knight of the Burning Pestle* and possibly *The White Devil*, would stand much chance of success now. Where audiences then and now would be more inclined to differ is over the plays which were the greatest successes of the early period. Judging by the number of editions printed, with *Faustus*, *Hamlet* and the *Henry IV* plays, the most popular pieces from the whole seventy years of playing were *The Spanish Tragedy*, *Mucedorus*, *Philaster*, Heywood's *If You Know Not Me*, and *Pericles*. The failures among the better plays of the period might be put down to the fickleness of individual audiences, but the successes among the better plays were made by the consistent judgements of a long series of audiences. They could hardly be called bad judges.

To conclude this section on audience behaviour it is instructive to put beside each other two pieces of evidence which come from the same time and more or less the same place, the Blackfriars at the end of the boy company's tenure in 1608. The first is Dekker's splendidly vivid set of burlesque advice to the ambitious gallant on how to behave in a playhouse. His remarks are meant to apply to any playhouse, but fit best at the leading private house:

let our Gallant. . . presently advance himselfe up to the Throne of the Stage. I meane not into the Lords roome (which is now but the Stages Suburbs): No, those boxes, by the iniquity of custome, conspiracy of waiting-women and Gentlemen-Ushers, that there sweat together, and the covetousness of Sharers, are contemptibly thrust into the reare, and much new Satten is there dambd, by being smothred to death in darknesse. But on the very Rushes where the Comedy is to daunce, yea, and under the state of *Cambises* himselfe, must our fethered *Estridge*, like a piece of Ordnance, be planted valiantly (because impudently) beating downe the mewes and hisses of the opposed rascality. . .

Present not your selfe on the Stage (especially at a new play) untill the quaking prologue hath (by rubbing) got culor into his cheekes, and is ready to give the trumpets their Cue, that hees upon point to enter: for then it is time, as though you were one of the *properties*, or that you dropt out of the *Hangings*, to creepe from behind the Arras, with your *Tripos* or three-footed stoole in one hand, and a teston mounted betweene a forefinger and a thumbe in the other: for if you should bestow your person upon the vulgar, when the belly of the house is but halfe full, your apparell is quite eaten up, the fashion lost, and the proportion of your body in more danger to be devoured then if it were served up in the Counter amongst the Powltry: avoid that as you would the Bastome. It shall crowne you with rich commendation, to laugh alowd in the middest of the most serious and saddest scene of the terriblest Tragedy: and to let that clapper (your tongue) be tost so high, that all the house may ring of it: your Lords use it; your Knights are Apes to the Lords, and do so too: your Inne-a-court-man is Zany to the Knights, and (mary very scurvily) comes likewise limping after it: bee thou a beagle to them all, and never lin snuffing, till you have scented them:. . .

Now sir, if the writer be a fellow that hath either epigrammed you, or hath had a flirt at your mistris, or hath brought either your feather, or your red beard, or your little legs &c. on the stage, you shall disgrace him worse then by tossing him in a blancket, or giving him the bastinado in a Taverne, if, in the middle of his play, (bee it Pastoral or Comedy, Morall or Tragedie) you rise with a screwd and discontented face from your stoole to be gone: no matter whether the Scenes be good or no; the better they are the worse do you distast them: and, beeing on your feet, sneake not away like a coward, but salute all your gentle acquaintance, that are spred either on the rushes, or on stooles about you, and draw what troope you can from the stage after you: the *Mimicks* are beholden to you, for allowing them elbow roome: their Poet cries, perhaps, a pox go with you, but care not for that, theres no musick without frets.

Mary, if either the company, or indisposition of the weather binde you to sit it out, my counsell is then that you turne plain Ape, take up a rush, and tickle the earnest eares of your fellow gallants, to make other fooles fall a laughing: mewe at passionate speeches, blare at merrie, finde fault with the musicke, whew at the childrens Action, whistle at the songs: and above all, curse the sharers, that whereas the same day you had bestowed forty shillings on an embrodered Felt and Feather, (Scotch-fashion) for your mistres in the Court, or your punk in the city, within two houres after, you encounter with the very same block on the stage, when the haberdasher swore to you the impression was extant but that morning.[26]

One can see the value of keeping audiences in darkness. Dekker's satire is of course an exaggeration, but as a burlesque of a gull's actions and motivations it is exactly parallel to other burlesques of gallant behaviour in the Induction to *Cynthia's Revels*, one of the earliest boy plays at the Blackfriars in 1601, and *The Isle of Gulls*, another private theatre play of 1606.

The other piece of evidence from the Blackfriars in 1608 tells of one effect of the kind of wilfulness described by Dekker. John Fletcher in 1608 wrote a careful and ambitious work, *The Faithful Shepherdess*, essentially an Arcadian pastoral drama of a type previously played only before Court or university audiences. It did not take at all on its first commercial appearance. As Fletcher angrily reported

It is a pastorall Tragic-comedie, which the people seeing when it was plaid, having ever had a singuler guift in defining, concluded to be a play of country hired Shepheards in gray cloakes, with curtaild dogs in strings, sometimes laughing together, and sometimes killing one another: And missing whitsun ales, creame, wassel and morris-dances, began to be angry.

The audience which received Fletcher's play with such lower-class expectation was at the Blackfriars watching a boy company. Shortly afterwards the King's Men took over the theatre and performed Beaumont and Fletcher's *Philaster*, a modified version of the same kind of play, which had an enormous success and created a fashion for tragicomedy to outlast the Stuart reign. Such apparent inconsistency on the part of the Blackfriars audiences should warn us first of the danger of making too absolute a distinction between the audiences at one kind of playhouse and another. Secondly the success of *Philaster* and the subsequent Beaumont and Fletcher plays should show that the playwrights were on occasion capable of forcing a new dramatic fashion on their wayward brethren. Catering to existing tastes was not the sole function of the Shakespearean dramatists.

The perspective that still remains to be laid down in this portrait of playhouse audiences is the chronological one. Plays such as *Faustus* and *The Spanish Tragedy* were popular at the Fortune until the theatres were closed, but the plays which were written for the Cockpit and Blackfriars in Caroline times were vastly different from the products of Shakespeare's Globe and the playhouses which preceded it. One group of theatres, the Curtain, Rose and Swan before 1600 and the Red Bull and Fortune afterwards, retained a fairly consistent repertory throughout the whole seventy years. The plays of Shakespeare's company on the whole kept in step with their fellows' public theatre plays until some time after 1610, when the private playhouses started moving away to end up with the Caroline fashion. One cannot really speak of a private playhouse style of repertory before the King's Men became themselves private players; it was rather a boy company repertory before that, one which was not taken up by the adults. To see the separate repertories in Harbage's term as 'rival traditions' before 1610, one middle class and the other aristocratic, is misleading, and even later it would be an over-simplification, though differences there certainly were.[27] The private theatre plays from the start had music and masquing compared with the public theatres' squibs and thunder. The private plays of the later Blackfriars did take over the tradition of wit and the aristocratic pastoral rather than rant and huffing parts, and the boys' Blackfriars plays had a good deal of sexual licence which soon returned under the King's company. But neither tradition was exclusive of features or even plays belonging to the other, and where Shakespeare's Globe fits into the picture before 1610 is a still unresolved question. Even after his company had moved into the Blackfriars they chose to play *Mucedorus*, perhaps the most popular of all the middle-class plays, and they performed it before the King. Burbage appears to have played Jeronimo in their version of *The Spanish Tragedy* until not long before his death in 1619.[28] The Untuned Kennel debate of 1630 suggests that so much great gulf as there was had been fixed between individual private houses as well as between private and public. Not unless we knew the complete repertory of all the major playhouses for much of the period should we be able to trace the chronology or even the degree of change with confidence and precision.

It takes a perspective of forty or fifty years to recognise real changes in repertories and audience fashions. Differences in due time there undoubtedly were: it is hard to visualise *Faustus* being put on in the private theatre repertory in 1620 quite as John Melton described it at the Fortune. By 1632 Jonson was looking back on the fashion still current at the Fortune as one belonging wholly to former days. In *The Magnetic Lady* he summarised the plot of an old play which sounds suspiciously like Beaumont's burlesque of the same fashion in 1607:

if a Child could be borne, in a Play, and grow up to a man, i' the first Scene, before hee went off the Stage; and then after to come forth a Squire, and bee made a Knight: and that Knight to travell betweene the Acts, and doe wonders i' the holy land, or else where; kill Paynims, wild Boores, dun Cowes, and other Monsters; beget him a reputation, and marry an Emperours Daughter for his Mistris; convert her Fathers Countrey; and at last come home, lame... These miracles would please, I assure you.[29]

Beaumont had fired first, and Cervantes before him; but it was still a living target in the public playhouses. One of Jonson's tribe of followers, Richard Brome, followed him in *The Antipodes* (1638) with a scene in which a lord reproves an actor for various old-fashioned tricks including extempore clowning:

> when you are
> To speake to your coactors in the Scene,
> You hold interloquutions with the Audients.
> *Bi[play]*. That is a way my Lord has bin allow'd
> On elder stages to move mirth and laughter.
> *Letoy*. Yes in the dayes of *Tarlton* and *Kempe*,
> Before the stage was purg'd from barbarisme,
> And brought to the perfection it now shines with. [II.ii.]

The distance which some companies had travelled by that year is signalled in Ford's complaint in the prologue to *The Lady's Trial* that the Caroline taste was only for wit; 'The Muses chatter, who were wont to sing':

> He who will venture on a jest, that can
> Raile on anothers paine, or idlely scan
> Affaires of state, Oh hee's the onely man.

What seems to have happened in the twilight of the Stuart Gods is that the public theatres soldiered on with an old repertory while the private theatres recruited the new plays. In such circumstances the gulf would inevitably widen. The analogy with the world of fashion in dress, where some keep up to date and others stick to the clothes of their youth, was recognised by Middleton in the Epistle to *The Roaring Girl*:

The fashion of play-making, I can properly compare to nothing, so naturally, as the alteration in apparell. For in the time of the Great-crop-doublet, your huge bombasted plaies, quilted with mighty words to leane purpose was onely then in fashion. And as the doublet fell, neater inventions beganne to set up. Now in the time of sprucenes, our plaies followe the nicenes of our Garments, single plots, quaint conceits, letcherous jests, drest up in hanging sleeves, and those are fit for the Times and the Tearmers.

Middleton's analogy was drawn up as early as 1611, and the fact that it was as pertinent in 1641 as in 1611 shows the slowness of the changes being mapped, and perhaps the thoroughness of the split which lasted so many years. The one play which according to Anthony Scoloker had managed to 'please all' was *Hamlet*; but that was at the Globe in 1600.[30] When the plays which had occupied the stage in the great years that followed were out of fashion then, by 1641, it was indeed, as Harison put it, good night to the players.

Appendix: A Select List of Plays

The following list is designed as a basis for reference from specific plays to their compan
and playhouse background. It includes only those plays which can reasonably positive
be assigned to particular playhouses and companies. The information has been compil
largely from *ES*, III–IV, *JCS*, III–V, and Harbage, *Annals of English Drama 975–170*
revised by S. Schoenbaum.

The same name was sometimes used by more than one company, chiefly the two Pau
companies, the various Queen's and Prince's companies, and the King's Revels. The dat
make it clear which Paul's company is intended; the Queens' companies are variously list
as Queen's (i.e. Elizabeth's), Queen Anne's, or Queen Henrietta's, The Jacobean Prince
company is called the Prince's, and the post-1615 companies are called Prince Charles's. A
the boy companies have the name 'Children' in their title; the King's Revels Children
1607–9 can thus be distinguished from the Salisbury Court King's Revels. Beeston's Bo
retain their title because the company was not strictly a boy company.

Some of the details in the list (notably those relating to Shakespeare) are more conjectur
than others. In particular the assignment of King's Company plays dating from after 16
to the Globe or the Blackfriars is a hazardous business. Where one or other of the playhous
is positively assigned, it means that the playhouse named has been specifically linked wi
the play in question. The naming of one playhouse only does not mean that a play w
necessarily performed only at that playhouse, of course.

AUTHOR	PLAY	DATE	COMPANY	PLAYHOUSE
Robert Armin	The Two Maids of Moreclacke	1607–8(?)	King's Revels Children	Whitefriars
Barnabe Barnes	The Devil's Charter	1607	King's	Globe
Lording Barry	Ram-Alley	1607–8	King's Revels Children	Whitefriars
Francis Beaumont	The Woman Hater	c. 1606	Paul's Children	Paul's
Francis Beaumont	The Knight of the Burning Pestle	1607	Queen's Revels Children	Blackfriars
Francis Beaumont and John Fletcher	Cupid's Revenge	1608	Queen's Revels Children	Blackfriars
Francis Beaumont and John Fletcher	The Coxcomb	1608–9	Queen's Revels Children (c. 1614 Lady Elizabeth's, 1622 King's)	Blackfriars?
Francis Beaumont and John Fletcher	Philaster	1609	King's	Globe/Blackfriars
Francis Beaumont and John Fletcher	The Maid's Tragedy	1610	King's	Blackfriars

AUTHOR	PLAY	DATE	COMPANY	PLAYHOUSE
Francis Beaumont and John Fletcher	*A King and No King*	1611	King's	Globe/Blackfriars
Sir William Berkeley	*The Lost Lady*	1637–8	King's	Blackfriars
Alexander Brome(?)	*The Cunning Lovers*	1632–9	Beeston's Boys	Cockpit
Richard Brome	*The Northern Lass*	1629	King's	Globe/Blackfriars
Richard Brome	*The Novella*	1632–3	King's	Blackfriars
Richard Brome and Thomas Heywood	*The Late Lancashire Witches*	1634	King's	Globe
Richard Brome	*The Sparagus Garden*	1635	King's Revels	Salisbury Court
Richard Brome	*The Queen and Concubine*	1635–9	King's Revels	Salisbury Court
Richard Brome	*The English Moor*	1637	Queen Henrietta's	Salisbury Court
Richard Brome	*The Antipodes*	1638	Queen Henrietta's	Salisbury Court
Richard Brome	*The Court Beggar*	1639–40	Beeston's Boys	Cockpit
Richard Brome	*A Jovial Crew*	1641	Beeston's Boys	Cockpit
J.C.	*The Two Merry Milkmaids*	1619–20	Red Bull Company	Red Bull
Lodowick Carlell	*The Deserving Favourite*	1622–9	King's	Blackfriars
Lodowick Carlell	*1 and 2 The Passionate Lovers*	1638	King's	Blackfriars
William Cavendish (Duke of Newcastle) and James Shirley	*The Country Captain*	1639–40	King's	Blackfriars
William Cavendish	*The Variety*	1641–2(?)	King's	Blackfriars
George Chapman	*The Blind Beggar of Alexandria*	1596	Admiral's	Rose
George Chapman	*An Humorous Day's Mirth*	1597	Admiral's	Rose
George Chapman	*The Gentleman Usher*	1602(?)	Chapel Children	Blackfriars
George Chapman	*Sir Giles Goosecap*	1602	Chapel Children	Blackfriars
George Chapman	*All Fools*	1604(?)	Queen's Revels Children	Blackfriars
George Chapman	*Monsieur D'Olive*	1604	Queen's Revels Children	Blackfriars
George Chapman	*Bussy D'Ambois*	1604	Paul's Children (c. 1606 Queen's Revels Children, 1634 King's)	Paul's?/Blackfriars
George Chapman, Ben Jonson and John Marston	*Eastward Ho!*	1605	Queen's Revels Children	Blackfriars

AUTHOR	PLAY	DATE	COMPANY	PLAYHOUSE
George Chapman	The Widow's Tears	c. 1605	Queen's Revels Children	Blackfriars
George Chapman	Charles Duke of Byron	1608	Queen's Revels Children	Blackfriars
George Chapman	May-Day	1609	Queen's Revels Children	Whitefriars?
George Chapman	The Revenge of Bussy	c. 1610	Queen's Revels Children	Whitefriars
George Chapman	Chabot	c. 1613?	Lady Elizabeth's (1635 Queen Henrietta's at Cockpit)	Whitefriars?/Hope
Henry Chettle and Antony Mundy	Robert Earl of Huntingdon	1598	Admiral's	Rose
Henry Chettle and John Day	1 The Blind Beggar of Bednal Green	1600	Admiral's (c. 1631 Prince Charles's, Salisbury Court, c. 1634 Prince Charles's, Red Bull)	Rose
Henry Chettle, Thomas Dekker and William Haughton	Patient Grissil	1600	Admiral's	Fortune
Henry Chettle	Hoffman	1602	Admiral's (c. 1630 Queen Henrietta's, Cockpit)	Fortune
Robert Daborne	The Poor Man's Comfort	1610–17	Queen Anne's (later at Cockpit)	Red Bull
Samuel Daniel	Philotas	1604	Queen's Revels Children	Blackfriars
William Davenant	The Cruel Brother	1627	King's	Blackfriars
William Davenant	The Just Italian	1629	King's	Blackfriars
William Davenant	Love and Honour	1634	King's	Blackfriars
William Davenant	The Wits	1634	King's	Blackfriars
William Davenant	News from Plymouth	1635	King's	Globe
William Davenant	The Platonic Lovers	1635	King's	Blackfriars
William Davenant	The Fair Favourite	1638	King's	Blackfriars
William Davenant	The Unfortunate Lovers	1638	King's	Blackfriars
William Davenant	The Distresses	1639	King's	Blackfriars?
Robert Davenport	The City Nightcap	1634	Lady Elizabeth's (later Beeston's Boys, Cockpit)	Cockpit
Robert Davenport	King John and Matilda	1628–34	Queen Henrietta's (later Beeston's Boys, Cockpit)	Cockpit
John Day	Law Tricks	1604	Revels Children	Blackfriars
John Day	The Isle of Gulls	1606	Queen's Revels Children	Blackfriars
John Day, William Rowley and George Wilkins	The Travels of the Three English Brothers	1607	Queen Anne's	Red Bull

AUTHOR	PLAY	DATE	COMPANY	PLAYHOUSE
John Day	Humour out of Breath	1607–8	King's Revels Children	Whitefriars?
Thomas Dekker	Old Fortunatus	1599	Admiral's	Rose
Thomas Dekker	The Shoemaker's Holiday	1599	Admiral's	Rose
Thomas Dekker	1 and 2 The Honest Whore	1604–5	Prince's (c. 1635 Queen Henrietta's, Cockpit)	Fortune
Thomas Dekker and John Webster	Westward Ho!	1604	Paul's Children	Paul's
Thomas Dekker and John Webster	Northward Ho!	1605	Paul's Children	Paul's
Thomas Dekker	The Whore of Babylon	1606	Prince's	Fortune
Thomas Dekker and Thomas Middleton	The Roaring Girl	c. 1608	Prince's	Fortune
Thomas Dekker	If It Be not Good, the Devil is in It	1611–12	Queen Anne's	Red Bull
Thomas Dekker and Philip Massinger	The Virgin Martyr	1620	Red Bull Company	Red Bull
Thomas Dekker, John Ford and William Rowley	The Witch of Edmonton	1621	Prince Charles's	Cockpit
John Denham	The Sophy	1641	King's	Blackfriars
Michael Drayton, Richard Hathway, Antony Mundy and Robert Wilson	1 Sir John Oldcastle	1599	Admiral's (1602 Worcester's, Rose)	Rose
Thomas Drue	The Duchess of Suffolk	1624	Palsgrave's	Fortune
Thomas Drue	The Bloody Banquet	1639	Beeston's Boys	Cockpit
Nathan Field	A Woman is a Weathercock	1609?	Queen's Revels Children	Whitefriars
Nathan Field	Amends for Ladies	1610–11	Lady Elizabeth's	Porter's Hall
Nathan Field and Philip Massinger	The Fatal Dowry	1616–19	King's	Globe/Blackfriars
John Fletcher	The Faithful Shepherdess	1608	Queen's Revels Children	Blackfriars
John Fletcher	The Captain	1609–12	King's	Globe?/Blackfriars?
John Fletcher	Valentinian	1610–14	King's	Globe?/Blackfriars?
John Fletcher	Bonduca	1611–14	King's	Globe?/Blackfriars?
John Fletcher	Thierry and Theodoret	1613–21	King's	Blackfriars
John Fletcher and William Shakespeare	The Two Noble Kinsmen	1613?	King's	Blackfriars
John Fletcher	The Chances	1613–25	King's	Blackfriars
John Fletcher (and Philip Massinger?)	The Beggars' Bush	1615–22	King's	Blackfriars

AUTHOR	PLAY	DATE	COMPANY	PLAYHOUSE
John Fletcher	*The Mad Lover*	1616?	King's	Blackfriars?
John Fletcher	*Love's Pilgrimage*	1616?	King's	Blackfriars
	(revised 1635)			
John Fletcher (and Philip Massinger? and Nathan Field?)	*The Queen of Corinth*	1616–18	King's	Blackfriars
John Fletcher and Nathan Field (and Philip Massinger?)	*The Knight of Malta*	1616–19	King's	Blackfriars
John Fletcher	*Rollo, Duke of Normandy (The Bloody Brother)*	1617?	King's	Globe/Blackfriars
John Fletcher	*The Loyal Subject*	1618	King's	Blackfriars
John Fletcher and Philip Massinger	*Sir John Van Olden Barnavelt*	1619	King's	Globe?
John Fletcher	*The Humorous Lieutenant*	1619(?)	King's	Blackfriars
John Fletcher	*The Island Princess*	1619–21	King's	Blackfriars
John Fletcher and Philip Massinger	*The Custom of the Country*	1619–23	King's	Blackfriars
John Fletcher and Philip Massinger	*The Double Marriage*	1619–23	King's	Blackfriars
John Fletcher and Philip Massinger	*The False One*	1619–23	King's	Blackfriars
John Fletcher? John Ford?	*The Laws of Candy*	1619–23	King's	Blackfriars
John Fletcher and Philip Massinger	*The Little French Lawyer*	1619–23	King's	Blackfriars
John Fletcher	*The Pilgrim*	1621?	King's	Blackfriars
John Fletcher	*The Wild Goose Chase*	1621?	King's	Blackfriars
John Fletcher (and Philip Massinger?)	*The Prophetess*	1622	King's	Blackfriars
John Fletcher (and Philip Massinger?)	*The Sea Voyage*	1622	King's	Globe/Blackfriars
John Fletcher (and Philip Massinger?)	*The Spanish Curate*	1622	King's	Blackfriars
John Fletcher and William Rowley	*The Maid in the Mill*	1623	King's	Blackfriars?
John Fletcher	*Rule a Wife and Have a Wife*	1624	King's	Blackfriars
John Fletcher	*A Wife for a Month*	1624	King's	Blackfriars
John Fletcher	*The Elder Brother*	1625?	King's	Blackfriars
John Fletcher	*The Fair Maid of the Inn*	1625	King's	Blackfriars

THOR	PLAY	DATE	COMPANY	PLAYHOUSE
n Ford	*The Lover's Melancholy*	1628	King's	Globe/Blackfriars
n Ford	*The Broken Heart*	1625–33	King's	Blackfriars
n Ford	*'Tis a Pity She's a Whore*	1629?–33	Queen Henrietta's (*c.* 1639 Beeston's Boys, Cockpit)	Cockpit
n Ford	*Perkin Warbeck*	1629–34	Queen Henrietta's	Cockpit
n Ford	*Love's Sacrifice*	1632(?)	Queen Henrietta's (*c.* 1639 Beeston's Boys, Cockpit)	Cockpit
n Ford	*The Lady's Trial*	1638	Beeston's Boys	Cockpit
nry Glapthorne	*Argalus and Parthenia*	1632–8	Beeston's Boys	Cockpit
nry Glapthorne	*Albertus Wallenstein*	1634–9	King's	Globe
nry Glapthorne	*The Lady Mother*	1635	King's Revels	Salisbury Court
nry Glapthorne	*The Hollander* (*Love's Trial*)	1636	Queen Henrietta's	Cockpit
nry Glapthorne	*Wit in a Constable* (revised 1639)	1636–8	Beeston's Boys	Cockpit
nry Glapthorne	*The Lady's Privilege*	1637–40	Beeston's Boys	Cockpit
bert Greene	*Friar Bacon and Friar Bungay*	1589	1592 Strange's 1594 Queen's/ Sussex's 1602 Admiral's Prince's	Rose Fortune
bert Greene	*Orlando Furioso*	*c.* 1591	Queen's Admiral's	Rose
lliam Heminges	*The Madcap*	1633	King's Revels	Fortune
lliam Heminges	*The Fatal Contract*	1638–9?	Queen Henrietta's	Salisbury Court
omas Heywood	*The Four Prentices of London*	*c.* 1600?	Admiral's Queen Anne's	Fortune? Red Bull
omas Heywood	*The Royal King and the Loyal Subject*	1602	Worcester's	Curtain
omas Heywood	*A Woman Killed with Kindness*	1603	Worcester's Queen Anne's	Curtain Red Bull
omas Heywood	*If You Know not Me, You Know Nobody*	1605	Queen Anne's (later at Cockpit)	Red Bull
omas Heywood	*The Rape of Lucrece*	*c.* 1607	Queen Anne's (after 1628 Cockpit)	Red Bull
omas Heywood 1 William Rowley	*Fortune by Land and Sea*	1607–9	Queen Anne's	Red Bull

AUTHOR	PLAY	DATE	COMPANY	PLAYHOUSE
Thomas Heywood	*The Golden Age*	1610?	Queen Anne's	Red Bull
Thomas Heywood	*The Silver Age*	1610–12	Queen Anne's (& King's?)	Red Bull
Thomas Heywood	*The Brazen Age*	1610–13	Queen Anne's	Red Bull
Thomas Heywood	*The Iron Age*	1612–13	Queen Anne's	Red Bull (later at Cockpit)
Thomas Heywood	*The Captives*	1624	Lady Elizabeth's	Cockpit
Thomas Heywood	*The English Traveller*	c. 1627?	Queen Henrietta's	Cockpit
Thomas Heywood	*A Maidenhead Well Lost*	1625–34	Queen Henrietta's	Cockpit
Thomas Heywood	*2 The Fair Maid of the West*	1630–1	Queen Henrietta's	Cockpit
Thomas Heywood	*Love's Mistress*	1634	Queen Henrietta's	Cockpit
Thomas Heywood	*A Challenge for Beauty*	1634–6	King's	Globe/Blackfriars
Ben Jonson	*Every Man in his Humour*	1598	Chamberlain's (1605 King's, Globe)	Curtain
Ben Jonson	*Every Man out of his Humour*	1599	Chamberlain's	Globe
Ben Jonson	*Cynthia's Revels*	1601	Chapel Children	Blackfriars
Ben Jonson	*Poetaster*	1601	Chapel Children	Blackfriars
Ben Jonson	*Sejanus*	1603	King's	Globe
Ben Jonson	*Volpone*	1606	King's	Globe
Ben Jonson	*Epicene*	1609	Queen's Revels Children	Whitefriars
Ben Jonson	*The Alchemist*	1610	King's	Blackfriars
Ben Jonson	*Catiline*	1611	King's	Globe?/Blackfriars
Ben Jonson	*Bartholomew Fair*	1614	Lady Elizabeth's	Hope
Ben Jonson	*The Devil is an Ass*	1616	King's	Blackfriars
Ben Jonson	*The Staple of News*	1626	King's	Blackfriars
Ben Jonson	*The New Inn*	1629	King's	Blackfriars
Ben Jonson	*The Magnetic Lady*	1632	King's	Blackfriars
Ben Jonson	*The Tale of a Tub*	1633	Queen Henrietta's	Cockpit
Thomas Killigrew	*The Prisoners*	1632–5	Queen Henrietta's	Cockpit
Thomas Killigrew	*Claracilla*	1635–6	Queen Henrietta's	Cockpit
Thomas Kyd	*The Spanish Tragedy*	c. 1587	1592–3 Strange's 1597–1602 Admiral's	Rose Fortune
Thomas Lodge	*The Wounds of Civil War*	c. 1588	Admiral's (before 1592)	Rose?
John Lyly	*Sapho and Phao*	1584	Chapel/Paul's Children	first Blackfriars
John Lyly	*Galathea*	1584–8	Paul's Children	Paul's
John Lyly	*Endymion*	1588	Paul's Children	Paul's

AUTHOR	PLAY	DATE	COMPANY	PLAYHOUSE
ohn Lyly	*Midas*	1589	Paul's Children	Paul's
ohn Lyly	*Mother Bombie*	c. 1589	Paul's Children	Paul's
ervase Markham and Lewis Machin	*The Dumb Knight*	1607–8	King's Revels Children	Whitefriars
ervase Markham nd William ampson	*Herod and Antipater*	1619–22	Red Bull Company	Red Bull
hristopher arlowe	1 *Tamburlaine*	c. 1587	1590 Admiral's	Rose
hristopher arlowe	2 *Tamburlaine*	1588	1590 Admiral's	Rose
hristopher arlowe	*Dr Faustus*	1588?	Admiral's	Bel Savage? Rose/Fortune
hristopher arlowe	*The Jew of Malta*	c.1589	1592–3 Strange's 1594 Sussex's 1594–1601 Admiral's c. 1632 Queen Henrietta's	Rose Rose Rose Cockpit
hristopher arlowe	*Edward II*	1592	Pembroke's (c. 1617 Queen Anne's, Red Bull)	Theatre?
nackerly Marmion	*Holland's Leaguer*	1631	Prince Charles's	Salisbury Court
nackerly Marmion	*A Fine Companion*	1632–3	Prince Charles's	Salisbury Court
nackerly Marmion	*The Antiquary*	1634–6	Queen Henrietta's	Cockpit
ohn Marston	*Antonio and Mellida*	1599	Paul's Children	Paul's
ohn Marston	*Antonio's Revenge*	1600	Paul's Children	Paul's
ohn Marston	*What You Will*	1601	Paul's Children	Paul's
ohn Marston	*The Dutch Courtesan*	1603–4	Queen's Revels Children	Blackfriars
ohn Marston	*The Malcontent*	1604	Queen's Revels Children King's	Blackfriars Globe
ohn Marston	*The Fawn*	1605	Queen's Revels Children	Blackfriars
ohn Marston	*Wonder of Women (Sophonisba)*	1605	Queen's Revels Children	Blackfriars
ohn Marston and illiam Barksted	*The Insatiate Countess*	1610–13	Queen's Revels Children	Whitefriars
ohn Mason	*The Turk*	1607	King's Revels Children	Whitefriars
hilip Massinger	*The Duke of Milan*	1621–2	King's	Blackfriars
hilip Massinger	*A New Way to Pay Old Debts*	1621–5	Prince Charles's (c.1633 Queen Henrietta's, Cockpit, 1639 Beeston's Boys, Cockpit)	Cockpit

7   GSS

AUTHOR	PLAY	DATE	COMPANY	PLAYHOUSE
Philip Massinger	*The Unnatural Combat*	1621–5	King's	Globe/Blackfriars
Philip Massinger	*The Maid of Honour*	c. 1621?	Red Bull Company	Red Bull
				(1632 Queen Henrietta's, Cockpit, 1639 Beeston's Boys, Cockpit)
Philip Massinger	*The Bondman*	1623	Lady Elizabeth's	Cockpit
				(1639 Beeston's Boys, Cockpit)
Philip Massinger	*The Renegado*	1624	Lady Elizabeth's	Cockpit
				(1630 Queen Henrietta's, Cockpit, 1639 Beeston's Boys, Cockpit)
Philip Massinger	*The Roman Actor*	1626	King's	Blackfriars
Philip Massinger	*The Great Duke of Florence*	1627?	Queen Henrietta's	Cockpit
				(1639 Beeston's Boys, Cockpit)
Philip Massinger	*The Picture*	1629	King's	Globe/Blackfriars
Philip Massinger	*Believe as You List*	1631	King's	Blackfriars?
Philip Massinger	*The Emperor of the East*	1631	King's	Globe/Blackfriars
Philip Massinger	*The City Madam*	1632?	King's	Blackfriars
Philip Massinger	*The Guardian*	1633	King's	Blackfriars
Philip Massinger	*The Bashful Lover*	1636	King's	Blackfriars
Thomas May	*The Heir*	1620	Red Bull Company	Red Bull
Jasper Mayne	*The City Match*	1637–8	King's	Blackfriars
Thomas Middleton	*Blurt Master Constable*	1601	Paul's Children	Paul's
Thomas Middleton	*The Phoenix*	1604	Paul's Children	Paul's
Thomas Middleton	*A Trick to Catch the Old One*	1605	Paul's Children	Paul's
				(c.1607 Queen's Revels Children, Blackfriars)
Thomas Middleton	*A Mad World, my Masters*	1604–6	Paul's Children	Paul's
				(c. 1640 Queen Henrietta's, Salisbury Court)
Thomas Middleton	*Michaelmas Term*	1606	Paul's Children	Paul's
Thomas Middleton	*The Witch*	1609–16	King's	Blackfriars
Thomas Middleton	*A Chaste Maid in Cheapside*	1611	Lady Elizabeth's	Swan
Thomas Middleton	*The Widow*	1615–17	King's	Blackfriars
Thomas Middleton and William Rowley	*A Fair Quarrel*	1615–17	Prince's	Hope/Red Bull
				(1639 Beeston's Boys, Cockpit)
Thomas Middleton	*Anything for a Quiet Life*	1620–1	King's	Blackfriars
Thomas Middleton and William Rowley	*The Changeling*	1622	Lady Elizabeth's	Cockpit
				(1639 Beeston's Boys, Cockpit)
Thomas Middleton and William Rowley	*The Spanish Gypsy*	1623	Lady Elizabeth's	Cockpit
				(1639 Beeston's Boys, Cockpit)

UTHOR	PLAY	DATE	COMPANY	PLAYHOUSE
homas Middleton	*A Game at Chess*	1624	King's	Globe
homas Nabbes	*Covent Garden*	1633	Queen Henrietta's	Cockpit
homas Nabbes	*Hannibal and Scipio*	1635	Queen Henrietta's	Cockpit
homas Nabbes	*Microcosmus*	1637	Queen Henrietta's	Salisbury Court
homas Nabbes	*The Bride*	1638	Beeston's Boys	Cockpit
eorge Peele	*The Battle of Alcazar*	c. 1589	Admiral's	Rose
enry Porter	1 *Two Angry Women of Abingdon*	c. 1598	Admiral's	Rose
homas Randolph	*Amyntas*	1630	King's Revels	Salisbury Court
homas Randolph	*The Muses' Looking Glass*	1630	King's Revels	Salisbury Court
homas Rawlins	*The Rebellion*	1629–39	King's Revels	Salisbury Court? (and Red Bull?)
athaniel Richards	*Messallina*	1634–6	King's Revels	Salisbury Court
amuel Rowley	*When You See Me, You Know Me*	1604	Prince's	Fortune
illiam Rowley	*All's Lost by Lust*	1619–20	Lady Elizabeth's (1633 Queen Henrietta's, 1639 Beeston's Boys,	Cockpit Cockpit, Cockpit)
illiam Rowley	*A Match at Midnight*	1621–3	Red Bull Company	Red Bull
oseph Rutter	*The Shepherd's Holiday*	1633–5	Queen Henrietta's	Cockpit
oseph Rutter	1 *The Cid* (trans. of Corneille)	1637–8	Beeston's Boys	Cockpit
S.	*The Honest Lawyer*	1614–15	Queen Anne's	Red Bull
illiam Shakespeare	1, 2 and 3 *Henry VI*	c. 1590	Pembroke's	Theatre?
illiam Shakespeare	*Titus Andronicus*	c.1592	Strange's Pembroke's Sussex's Chamberlain's	Rose Globe
illiam Shakespeare	*Richard III*	1593	Pembroke's 1594 Chamberlain's	Theatre?
illiam Shakespeare	*The Taming of the Shrew*	1593?	Pembroke's Chamberlain's	Theatre?
illiam Shakespeare	*Romeo and Juliet*	1594?	Pembroke's Chamberlain's	Theatre?
illiam Shakespeare	*A Midsummer Night's Dream*	1594	Chamberlain's	Theatre?

AUTHOR	PLAY	DATE	COMPANY	PLAYHOUSE
William Shakespeare	The Merchant of Venice	1594?	Chamberlain's	Theatre?
William Shakespeare	Richard II	1595?	Chamberlain's	Theatre?
William Shakespeare	1 and 2 Henry IV	1596–7	Chamberlain's	Theatre?
William Shakespeare	Much Ado About Nothing	1598?	Chamberlain's	Curtain?
William Shakespeare	Henry V	1599	Chamberlain's	Curtain?/Globe?
William Shakespeare	Julius Caesar	1599	Chamberlain's	Curtain?/Globe?
William Shakespeare	As You Like It	1599–1600	Chamberlain's	Globe
William Shakespeare	Twelfth Night	1600	Chamberlain's	Globe
William Shakespeare	Hamlet	1600	Chamberlain's	Globe
William Shakespeare	The Merry Wives of Windsor	1600	Chamberlain's	Globe
William Shakespeare	All's Well that Ends Well	1602?	Chamberlain's	Globe
William Shakespeare	Measure for Measure	1603	King's	Globe
William Shakespeare	Othello	1603?	King's	Globe
William Shakespeare	King Lear	1605	King's	Globe
William Shakespeare	Coriolanus	1606?	King's	Globe
William Shakespeare	Macbeth	1606	King's	Globe
William Shakespeare	Pericles	1606–7?	King's	Globe
William Shakespeare	Antony and Cleopatra	1607?	King's	Globe
William Shakespeare	Cymbeline	1609?	King's	Globe
William Shakespeare	The Winter's Tale	1610?	King's	Globe?/Blackfriars
William Shakespeare	The Tempest	1611?	King's	Globe?/Blackfriars
William Shakespeare	Henry VIII	1613	King's	Globe
Lewis Sharpe	The Noble Stranger	1638–40	Queen Henrietta's	Salisbury Court
Edward Sharpham	The Fleer	1606	Queen's Revels Children	Blackfriars
James Shirley	Love Tricks (The School of Compliment)	1625	Lady Elizabeth's (1631 Queen Henrietta's, 1639 Beeston's Boys, Cockpit)	Cockpit
James Shirley	The Maid's Revenge	1626	Queen Henrietta's (1639 Beeston's Boys, Cockpit)	Cockpit
James Shirley	The Wedding	1626–9	Queen Henrietta's (1639 Beeston's Boys, Cockpit)	Cockpit
James Shirley	The Witty Fair One	1628	Queen Henrietta's (1639 Beeston's Boys, Cockpit)	Cockpit
James Shirley	The Grateful Servant	1629	Queen Henrietta's (Beeston's Boys, Cockpit)	Cockpit

AUTHOR	PLAY	DATE	COMPANY	PLAYHOUSE
ames Shirley	*The Humorous Courtier*	1631	Queen Henrietta's	Cockpit
ames Shirley	*Love's Cruelty*	1631	Queen Henrietta's	Cockpit
				(1639 Beeston's Boys, Cockpit)
ames Shirley	*The Traitor*	1631	Queen Henrietta's	Cockpit
				(1639 Beeston's Boys, Cockpit)
mes Shirley	*Hyde Park*	1632	Queen Henrietta's	Cockpit
				(1639 Beeston's Boys, Cockpit)
mes Shirley	*The Ball*	1632	Queen Henrietta's	Cockpit
mes Shirley	*The Bird in a Cage*	1633	Queen Henrietta's	Cockpit
mes Shirley	*The Gamester*	1633	Queen Henrietta's	Cockpit
mes Shirley	*The Young Admiral*	1633	Queen Henrietta's	Cockpit
				(1639 Beeston's Boys, Cockpit)
mes Shirley	*The Example*	1634	Queen Henrietta's	Cockpit
				(1639 Beeston's Boys, Cockpit)
mes Shirley	*The Opportunity*	1634	Queen Henrietta's	Cockpit
				(1639 Beeston's Boys, Cockpit)
mes Shirley	*The Coronation*	1635	Queen Henrietta's	Cockpit
				(1639 Beeston's Boys, Cockpit)
mes Shirley	*The Lady of Pleasure*	1635	Queen Henrietta's	Cockpit
				(1639 Beeston's Boys, Cockpit)
mes Shirley	*The Duke's Mistress*	1636	Queen Henrietta's	Cockpit
mes Shirley	*The Imposter*	1640	King's	Blackfriars
mes Shirley	*The Cardinal*	1641	King's	Blackfriars
mes Shirley	*The Brothers*	1641?	King's	Blackfriars
mes Shirley	*The Sisters*	1642	King's	Blackfriars
r John Suckling	*Aglaura*	1637	King's	Blackfriars
r John Suckling	*The Goblins*	1637–41	King's	Blackfriars
r John Suckling	*Brennoralt*	1639–41	King's	Blackfriars
ohn Webster	*The White Devil*	1612	Queen Anne's	Red Bull
				(*c.* 1630 Queen Henrietta's, Cockpit)
ohn Webster	*The Duchess of Malfi*	1614	King's	Globe/Blackfriars
ohn Webster	*The Devil's Law-Case*	1610–19	Queen Anne's	Red Bull

AUTHOR	PLAY	DATE	COMPANY	PLAYHOUSE
George Wilkins (and Thomas Heywood?)	The Miseries of Enforced Marriage	1606	King's	Globe
Arthur Wilson	The Swisser	1631	King's	Blackfriars
Anon	The Famous Victories of Henry V	c. 1588?	Queen's	Bull Inn
Anon	Fair Em	c. 1590	Strange's	Rose?
Anon	A Knack to Know a Knave	1592	Strange's/ Admiral's	Rose
Anon	A Knack to Know an Honest Man	1594	Admiral's	Rose
Anon	Captain Thomas Stukeley	1596	Admiral's	Rose
Anon	A Warning for Fair Women	c. 1599	Chamberlain's	Curtain?
Anon	Look About You	1599(?)	Admiral's	Rose
Anon	The Wisdom of Dr Dodypoll	1599	Paul's Children	Paul's
Anon	An Alarum for London	1600	Chamberlain's	Globe
Anon	The Merry Devil of Edmonton	c. 1602	Chamberlain's	Globe
Anon	The Fair Maid of Bristow	c. 1604	King's	Globe
Anon	1 Jeronimo	c. 1604	King's	Globe?
Anon	The London Prodigal	1604	King's	Globe
Anon	The Yorkshire Tragedy	c. 1606	King's	Globe
Anon	The Revenger's Tragedy	1606	King's	Globe
Anon	The Puritan	1606	Paul's Children	Paul's
Anon	Swetnam the Woman-Hater	1617–18?	Queen Anne's	Red Bull
Anon	The Two Noble Ladies	1619–23	Red Bull Company	Red Bull
Anon	The Costly Whore	1619–32	Red Bull Company	Red Bull

Notes

The following abbreviations have been used in the notes:

Dramatic Documents   W. W. Greg, ed. *Dramatic Documents from the Elizabethan Playhouses*, 2 vols. (Oxford 1931).
ES   E. K. Chambers, *The Elizabethan Stage*, 4 vols. (Oxford 1923).
Henslowe's Diary   R. A. Foakes and R. T. Rickert, eds., *Henslowe's Diary* (Cambridge 1961).
Henslowe Papers   W. W. Greg, ed., *Henslowe Papers* (London 1907).
Herbert   J. Q. Adams, ed., *The Dramatic Records of Sir Henry Herbert* (New Haven 1917).
JCS   G. E. Bentley, *The Jacobean and Caroline Stage*, 7 vols. (Oxford 1941–68).
MLN   *Modern Language Notes.*
MLR   *Modern Language Review.*
NQ   *Notes and Queries.*
Nungezer   E. Nungezer, *A Dictionary of Actors* (New Haven 1929).
RES   *Review of English Studies.*
SB   *Studies in Bibliography.*
SEL   *Studies in English Literature* (Rice University).
ShAB   *Shakespeare Association Bulletin.*
ShS   *Shakespeare Survey.*
SP   *Studies in Philology.*
SQ   *Shakespeare Quarterly.*
ThN   *Theatre Notebook.*
WS   E. K. Chambers, *William Shakespeare*, 2 vols. (Oxford 1930).

References to plays of Shakespeare are to the New Cambridge editions, under the general editorship of J. Dover Wilson. References to Jonson are to the edition of C. H. Herford, P. and E. Simpson, 11 vols. (Oxford 1925–52).

I INTRODUCTION (pp. 1–18)

There are two general works which deal with the background to the Shakespearean stage: A. M. Nagler's short book *Shakespeare's Stage* (New Haven 1958), and K. J. Holzknecht's *The Backgrounds of Shakespeare's Plays* (New York 1950). There is no background study of the whole period up to 1642. The four volumes of *ES* contain the bulk of the information on the theatre background up to about 1616 which was available by 1920. The first two volumes of *JCS*, published in 1941, describe the history of the playing companies and print some important background documents; Vols. III–V list the extant information about the dramatists and their plays, as it was known in 1954; Vol. VI gives the information about the playhouses, correct up to 1966, and Vol. VII gives an index of all seven volumes. A few of the other works which throw light on the background to the plays are listed in the notes below.

1 See George F. Reynolds, '*Hamlet* at the Globe', *ShS*, 9 (1956), 50.
2 *ES*, IV, 269.
3 *JCS*, VI, 49–50.
4 *ES*, IV, 273–4.
5 *JCS*, VI, 29.
6 John Burnett, *A History of the Cost of Living* (London 1969), p.71. The figures of Shakespearean prices are taken largely from this work. A more concise statement of relative prices can be found in a letter by Giles E. Dawson, quoted by Irwin Smith, *Shakespeare's Blackfriars Playhouse* (London 1964), pp. x–xi.
7 L. C. Knights, *Drama and Society in the Age of Jonson* (London 1937), p. 174.
8 Burnett, *History of the Cost of Living*, p. 112.
9 See C. C. Mish, 'Comparative Popularity of Early Fiction and Drama', *NQ*, CXCVII (1952), 269–70.
10 John Doebler, 'Beaumont's *Knight of the Burning Pestle* and the Prodigal Son Plays', *SEL*, V (1965), 333–44.
11 Alfred Harbage's *Shakespeare and the Rival Traditions* (New York 1952), analyses the differences between the private- and public-theatre repertories. It is now usually thought to overstate its case. See R. Ornstein, *The Moral Vision of Jacobean Tragedy* (Madison 1962), p. 12.
12 *ES*, IV, 332.
13 Valerie Pearl, *London and the Outbreak of the Puritan Revolution* (London 1961), p. 41.
14 *JCS*, VI, 54.
15 Jonson, VII, 735.
16 *JCS*, IV, 555.
17 *Drummond of Hawthornden's Conversations with Ben Jonson*, ed. G. B. Harrison (London 1927), p. 61.
18 See B. de Luna, *Jonson's Romish Plot* (Oxford 1968).
19 See Jonson, I, 24–31.
20 *Ibid.* VIII, 601.

2 THE COMPANIES (pp. 19–59)

A complete history of the playing companies up to 1642 has not yet been written. The extant information on each company up to 1616 is set out in *ES*, II, and from about that time to 1642 in *JCS*, I. The major documents for the period are reprinted in *ES*, IV, *Henslowe's Diary*, and *Herbert*. *ES*, IV prints the Privy Council and other documents for the control of the companies and playhouses, together with a selection of contemporary comments. *Henslowe's Diary*, and the supplementary *Henslowe Papers*, is a rich mine of information on the day-to-day running of one of the two leading enterprises of Shakespeare's own time. The papers of the last and most industrious Master of the Revels (*Herbert*) provide a detailed record of the day-to-day business of supervising the companies after 1623.

The most substantial analysis of the various records, apart from *ES* and *JCS*, is in T. W. Baldwin's *The Organisation and Personnel of the Shakespearean Company* (Princeton 1927). Some of the interpretations in this work are open to question, but it is none the less the most detailed history of the longest-lived of all the playing companies. Studies of more limited aspects of the material for this chapter are listed in the notes.

1   *ES*, IV, 270.
2   *ES*, IV, 324 and 337.
3   See note on playhouse origins, Chap. 4.
4   *ES*, II, 86.
5   *ES*, II, 87–8.
6   *ES*, IV, 200.
7   *ES*, II, 462.
8   *ES*, II, 104–5.
9   *ES*, IV, 302.
10 *ES*, IV, 202
11 H. M. Hillebrand, *The Child Actors* (Urbana 1926), p. 85.
12 *ES*, II, 36.
13 *Dramatic Documents*, p. 19.
14 *ES*, II, 123.
15 *Dramatic Documents*, p. 12.
16 *WS*, I, 42.
17 *Dramatic Documents* p. 47.
18 See above, n. 16.
19 See J. Dover Wilson, ed., *2 Henry VI*, p. xi.
20 *ES*, IV, 311–12.
21 J. T. Murray, *English Dramatic Companies*, II, 293.
22 *ES*, II, 124.
23 The appearance of players' names in play-texts does not necessarily mean that they were members of the company for whom the play was originally written. The names may have been inserted later, as for instance Will Kempe's must have been in the second quarto of *Romeo and Juliet*. Kempe was in Strange's before 1594, when the play, to judge by echoes of it in the Pembroke pirated texts, was being performed by Pembroke's. See A. S. Cairncross, 'Pembroke's Men and some Shakespearian Piracies', *SQ*, XI (1960), 335 and 345.
24 Henslowe's 'harey the vi' is the only Strange's play which might be identified as Shakespeare's, but it is in fact unlikely to have been his. See Cairncross, ed., *1 Henry VI*, p. xxxv.
25 In September 1594 the Chamberlain's are recorded asking for leave to play at the Cross Keys inn, in the City. They probably wanted it as a winter house, to supplement the Theatre's summer accommodation. See *ES*, II, 194.
26 *ES*, II, 152.
27 But see *Henslowe's Diary*, p. xxxix.
28 *ES*, II, 158.

29 T. W. Baldwin, *The Organisation and Personnel of the Shakespearean Company* (New York 1927), p. 52.

30 *ES*, II, 173.

31 *ES*, II, 225.

32 *ES*, II, 231.

33 *ES*, II, 44, 52.

34 Mark Eccles, 'Martin Peerson and the Blackfriars', *ShS*, 11 (1958), 101.

35 See *ES*, III, 257–8.

36 The full text is printed by J. J. Jusserand, 'Ambassador la Boderie and the "Compositeur" of the Byron Plays', *MLR*, VI (1911), 203–5.

37 *ES*, III, 258.

38 For a concise account of the war see Jonson, I, chapter on *Poetaster*.

39 *JCS*, I, 151. The loss of their playbooks and apparel in the fire was the first of a series of disasters which led to their eclipse in 1625.

40 C. J. Sisson, 'Notes on Early Stuart Stage History', *MLR*, XXXVII (1942), 34. The records of Red Bull litigation are summarised in Sisson, pp. 30–6 and in *ES*, II, 236–40.

41 *ES*, II, 238.

42 *Herbert*, p. 65.

43 *Ibid.* p. 62.

44 *JCS*, I, 201.

45 *JCS*, I, 4–5.

46 *JCS*, I, 226.

47 *JCS*, I, 328.

48 *JCS*, I, 237.

49 *JCS*, II, 684.

50 *JCS*, I, 234.

51 *Herbert*, p. 67.

52 *JCS*, I, 332–3.

53 See A. H. Nethercot, *Sir William D'Avenant* (New York 1938), revised ed. 1967, Chap. XI.

54 *JCS*, VI, 104–5.

55 See below, p. 53, and n. 72.

56 See *Dramatic Documents*, p. 170.

57 Sisson, 'Notes on Early Stuart Stage History', p. 33.

58 *ES*, I, 352, *JCS* I, 43.

59 *ES*, II, 256–7.

60 *ES*, I, 357.

61 *ES*, I, 356.

62 *ES*, I, 372.

63 Burnett, *History of the Cost of Living*, p. 71 and A. Harbage, *Shakespeare's Audience* (New York 1941), p. 55.

64 A. Thorndike, *Shakespeare's Theater* (New York 1919), p. 311.

65 *ES*, I, 369.

66 Sisson, 'Notes on Early Stuart Stage History', p. 33.

67 *JCS*, VI, 243.

68 *ES*, I, 373, and note.

69 See *ES*, I, 71.

70 *ES*, IV, 263.

71 *Herbert*, pp. 5–6.

72 *JCS* I, 178.
73 *Herbert*, pp. 44–5.
74 *ES*, IV, 263.
75 *ES*, IV, 338–9.
76 *Herbert*, p. 22.
77 *Ibid.* pp. 18–19.
78 *Ibid.* p. 23.
79 See below, p. 63. Cuthbert Burbage was one of Charles's victims.
80 *ES*, IV, 267.
81 *ES*, IV, 336.
82 G. E. Bentley, 'Lenten Performances in the Jacobean and Caroline Theaters', *Essays on Shakespeare and Elizabethan Drama*, ed. R. Hosley (New York 1963), pp. 351–60.
83 *JCS*, II, 690.
84 Baldwin, *Organisation and Personnel of the Shakespearean Company*, Chap. VII and pp. 175–6.
85 Some of his earlier parts are noted by Baldwin Maxwell, *Studies in Beaumont, Fletcher and Massinger* (Chapel Hill 1939), pp. 74–83.
86 Nungezer, p. 367.

3 THE PLAYERS (pp. 60–81)

The best general account of Elizabethan players is M. C. Bradbrook's *The Rise of the Common Player* (London 1962). Nungezer's *Dictionary of Actors* is a dictionary of all the known English players up to 1642, with the contemporary references to them supplied in full. *ES*, II contains a list with more cursory detail, and *JCS*, II gives a comparably detailed list of players between 1616 and 1642. On acting, R. A. Foakes has a useful article, 'The Player's Passion', in *Essays and Studies*, n.s. VIII (1954), 62–77. B. L. Joseph's monograph *Elizabethan Acting* (London 1951), revised ed. 1964, has some information, chiefly about gesture. The edition of 1964 has been considerably revised, and wisely so.

1 The social origins of players are described in detail in Bradbrook, *Rise of the Common Player*.
2 J. Stephens, *Essayes and Characters* (1615), V6r–X1r. Cocke revised his essay for the second edition of Stephens's collection, which was also printed in 1615. See *ES*, IV, 255–7.
3 J. Overbury, *New Characters* (1615), M5v–M6v. See *ES*, IV, 258–9.
4 The Dulwich Collection has a painting allegedly by Burbage. See Nungezer, p. 77.
5 Harbage, *Shakespeare and the Rival Traditions*, p. 19.
6 Bradbrook, *Rise of the Common Player*, p. 203.
7 Alexandra Mason, 'The Social Status of Theatrical People', *SQ*, XVIII (1967), 429–30.
8 Nungezer, p. 73.
9 *Ibid.* p. 219.
10 *Ibid.* pp. 347–54.
11 Nungezer, p. 360.
12 *Ibid.* p. 363.

13 *Thalia's Banquet* (1620), quoted in Nungezer, pp. 362–3.

14 Quoted in Nungezer, pp. 356–7.

15 A reference to Wilson by Thomas Lodge, in his *Defence of Poetry, Musick, and Stage Plays* (1580) has been taken as a compliment to his learning.

16 See R. C. Bald, 'Will, My Lord of Leicester's Jesting Player', *NQ*, CCIV (1959), 112, and J. A. Bryant jr, 'Shakespeare's Falstaff and the Mantle of Dick Tarlton', *SP*, LI (1954), 149–62.

17 H. D. Gray, 'The Roles of William Kemp', *MLR*, XXV (1930), 261–73.

18 C. S. Felver, *Robert Armin, Shakespeare's Fool*, Kent State University Bulletin Research Series V (Kent 1961).

19 Nungezer, p. 8.

20 Bradbrook, *Rise of the Common Player*, p. 196.

21 Nungezer, p. 6.

22 *Ibid.* p. 11.

23 *Ibid.* pp. 67–8.

24 See above, p. 31.

25 Nungezer, p. 70.

26 *Ibid.* pp. 140–1.

27 *Ibid.* p. 140.

28 *JCS*, II, 563.

29 *JCS*, II, 401.

30 *JCS*, II, 541.

31 Nungezer, p. 68.

32 Bradbrook, *Rise of the Common Player*, p. 238.

33 Harbage, *Shakespeare and the Rival Traditions*, pp. 44–5.

34 See Joseph, *Elizabethan Acting*, and Andrew Gurr, 'Elizabethan Action', *SP*, LXIII (1966), 144–56.

35 For an indication of the pressure that was put on the boy company managers to prove their respectability by maintaining the educational and chorister functions, see Bradbrook, *Rise of the Common Player*, p. 238.

36 Compare Shakespeare's Latin in 2 and 3 *Henry VI* with the versions transcribed in the pirated texts.

37 Bradbrook, *Rise of the Common Player*, p. 205.

38 Jonson, IV, 63.

39 We cannot understand the following passage in Chapman's *Gentleman Usher* (1601) unless we have some knowledge of the niceties of academic theory and the need for the orator to stir up in himself the actual passion he is to convey. Sarpego, a 'fustian lord', first ventures to display his talents:

> when I in Padua schoolde it,
> I plaid in one of *Plautus* Comedies,
> Namely *Curculo*, where his part I acted,
> Projecting from the poore summe of foure lines,
> Forty faire actions...
>
> *Alp.* How like you Lords, this stirring action?
> *Stro.* In a cold morning it were good my Lord...

176

> *Med.* My Lord, away with these scholastique wits,
>> Lay the invention of your speech on me,
>> And the performance too; ile play my parte,
>> that you shall say, Nature yeelds more then Art.
> *Alp.* Bee't so resolv'd; unartificiall truth
>> An unfaind passion can decipher best.

40 Gurr, 'Elizabethan Action', p. 144.

41 The following passage, in the anonymous *Nero* of 1623, is typical in its terminology:
>> *Nero.* Come Sirs, I faith, how did you like my acting?
>> What? wast not as you lookt for?
>> *Epaph.* Yes my Lord, and much beyond.
>> *Nero.* Did I not doe it to the life?
>> *Epaph.* The very doing never was so lively
>> As now this counterfeyting.

42 BM.MS.Sloane 3709, fol. 8r.

43 See also B. L. Joseph, *Elizabethan Acting*, pp. 47–71.

44 See M. C. Bradbrook, *Themes and Conventions in Elizabethan Tragedy* (Cambridge 1936).

45 See Lawrence Babb, 'Sorrow and Love on the Elizabethan Stage', *ShAB*, XVIII (1943), 140.

46 Richard Brome, *The Antipodes* (1638), II.ii.

47 S. L. Bethell, *Shakespeare and the Popular Dramatic Tradition* (London 1944), pp. 87–9.

48 *Shakespeare at the Globe* (New York 1962), p. 130.

49 W. W. Greg, *Two Elizabethan Stage Abridgements* (Oxford 1923).

50 *Ibid*, pp. 133–4.

51 Harold Jenkins, 'Playhouse Interpolations in the Folio Text of *Hamlet*', *SB*, XIII (1960), 31–48.

52 J. H. Walter, ed, *Henry V* (London 1954).

53 See below, p. 146.

54 Nungezer p. 32.

55 Andrew Gurr, 'Who Strutted and Bellowed?', *ShS*, 16 (1963), 95–102.

56 Nungezer, p. 74.

57 Jenkins, 'Playhouse Interpolations in the Folio Text of *Hamlet*', p. 32.

4 THE PLAYHOUSES (pp. 82–111)

The basic information on playhouses, together with a judiciously limited amount of speculation, is in *ES*, II and *JCS*, VI. The lack of tangible information about such tangible structures as playhouses makes loose hypothesising all too tempting, and much of the scholarship of the last thirty years has been devoted to destroying the syncretic conjectures of writers such as J. Cranford Adams, and his follower Irwin Smith, and the elaborate hypotheses of Leslie Hotson. The first book which made a properly restrained use of the available evidence was G. F. Reynolds's *The Staging of Elizabethan Plays at the Red Bull Theater* 1605–25 (London 1940). Since then Richard Hosley in particular has used Occam's Razor to good effect on the evidence, but apart from A. M. Nagler's short study, no complete survey has yet been made in book form.

1   *ES*, II, 532.
2   See R. Hosley, 'The Origins of the Shakespearian Playhouse', *Shakespeare 400*, ed. James G. McManaway (New York 1964), pp. 29–39.
3   *JCS*, VI, 183.
4   *ES*, III, 523.
5   *ES*, II, 382.
6   *JCS*, VI, 140.
7   G. F. Reynolds, *The Staging of Elizabethan Plays*, p. 9.
8   *ES*, II, 373.
9   *ES*, II, 358.
10 *ES*, II, 359.
11 Notwithstanding contemporary illustrations, some of which show the playhouses as perfectly circular structures, it is thought that they could not have been, because the Elizabethans could not bend oak, and a circular construction based on a series of closely-spaced verticals would have impeded the view from the galleries. See Rennie Barker, 'The Structure of the first Globe Theatre', *ShAB*, XXIV (1944), 106–11.
12 *ES*, II, 409.
13 *ES*, II, 393 ff.
14 See Richard Southern, 'Colour in the Elizabethan Theatre', *ThN*, VI (1951–2), 57–8.
15 *ES*, II, 529–30, 545–6.
16 The best reproduction of the sketch is in *ShS*, I (1948), Plate III; a transcription of the accompanying text is in *ThN*, XX (1965–6), 73.
17 See D. F. Rowan, 'The "Swan" Revisited', *Research Opportunities in Renaissance Drama*, X (1967), 42–5.
18 R. Hosley, 'The Gallery over the Stage in the Public Playhouse of Shakespeare's Time', *SQ*, VIII (1957), 31.
19 The plot of *England's Joy* stipulated 'beneath under the Stage set forth with strange fireworkes, divers blacke and damned Soules' (*ES*, III, 501).
20 R. C. Bald, 'The Entrance to the Elizabethan Theatre', *SQ*, III (1952), 20.
21 Quoted in *ES*, II, 436–9.
22 *ES*, II, 436.
23 *JCS*, VI, 156.
24 *JCS*, VI, 154.
25 *ES*, II, 393.
26 For an examination of the technique as it can be seen at Tyrell's End Farm, Bedfordshire, see Nicholas Wood, 'Fifteenth-century Prefab', *Architectural Review* 144, no. 858 (August 1968), 140–1.
27 Contemporary 'Views' of London depicting the Bankside do not offer conclusive evidence either way. See I. A. Shapiro, 'The Bankside Theatres: Early Engravings', *ShS*, I (1948), 25–37.
28 *ES*, II, 420.
29 *JCS*, VI, 178n, and see Ernest Schanzer, 'Hercules and his Load', *RES*, n.s. XIX (1968), 51–3.
30 R. Hosley, 'The Discovery-Space in Shakespeare's Globe', *ShS*, 12 (1959), 35; B. Beckerman, *Shakespeare at the Globe*, pp. 69–70; J. W. Saunders, 'Staging at the Globe, 1599–1613', *SQ*, XI (1960), 406.
31 Beckerman, *Shakespeare at the Globe*, p. 92; Hosley, 'The Gallery over the Stage', p. 27.

32 Beckerman, *Shakespeare at the Globe*, p. 90; Hosley, 'Shakespeare's Use of a Gallery over the Stage', *ShS*, 10 (1957), 78.

33 Hosley, *ibid.* pp. 78, 85.

34 I. A. Shapiro, 'Robert Fludd's Stage-Illustration', *Shakespeare Studies*, II (1966), 204.

35 See R. Hosley, 'Was there a Music-Room in Shakespeare's Globe?', *ShS*, 13 (1960), 113.

36 *ES*, II, 47.

37 Hosley, 'Was there a Music-Room', p. 115.

38 W. F. Rothwell, 'Was there a Typical Elizabethan Stage?', *ShS*, 12 (1959), 16.

39 W. T. Jewkes, *Act Division in Elizabethan and Jacobean Plays* (New York 1958), pp. 100–1.

40 Hosley, 'Was there a Music-Room', pp. 113–14.

41 *Ibid.* pp. 115–16.

42 *ES*, III, 96.

43 Hosley, 'The Discovery-Space in Shakespeare's Globe', p. 36.

44 See Beckerman, *Shakespeare at the Globe*, pp. 82–4.

45 *Ibid.* pp. 85–7; Hosley, 'The Discovery-Space', p. 45.

46 Reynolds, *Staging of Elizabethan Plays*, p. 188. Elsewhere (p. 109) Reynolds suggests that the third entry might have been through the hangings concealing the discovery-space.

47 *JCS*, VI, 215.

48 See Lupold von Wedel, quoted in *ES*, II, 455.

49 *ES*, II, 466–8.

50 *ES*, II, 434.

51 *JCS*, VI, 207–10.

52 *JCS*, VI, 223.

53 *ES*, II, 477–81.

54 *ES*, II, 503.

55 *ES*, IV, 320.

56 *JCS*, VI, 5.

57 *JCS*, VI, 5–6.

58 *JCS*, VI, 6.

59 *ES*, II, 513.

60 *ES*, II, 513.

61 *The Dutch Courtesan*, v.iii, and G. Fitzgeoffery, *Observations at Black-friars* (1617), G 3r.

62 *JCS*, VI, 7. The prices quoted are not consistently supported by the evidence, and there may well have been some variation in the forty or so years of the playhouse's existence. See Irwin Smith, *Shakespeare's Blackfriars Playhouse*, pp. 299–301. That stool-holders reached the stage through the tiring-house is indicated by a reference in Fitzgeoffery to a gallant emerging from there, and by the difficulty the Wife in *The Knight of the Burning Pestle* had climbing on to the stage–there were evidently no steps up from the auditorium.

63 The illustration is reproduced and discussed by Frances Yates, *The Art of Memory* (Oxford 1966), pp. 342–67. Miss Yates allocates it to the Globe. I. A. Shapiro, 'Robert Fludd's Stage-Illustration', pp. 192–209, suggests more plausibly that it portrays the Blackfriars.

64 *ES*, III, 144.
65 *JCS*, VI, 54.
66 *JCS*, VI, 50.
67 See T. J. King, 'Staging of Plays at the Phoenix in Drury Lane, 1617–42', *ThN*, XIX (1965), 146–66.
68 *JCS*, VI, 269.
69 Such information as exists is collected in *JCS*, VI, 255–8.
70 *JCS*, VI, 264; Per Palme, *Triumph of Peace* (London 1957), p. 143.
71 Per Palme, *Triumph of Peace*, p. 143.
72 *Ibid.* p. 199.
73 *JCS*, VI, 266–7.
74 *JCS*, VI, 285.
75 Reproduced in *JCS*, VI, 276.
76 *JCS*, VI, 272–3.

5 THE STAGING (pp. 112–39)

ES, III contains a survey of the evidence for staging in the sixteenth and seventeenth centuries, and at Court. W. J. Lawrence supplemented the work of Chambers in his *Pre-Restoration Stage Studies* (Cambridge (Mass.) 1927), though his reliance on printed texts of the plays which were not as faithful copies of the first editions as they should have been has on occasions led him astray. Other studies have concentrated on the staging at particular playhouses: Reynolds at the Red Bull, Beckerman at the Globe, and T. J. King at the Cockpit. The most useful general studies have been confined to particular aspects of staging. C. R. Baskervill, *The Elizabethan Jig* (Chicago 1929); W. T. Jewkes, *Act Division in Elizabethan and Jacobean Plays 1583–1616*; M. C. Linthicum, *Costume in the Drama of Shakespeare and his Contemporaries* (Oxford 1936); Dieter Mehl, *The Elizabethan Dumb-Show* (London 1965); and Allardyce Nicoll, *Stuart Masques and the Renaissance Stage* (London 1938), are all useful.

1 Kenneth R. Richards, 'Changeable Scenery for Plays on the Caroline Stage', *ThN*, XXIII (1968), 20.
2 T. J. King, 'Staging of Plays at the Phoenix', p. 166.
3 Quoted in C. R. Baskervill, *The Elizabethan Jig*, p. 102.
4 *Ibid.* p. 99.
5 *Attewell's Jig* is reprinted in Baskervill, pp. 450–64, and *Singing Simkin*, pp. 444–9.
6 Baskervill, *Elizabethan Jig*, p. 115.
7 *Turners dish of Lentten stuffe* (1613?), in H. E. Rollins, ed., *A Pepysian Garland* (Cambridge 1922), p. 35.
8 *JCS*, II, 354.
9 *Dramatic Documents*, p. 19.
10 Beaumont's *Knight of the Burning Pestle* has inter-act performances of music with a boy dancing after Acts I and III, music (fiddlers) after Act II, and a burlesque Maylord speech after Act IV.
11 Warren D. Smith, 'New Light on Stage Directions in Shakespeare', *SP*, XLVII (1950), 173.
12 Jonson, VI, 15. See David Klein, 'Time Allotted for an Elizabethan Performance', *SQ*, XVIII (1967), 434–8.

13 *ES*, III, 126.
14 Hosley, 'Gallery over the Stage', p. 78; T. J. King, 'Staging of Plays at the Phoenix', p. 166.
15 For a history of the recognition of the open Elizabethan stage, see G. F. Reynolds, 'The Return of the Open Stage', *Essays on Shakespeare and Elizabethan Drama in honour of Hardin Craig* (London 1963), pp. 361–8.
16 Quoted in *ES*, III, 40–1.
17 W. J. Lawrence, *Pre-Restoration Stage Studies*, p. 221.
18 *Ibid.* p. 204.
19 Noted by G. F. Reynolds, *The Staging of Elizabethan Plays at the Red Bull*, p. 43.
20 Quoted in *ES*, III, 72.
21 John Melton, *Astrologaster* (1620), E 4r.
22 *ES*, II, 455.
23 *ES*, III, 79 n. 3.
24 See J. H. Long, *Shakespeare's Use of Music* (Miami 1955); W. R. Bowden, *The English Dramatic Lyric*, 1603–42 (New Haven 1951).
25 See G. Wickham, *Early English Stages* (London 1959–63), II.i. pp. 206–44.
26 T. J. King, 'Staging of Plays at the Phoenix', p. 162.
27 Allardyce Nicoll, 'Passing over the Stage', *ShS*, 12 (1959), 47–55.
28 Inter-act IV. There are two other similar dumb-shows in the play.
29 Beckerman, *Shakespeare at the Globe*, p. 106.
30 Lawrence, *Pre-Restoration Stage Studies*, p. 314.
31 *Ibid.* p. 23. Lawrence cites the second of these passages in a text in which only one man carries the scaffold.
32 K. J. Holzknecht, *The Backgrounds of Shakespeare's Plays*, p. 131.
33 *Thomas Platter's Travels in England, 1599*, trans. Clare Williams (London 1959), p. 167.
34 M. C. Linthicum, *Costume in the Drama of Shakespeare*, p. 14.
35 Holzknecht, *Backgrounds of Shakespeare's Plays*, p. 135.
36 Eldred Jones, 'The Physical Representation of African Characters on the Elizabethan Stage During the 16th and 17th Centuries', *ThN*, XVII (1962), 18.
37 *Ibid.* p. 18.
38 Sir Ralph Winwood, *Memorials of Affairs of State*, quoted by Jones, 'The Physical Representation of African Characters', p. 20.
39 Quoted by Richards, 'Changeable Scenery', p. 11.
40 *JCS*, VI, 107–9; and see T. J. King, 'Staging of Plays at the Phoenix', pp. 147–8.
41 William E. Miller, '*Periaktoi* in the Old Blackfriars', *MLN*, LXXIV (1959), 1–3; and '*Periaktoi*: Around Again', *SQ*, XV (1964), 61–5.
42 *JCS*, VI, 283.
43 Jonson, VIII, 404.
44 *Calender of State Papers, Venetian 1617–19*, pp. 111–14.
45 Richards, 'Changeable Scenery', p. 18.
46 Holinshed, *Chronicles*, III (1578), 760. See also p. 735: 'Where he went abroad, his eies whirled about, his bodie privilie fenced, his hand ever upon his dagger.'

The best single work on audiences is Alfred Harbage's *Shakespeare's Audience* (New York 1941). Clifford Leech has an illuminating article, 'The Caroline Audience', in *MLR*, XXXVI (1941), 304–19, and W. A. Armstrong has written on private-theatre audiences in *RES*, n.s. X (1959), 234–49.

1   Quoted in Harbage, *Shakespeare's Audience*, p. 71.
2   *Ibid*, pp. 22–34.
3   *Ibid*. p. 30.
4   Irwin Smith, *Shakespeare's Globe Playhouse* (New York 1956), p. 65.
5   Quoted in Harbage, *Shakespeare's Audience*, p. 91.
6   *Thomas Platter's Travels in England*, pp. 166–7.
7   W. A. Armstrong, 'The Audience of the Elizabethan Private Theatres', *op cit*. pp. 240–1.
8   Harbage, *Shakespeare's Audience*, p. 56. See his tables of comparative prices, p. 59.
9   *JCS*, II, 673–81.
10 *Historia Histrionica* (1699), p. 5.
11 Verses by Thomas Craford.
12 The full quarrel is analysed by Georges Bas, 'James Shirley et "Th' Untun'd Kennell" Une petite guerre des théâtres vers 1630', *Etudes Anglaises*, XV (1963), 11–22. Bas does not perhaps make enough of the fact that Heywood had moved from the Red Bull to the Cockpit.
13 *WS*, II, 233.
14 *Shakespeare's Audience*, p. 17.
15 S. P. Zitner, 'Gosson, Ovid, and the Elizabethan Audience', *SQ*, IX (1958), 206–8.
16 See David Klein, *The Elizabethan Dramatists as Critics* (London 1962), pp. 173–84.
17 *ES*, I, 264–5.
18 Herbert Berry, 'The Stage and Boxes at the Blackfriars', *SP*, LXIII (1966), 163–86.
19 *Shakespeare's Audience*, p. 93.
20 *JCS*, VI, 147.
21 See W. J. Lawrence, *Those Nut-cracking Elizabethans* (London 1926), pp. 1–9.
22 *Works*, II, 334.
23 Quoted by G. Tillotson, *Times Literary Supplement*, 20 July 1933, p. 494.
24 See p. 75.
25 Jonson, VI, 283.
26 *The Gull's Hornbook* (1609), Chap. 6: 'How a Gallant should behave himself in a Play-house.'
27 See above, Chap. I, n. II.
28 See above, p. 81.
29 Jonson, VI, 527–8.
30 Antony Skoloker, *Daiphantus* (1604), A2r.

Index

Cockpit-at-Court, 108, 109–11
Cockpit players, 37, 43–5, 137, 146–7
Cockpit playhouse, 3, 13–14, 37, 39, 42, 43, 44, 45, 84, 85, 87, 102, 107, 112, 117, 126, 127, 143, 144, 146–7, 152, 155, 159–70 passim
colour symbolism, 10, 131
companies, 19–59 passim. See also under individual titles
company finances, 30–1, 38–9, 46–51
company organisation, 20, 46–8, 69
Condell, Henry, 27, 28, 29, 31, 119
continuous staging, 116–18
Cooke, Alexander, 27, 29, 31
Coriolanus, 168
Coronation, The, 169
cost of living, 7, 9
Costly Whore, The, 170
costumes. See apparel
Country Captain, The, 159
Court Beggar, The, 44, 138, 159
Covent Garden, 167
Coventry, 26
cover. See 'heavens'
Cowley, Richard, 24, 25, 26, 27, 29, 31
Coxcomb, The, 158
crackropes, 72
Cross Keys Inn, 85, 173
Cruel Brother, The, 160
Cuckqueans and Cuckolds Errant, 128
Cunning Lovers, The, 159
Cupid's Revenge, 158
Curtain playhouse, 13, 22, 23, 33, 83, 84, 85, 86, 89, 114–15, 142, 150, 155, 163, 164, 168, 170
curtains. See hangings
Custom of the Country, The, 162
Cutlack, 81
Cymbeline, 125, 168
Cynthia's Revels, 72, 73, 106, 118, 133, 138, 154, 164
Cyprian Conqueror, The, 74

Daborne, Robert, 40, 160
Damon and Pithias, 73
Daniel, Samuel, 35, 160
Davenant, William, 44–5, 53, 54, 80, 106, 109, 142, 145–7, 148, 160
Davenport, Robert, 160
Davies, John, of Hereford, 60
Davies, Sir John, 4
Dawes, Robert, 40, 48
Day, John, 11, 35, 160, 161
Dead Man's Fortune, The, 25, 116
Defence of Conny-Catching, A, 76
Defence of Poesy, A, 119
'degrees', 107, 108
Dekker, Thomas, 10, 34, 51, 67, 114, 122, 149, 150, 153–4, 161
Denham, John, 161
Deserving Favourite, The, 159
Devil is an Ass, The, 106, 164

Devil's Charter, The, 99, 100, 123, 125, 158
Devil's Law-case, The, 123, 169
de Witt, Johannes, 83, 89–92, 96, 97, 141
Digges, Leonard, 147
directing, 137–9
discoveries, 90, 98–9, 100, 106, 107, 123, 124, 127
discovery-space, 2, 90, 91, 96, 98–100, 105, 106, 107, 127, 179
Dish of Lenten Stuffe, A, 114–15
Distresses, The, 160
Dogberry, 66
Don Pedro, 55
Don Quixote, 11
Donne, John, 63, 71
Double Marriage, The, 162
Doubtful Heir, The, 148
Downton, Thomas, 27, 29, 30, 31
Drake, Sir Francis, 9
Drayton, Michael, 152, 161
Drue, Thomas, 54, 161
Drummond, William, of Hawthornden, 16–17
drums, 64, 97, 103, 113, 119, 121, 122, 123
Duchess of Malfi, The, 58, 62, 67, 122, 169
Duchess of Suffolk, The, 54, 161
Duke, John, 27, 28, 29, 33
Duke of Milan, The, 165
Duke's Mistress, The, 169
Dulwich Collection, vi, 24, 25, 39
Dulwich College, 63, 67
Dumb Knight, The, 127, 165
dumb-show, 2–3, 75, 116, 125–6
duration of performances, 116–17
Dutch Courtesan, The, 120, 165
Dutton, Edward, 29
Dutton, John, 22

Earle, John, 145
East India Company, 9
Eastward Ho!, 17, 35, 106, 159
Ecclestone, William, 39, 40
Edward I, 26
Edward II, 26, 165
Edwardes, Richard, 73
Elder Brother, The, 162
Elizabeth I, 4, 6, 7, 21, 22, 23, 32, 33, 107
Elsinore, 24
Emperor of the East, The, 166
Endymion, 164
England's Joy, 91, 178
English Moor, The, 159
English Traveller, The, 164
entrances, gallery, 87, 89, 90, 92
entrances, playhouse, 87, 88, 89, 90, 91, 92, 104
entrances, stage, 88, 89, 90, 95–6, 98–9, 106, 107, 109, 118, 125
Epicene, 164
Essex, Captain, 150, 151
Essex's Men, 22
Evans, Henry, 23, 33–6, 70, 104

185

Henslowe, Phillip, 16, 26, 27, 28, 29, 30, 31, 32, 33, 39–41, 47, 48, 49, 50, 51, 57, 58, 63, 66, 76, 85, 92–4, 100–2, 121, 123–4, 128, 129, 131, 132, 141

Herbert, Henry (Master of the Revels), 44, 45–6, 53–5, 173

Herod and Antipater, 165

Heton, Richard, 44, 46

Heywood, Thomas, 10, 16, 33, 37, 46, 62, 70–1, 73, 122, 126, 137, 147, 149, 163–4

Hierarchy of the Blessed Angels, The, 147

hired men, 20, 27, 31, 41, 46, 47, 48, 50, 121, 124, 127

Histriomastix (Marston's), 2, 48, 126

Histrio-mastix (Prynne's), 3, 63

Hoffman, 160

Holinshed, 138, 181

Holland, John, 26, 27, 28, 29

Hollander, The, 163

Holland's Leaguer, 165

Hollar, Wenceslas, vi, 8, 92

Holmes, Martin, vi

Honest Lawyer, The, 167

Honest Whore, 1 & 2 The, 161

Hope building contract, 100–1, 105

Hope playhouse, 84, 86, 87, 88, 90, 92, 100–2, 105, 164, 166

housekeepers, 32, 49

Howes, Edmond, 22, 64, 87

Humorous Courtier, The, 169

Humorous Day's Mirth, An, 159

Humorous Lieutenant, The, 162

Humour out of Breath, 161

Hunnis, William, 23

Hunt, Thomas, 29

hut, above the stage-cover, 88, 89, 96

Hyde Park, 169

If It Be Not Good, the Devil is in It, 122, 123, 161

If You Know Not Me, You Know Nobody, 153, 163

Imposter, The, 169

incomes, 7–9

inner-stage. *See* discovery-space

Inns of Court men, 9, 13, 144, 145, 148, 149, 154, 157

innyard playing-places, 4, 56, 82, 83, 85–6, 94

Insatiate Countess, The, 75, 120, 165

inter-act music, 97

internal staircases, 90, 91–2

Ipswich, 26

Iron Age, The, 46, 164

Island Princess, The, 162

Isle of Dogs, The, 30

Isle of Gulls, The, 35, 54, 154, 160

Jack Drum's Entertainment, 144

James I, 7, 17, 19, 31, 33, 35, 36, 37, 43, 53, 56, 67, 86, 107, 133–6

James IV, 113, 116

Jeffes, Anthony, 30, 31, 47

Jeffes, Humphrey, 28, 30, 31, 53

Jenkins, Harold, 79

Jeronimo, 67, 81, 156, 170

Jew of Malta, The, 30, 57, 66, 81, 124, 151, 165

jigs, 66, 100, 113–15, 116, 122, 143, 148, 151

Jocasta, 126

Johnson, William, 21

Jones, Inigo, vi, 108, 109, 110, 112, 125, 132, 133, 137

Jones, Richard, 29, 30, 31, 32, 36, 50

Jonson, Ben vi, 14, 16–17, 30, 34, 35, 59, 63, 68, 72, 73, 91, 97, 98, 102, 106, 108, 114, 118, 119, 122, 127, 133, 137, 138, 144, 146, 149–50, 153, 156, 164

Jovial Crew, A, 159

Juby, Edward, 29, 31, 47

Jugurtha, 151

Julius Caesar, 100, 168

Just Italian, The, 80, 145–6, 160

Kempe, Will, 24, 27, 29, 31, 32, 64, 66, 80, 113–14, 156, 173

Kempe's Nine Days' Wonder, 113

Kendall, Thomas, 35

Kendall, William, 50

Kenilworth, 21

Keysar, Robert, 36

Kiechel, Samuel, 87

Killigrew, Thomas, 51, 164

King and No King, A, 159

King and the Subject, The, 55

King John and Matilda, 160

King Lear, 67, 124, 168

King's and Queen's Young Company. *See* Beeston's Boys

King's Men (Shakespeare's Company), 16, 17, 31, 36, 37, 39, 42, 43, 44, 47, 49, 50, 53, 54, 56, 58–9, 62, 63, 68, 71, 73, 86, 97, 102, 115, 122, 132, 137, 138, 143, 145, 146–7, 147–9, 152, 155–6, 158–70. *See also* Chamberlain's Men

King's Revels Children, 158, 161, 165

King's Revels Company, 44, 125, 159, 163, 167

Kirkham, Edward, 34, 35

Knack to Know a Knave, A, 25, 170

Knack to Know an Honest Man, A, 170

Knell, William (?), 64

Knight of Malta, The, 162

Knight of the Burning Pestle, The, 11–12, 70, 106–7, 118, 125, 144, 153, 156, 158, 179, 180

Knolles, Richard, vi

Kyd, Thomas, 16, 164

Lady Elizabeth's Men, 39, 43, 102, 158, 160, 161, 164, 166, 167, 168

Lady Mother, The, 163

Lady of Pleasure, The, 169

New Way to Pay Old Debts, A, 10, 165
Newington Butts playhouse, 87
News from Plymouth, 148, 160
No Wit, No Help like a Woman's, 152
Noble Stranger, The, 168
Northern Lass, The, 159
Northward Ho!, 161
Norwich, 53, 113
Novella, The, 159
nut-cracking, 143, 151–2, 153

Observations at Black-Fryers, 145
Old Fortunatus, 161
Opportunity, The, 169
Orlando Furioso, 66, 76, 81, 116, 163
Ormond, Duke of, 150
Ostler, William, 36, 58, 71
Othello, 67, 152, 168
Ovid, 149
Oxford's Men, 22, 32
Oxford University, 137

palings, 91, 93, 94
Pallant, Robert, 33, 40, 41
Palmer, Thomas, 152
Palsgrave's Men, 38, 42, 43, 47, 53, 54, 68, 81, 161
Paris Garden, 22. See also Beargarden
Parnassus plays, 15, 71
Parr, William, 53
Passionate Lovers, 1 & 2 The, 159
patents, 18, 21, 33, 35, 42, 52, 56. See also licensing of companies
Patient Grissil, 160
patronage of playing companies, 19, 20–1
Paul's Boys, 23, 24, 34, 36, 70, 71, 87, 107, 118, 122, 126, 127–8, 144, 158–70 passim
Payne, Robert, 35
Peacham, Henry, vi, 65, 131
Pearce, Edward, 33
Peele, George, 113, 131, 167
Peerson, Martin, 122
Pembroke, third Earl of, 27, 64
Pembroke, fourth Earl of, 14–15, 64, 137
Pembroke's Company, 26, 27, 28, 29, 30, 31, 67, 139, 165, 167, 173
Pepys, Samuel, 51
Perambulation of Kent, 142
Percy, William, 127–8
periaktoi, 132
Pericles, 95–6, 144, 153, 168
Perkin, John, 21
Perkin Warbeck, 163
Perkins, Richard, vi, 33, 39, 43, 44, 64
Perry, William, 53
'personation', 54–5, 73–4, 76, 80, 81, 121
perspective staging, 108, 112, 118, 132–3, 135
Philaster, 99, 153, 155, 158
Phillips, Augustine, 24, 25, 26, 27, 31, 32
Philotas, 35, 160
Phoenix, The, 166

Phoenix playhouse. See Cockpit
Picture, The, 166
Pierce Penilesse, 65
Pilgrim, The, 120, 162
pillars (stage), 88, 89, 95, 100, 101, 106
pirating of playbooks, 26, 28, 71, 76, 79–80, 139, 173
Pistol, 80
pit, 105, 142, 149
plague, 6, 20, 21, 23, 43–4, 55–6, 103
Platonic Lovers, The, 160
Platter, Thomas, 128–9, 142
players, 22, 60–81 passim
playwriting, 15–18, 51, 61–2, 71, 140
Pleasure Reconciled to Virtue, 137
Poetaster, 106, 164
Pollard, Thomas, 58
Poor Man's Comfort, The, 160
Pope, Thomas, 24, 25, 26, 27, 29, 31
population of London, 141
Porter, Endymion, 54
Porter, Henry, 167
Porter's Hall playhouse, 53, 85, 86, 107, 122, 161
Prince Charles's Men, 39, 41, 42, 43, 44, 49, 53, 56, 144, 160, 161, 165
Prince's Company (Admiral's), 161, 163, 166, 167. See also Palsgrave's
Prisoners, The, 164
'private' playhouses, 6, 7, 10, 11, 12, 13, 36, 50, 83, 85, 86, 95, 102, 107, 112, 115, 116, 117, 118, 120, 122, 125, 137, 141, 142, 143, 144, 146–7, 151–2, 153–5, 157
Privy Council, 4–5, 13, 14, 25, 27, 29, 32, 33, 37, 44, 51, 52, 56, 57, 103, 134, 141, 172
processions, 125–6
prohibitions on playing, 21, 30, 36, 43–4, 52, 55, 56, 57
prompt. See book-keeper
properties, stage, 90, 98, 99, 100, 111, 112, 118, 123–4, 125, 127, 128, 138
Prophetess, The, 162
proscenium arch, 1, 108, 118
Prynne, William, 3, 63, 102
'public' playhouses, 6, 7, 10–11, 82, 83, 85, 97, 102, 106, 107, 112, 115, 116, 117, 118, 120, 121, 122, 123, 141, 142, 143, 144, 147–9, 155–7
Puritan, The, 170
Puritans, 3, 6, 14, 22, 23, 63, 88, 140, 141, 149

Queen and the Concubine, The, 159
Queen Anne's Men (Worcester's), 13, 16, 33, 38–9, 42, 47, 62, 63, 85–6, 102, 128, 158, 160, 161, 163, 164, 167, 169, 170
Queen Henrietta's Men, 43, 44, 46, 54–5, 144, 158–69 passim
Queen of Corinth, The, 162
Queen's Men, 22, 23, 24, 25, 27, 28, 56, 64, 65, 76, 77, 85, 158, 163, 170